Imperfect Past

Volume II

More History in a New Light

ESSAYS BY

Chles F. Bryp.

Charles F. Bryan, Jr., Ph.D.

With five essays by John Bryan

Foreword by Pamela Stallsmith

DEMENTI MILESTONE PUBLISHING

First Printing

Publisher and Design
Wayne Dementi
Dementi Milestone Publishing, Inc.
Manakin-Sabot, VA 23103
www.dementimilestonepublishing.com

The Library of Congress Control Number:

ISBN: 978-1-7368989-8-7

Cover design: Sarah Lapallo, Inkwell Book Company

Page Layout: Dianne Dementi

Printed in the United States

A full good faith effort has been made to trace copyright holders and to obtain their permission for the use of copyright material. The publisher apologizes for any omissions or errors and would appreciate notification of any corrections that should be incorporated in future reprints or editions of this book.

DEDICATION

In memory of Professors Paul H. Bergeron and Milton M. Klein, mentors extraordinaire, who taught me to love history's complexity, and to see that there is no simple "truth" in the past.

ACKNOWLEDGEMENTS

Much as I benefitted from the help of many people in producing Volume I of *Imperfect Past,* the same holds true for Volume II. First and foremost is the Richmond *Times-Dispatch,* publisher of my columns beginning in earnest in 2010. With rare exception, its editors have prominently featured my essays above the fold on the front page of the commentary section of the Sunday edition. Many of them are accompanied by one of Dwayne Carpenter's marvelous cartoons. President and Publisher Tom Silvestri, followed upon his retirement by Paige Mudd, not only allowed, but encouraged me to reprint my essays in book form. I thank them both for supporting this project from the beginning.

I offer a special word of gratitude to both of my editors at the *Times-Dispatch*—Bob Rayner and Pam Stallsmith. Until his retirement in 2019, Bob carefully read and edited all of my commentary pieces, only to be succeeded by Pam, as Commentary Editor. Like any good editor, both of them carefully read all of my submissions, catching any errors that may have slipped into them and making sure that I didn't confuse the use of certain words such as "affect" for "effect," or "further" for "farther.

Wayne Dementi, President of Dementi Milestone Publishing, continued his essential role as the book's publisher. I cannot remember a single time when I was with Wayne that he wasn't smiling. As he did with Volume 1, Wayne has had to gently prod me to stay on schedule, and he also has given me encouragment and useful suggestions throughout the process.

Once again, I owe my wife and best friend, Cammy, my sincere gratitude, for being the first "editor" to read the initial draft of each of my columns. Without fail, she has saved me from embarrassment by pointing out the inevitable errors and contradictions that somehow manage to slip into a draft essay, even though I may have read it numerous times.

Last, I want to thank the thousands of *Times-Dispatch* subscribers who have faithfully read my columns, providing me with encouragement, but also letting me know when they disagreed with my views. I hope they will enjoy re-reading some of my columns and appreciating others they read for the first time.

Charles F. Bryan, Jr., Ph.D.
Richmond, Virginia

CONTENTS

V. Running a Country for Better and for Worse

VI. Fall In: How the Military has Shaped America and Americans

VII. Living and Dying

FOREWORD

"Dr. Bryan's articles are among my favorite reads in the *Times-Dispatch*."

"Thank you for publishing his insightful pieces."

"His columns offer valuable lessons from little-known parts of history."

These are among the many comments I've heard over the years regarding Dr. Charles F. Bryan Jr.'s regular columns in the Sunday Commentary section in the Richmond *Times-Dispatch*. They are indeed a highlight of the newspaper.

Charlie helps readers unravel history's complexities through his clear narrative. His deep knowledge of history – whether it's Virginia, American or global – brings the past alive and offers valuable lessons for the future.

That's why his columns continue to be among the most popular pieces in the *Times-Dispatch*. Charlie skillfully frames a contemporary issue in a historical context and makes it relevant – and, most importantly, readable. His pieces anchor our pages, both in terms of presentation and intellectual heft.

The *Times-Dispatch* has benefited from Charlie's contributions for decades. As the retired, highly respected president of the Virginia Historical Society (now the Virginia Museum of History & Culture) Charlie brings an unparalleled understanding of the commonwealth and the South — in particular — to his commentary.

We live in an extraordinary time, a disharmonic convergence of racial reckoning, political polarization and the COVID-19 pandemic. Charlie's columns have helped our readers better understand the journalistic who-what-where-why-and-how behind a broad range of subjects, ranging from Confederate statuary, to best books, to Southern culture, to presidential politics through the centuries – but relayed through his keen historical analysis.

As Charlie wrote in his December 8, 2019, column, "Conspiracy theories and 'fake history'": "Manipulating or fabricating the facts of history to suit one's argument is unethical, according to the principles of scholarship proclaimed by the American Historical Association. These standards are notably similar to those prescribed to journalists. It was one of the first things we learned in graduate school, along with several other ethical canons."

His columns are unassailable, his voice authentic and his passion for history undeniable. Perhaps his most poignant columns involve his beloved alma mater, the Virginia Military Institute. Charlie, Class of 1969, offers unparalled insights into the college through his explanations of its traditions and the legacy of remarkable cadets such as Jonathan Daniels, the Episcopal seminarian and valedictorian of the Class of 1961 who died a civil rights martyr.

Charlie's most moving column about VMI told the powerful family story of how the brass buttons from his dress uniform became symbols of strength and resilience – first to his daughter, as she entered the U.S. Naval Academy, then to his son, as he became a fellow Rat, followed by other incoming cadets Charlie helped. Were they magic, he wondered? "No, but I think it serves as a reminder to never quit and as a result, you will never regret the decision to stay the course."

He has stayed the course as a top-notch historian and author, one whom the *Times-Dispatch* is fortunate to count as a regular contributor. It has been my privilege to work with Charlie and edit his masterful columns during my time as Opinions editor of the newspaper.

As English author and poet Rudyard Kipling wrote, "If history were taught in the form of stories, it would never be forgotten." Through his story telling, Charlie makes history memorable. How can you forget the horrors of trench warfare during World

War I or the crowded hospitals of the 1918 influenza pandemic after reading his powerful pieces?

You can't. Charlie brings you there and opens the doors to reflection, knowledge and understanding. His readers are better for it.

Pamela Stallsmith

About the Foreword author

Pamela Stallsmith was Opinions editor of the Richmond *Times-Dispatch* from 2019 to 2021. She previously was a state and political reporter for the Richmond *Times-Dispatch*, and also has worked in corporate and university communications. She is a longtime resident of Henrico County.

INTRODUCTION

Last year, I began to think about publishing another volume of the essays I had written since the release of my book, *Imperfect Past: History in a New Light* in 2016. It consisted of the first eighty columns I had published in the Richmond *Times-Dispatch* since 2011. At first, I was concerned that I would not have enough essays to justify a second volume because I have never kept a running count on just how many I had written. But much to my surprise when I added up the second group, I discovered that I had produced nearly eighty more columns.

The sales numbers for *Imperfect Past* had generated a small profit, and with the positive response I received from its readers and reviewers, I thought that a second volume would also be welcomed by the reading public.

When I presented the idea to my publisher, Wayne Dementi, president of Dementi Milestone Press, he endorsed the idea with his usual enthusiasm, and agreed to work with me in publishing another one. Therefore, I present all of my published essays in the Richmond *Times-Dispatch* since late 2016.

Much like I did with the first volume, I have arranged my essays by broad categories such as issues relating to health, politics, the military, education, and several others. I also have provided study questions to stimulate discussion in book clubs or in the classroom.

People frequently ask me how I choose the topics I write about. As I explained in Volume I, ideas come from a variety of sources: suggestions from friends and family, a newspaper or journal article that sparks my interest, and any number of topics that come to me from lectures I gave when I taught at the University of Tennessee and the University of Missouri-St. Louis.

The piece I wrote on the unusually cool summer of 1814, for example, came from a lecture I gave on how climate and weather have affected history.

I might be accused of being a jack of all trades, master of none when it comes to history, an accusation I accept. I particularly enjoyed teaching the survey course in American history because it forced me to study in greater depth subjects that fell outside of my specialty (Civil War and Reconstruction). As you will see, one of the smallest sections in this book is about the Civil War.

Included also are five essays that were originally published in the *Times-Dispatch* by my cousin, John Bryan. John grew up in Nashville, but he and his family (Janet, Kelly, and Thomas) have lived in Richmond for nearly 40 years. As you will read, he is a gifted writer who has devoted most of his career to finding and developing the resources to support the arts and the humanities in Virginia and beyond.

I hope that his columns, added to mine, will make for an interesting and pleasant learning experience for our readers.

Charles F. Bryan, Jr.
Richmond, Virginia

PART I

PEOPLE: WARTS AND ALL

The essays in this section tell the stories of a genuine war hero, hypocritical religious figures, a controversial person from the world of sports, and people who have escaped famine only to be discriminated against once they arrived on American shores. For better or worse, on a scale both large and small, these people have made a difference in shaping our nation's history.

1

REMEMBERING A REAL AMERICAN HERO: BOBBY RAY

The word "hero" is overused now, especially when applied to anyone in the military. Don't misunderstand me; people who voluntarily serve their country in the armed forces today are special, particularly if they have experienced combat and multiple deployments. But are they genuine heroes? Most people who have been engaged in actual fighting do not think so.

To me, a real hero is someone like David R. (Bobby) Ray. I went to school with Bobby in McMinnville, Tennessee, in the 1960s.

Tall, skinny, gangly, and almost always smiling and laughing, it was sometimes difficult to take Bobby seriously. He was anything but athletic. Instead he played trombone in the City High Rebel marching band. Although the term wasn't used then, today he would be considered a "band geek."

His personality and physical appearance, however, masked another side of him. He was very bright, and when he graduated near the top of his class, the University of Tennessee awarded him a full scholarship.

Going to UT was Bobby's first extended time away from home. Whether it was more freedom than he could handle or simply too high a jump from a small high school to a large university, he did not thrive there. He struggled to keep his scholarship and stay in school, which could have profound consequences, especially if you were a young male with a low draft number.

***

For any able-bodied man between the ages of 18 and 30, the prospect of conscription into the armed services was a fact of life in the 1960s. With the United States locked in an ongoing Cold War with the Soviet Union, and heavily involved in a civil war raging in Vietnam, the demand for men to serve in uniform was the highest it had been since World War II. By the thousands, young Americans with low draft numbers fled to Canada to avoid serving in the military.

Using a lottery system that had been employed in previous wars, the Selective Service Administration randomly assigned numbers to young men throughout the country. The way the system operated, the lower your draft number, the greater your chances of being called up.

As in previous wars, there were numerous ways to be exempted from serving - being married, teaching, pursuing certain types of education or the ministry - and staying in college with good grades. Many a person alive today used every means possible to avoid military service. Bobby Ray's low draft number made him a prime candidate to be called up in 1966.

But when I was home during spring furlough from the Virginia Military Institute, I ran into his mother, and she was excited that Bobby had just qualified for the Navy. To her, it was a safer alternative than having her only son get drafted into the Army.

Then Bobby did the first of several extraordinary things that would define the rest of his life. Rather than serving as a regular sailor in the fleet after completing boot camp, my friend signed up to be a corpsman (He would have been called a medic in the Army), potentially one of the most dangerous jobs in the armed forces.

After taking a rigorous training course, Bobby became a corpsman, first assigned to a hospital ship and then the large Navy hospital in Long Beach, California, where he treated wounded Marines from Vietnam.

***

Not content to stay safely in the States, he requested service in Vietnam with the Marines. After another round of training, in July 1968, Bobby was assigned to Battery D, second battalion, of the11th Marine Regiment based near An Hoa in Quang Nam province.

He quickly became one of the most popular men in the unit because of his deadpan humor and his skills in treating Marines. "Doc Bobby" told some of his buddies that after the Navy he wanted to finish his degree and become a doctor.

Early in the morning of March 19, 1969, a battalion of crack North Vietnamese soldiers launched a furious assault on the artillery base, catching the outnumbered Americans by surprise. Bobby Ray jumped immediately into action.

Amid a hail of enemy bullets, he dashed from one position to another tending to wounded and dying Marines. Within minutes, Bobby was seriously wounded, but he refused to stop. When two enemy soldiers rushed his position as he worked on a Marine, he grabbed a rifle and killed one and wounded the other.

Ignoring pleas of others to take care of himself, he continued to treat the wounded. It seemed that no one could prevent him from doing his duty.

While he was trying to assist another Marine, he heard the thud of a metallic object nearby - an enemy grenade. Bobby instinctively threw himself over the wounded Marine, saving the man's life but sacrificing his own.

The Americans eventually prevailed, but Bobby was one of 15 Americans killed in the action.

***

I will never forget how stunned I was when I received the news of Bobby Ray's death as I sat in my room in the VMI barracks reading my hometown newspaper. This was the spring of 1969, and I had almost grown numb from frequent announcements of VMI alumni killed in Vietnam over the past four years. They had come to VMI knowing full well they could serve in the line of fire and risk their lives.

But Bobby Ray, the geeky trombone player? The same Bobby Ray I exchanged lines with in our school's production of "Arsenic and Old Lace"? Who was always laughing and cutting up?

His unfathomable act of courage led to his being awarded the Congressional Medal of Honor. The Navy honored him by naming a Spruance-class destroyer after him and a medical clinic at the Marine Corps base at Quantico.

What Bobby did made me realize for the first time that a person's outward appearance can obscure a much different being underneath, one who is capable of making the ultimate sacrifice and becoming a real hero.

Richmond *Times-Dispatch*, May 24, 2015

2

CELEBRITIES GALORE IN 1964 EUROPEAN TRIP

Three weeks in the summer of 1964 arguably proved to be some of the most eventful in my life. As a rising high school senior from a small town in Tennessee, I had things happen to me that few people experience in a lifetime. What made those three weeks so special?

I had an uncle and aunt who loved to travel, so much so that my uncle left the Baptist ministry mid-career, and along with my aunt, started a travel agency in Mississippi that eventually blossomed into one of the largest in the South.

In the summer of 1964, they put together their first group tour to Europe. Fortunately, they had room for me to join the group of mostly of older women from the Magnolia State, along with my cousin Bill, who was my age and more like a brother than a cousin to me.

Like most teenage males of any time, we had an eye out for girls, and we had a share of mischief about us. But dropping water balloons from our ninth story hotel window to the empty alley below and making inappropriate bodily sounds in inappropriate places was about as malicious as we got.

I kept a diary for much of the trip. In retrospect, my entries did not do justice to the experience. Without fail, I mentioned virtually every meal I ate, good and bad alike.

The mushrooms, stewed tomatoes, and pork and beans served with breakfast in London struck me as odd. I loved the green pasta served in Florence, even though I didn't realize that it was made from spinach, a vegetable I could not abide then.

***

The diary was spare on details, and I have to draw on 55-year old memories to fill in the blanks. Here are some highlights, as recorded in my diary with all of its spelling errors and overuse of exclamation points.

June 1: "Flew to New York [from Nashville] on an American Airlines Boeing 707 jet, my first airplane trip ever. Neat!"June 2: "Billy and I got up early and went down to the TODAY program. [We] waved in the window and [the show's host] Jack Lescoulie came out on the street to interview the people. He enterviewed [sic] us. It was really great!"June 3: "Billy and I went to bed as soon as we got to the hotel [in London] about 8 in the morning. Big mistake! After we woke up, we went downstairs thinking it was morning and tried to order breakfast. The waiter laughed when he handed us a dinner menu and told us that we had 'jet lag,' which means getting your days and nights mixed up after flying a long way in a short time."June 6: "We saw the Beatles today! Just after leaving Amsterdam on our way to Germany, this big black lemosine [sic] passed our bus and someone shouted 'Look it's the Beatles.' It sure was! Three of them looked like they were sleeping, but George [Harrison] waved to us. Neat!" June 9: "Billy and I think that Jules [our tour guide] has something going on at night with [a lady in our group], who recently divorced!" June 17: [Our group rode by train from Rome to Nice, France, and once we crossed the French border we saw something that resulted in the following entry.] "All of a sudden, some women in our group started laughing and giggling, and one said: 'That's disgusting!' Billy and I looked out the window and saw a lot people standing around totally naked! Most of them were old and ugly. Jules told us later that it was a nudist beach. Weird!" June 23: "What a day! Spent a long time with Cassius Clay, who was on our plane back to New York [more later]. When we finally got to New York, Billy and I went to dinner near Broadway. As we walked back to the hotel, a big black lemosine [sic] pulled up in front of a theater. Out came Elizabeth Taylor and Richard Burtin [sic] who got in the car and drove away. They were only a few feet from where we stood!" June 24 - "Got home about 6:30 P.M. It was the greatest trip I have ever taken. I will never forget it."

***

About that hour with Cassius Clay: The air traffic controllers in Paris were on strike, and were allowing only one plane to take off only every half hour. Once we boarded our flight, we sat so long without taking off that the pilot eventually let us disembark and walk around the plane.

Bill and I were standing around talking to a few of our fellow passengers, when someone said: "Look!" We turned around, and standing in the doorway of the first-class section of the plane was the world heavyweight champion, Cassius Clay.

Always the showman, Clay bounded down the stairway, then for some reason he strode up to our small huddle.

Initially we were speechless as we stood in front of perhaps the world's most famous athlete. At 6'3", he towered over us. But he quickly disarmed us by regaling us with his poetry and jokes.

He was incredibly funny, and soon we began peppering him with questions about defeating Sonny Liston earlier in the year and winning a gold medal in the 1960 Olympics.

Only 22 years old and brimming over with hubris, he was truly the world champion, and he knew it. Someone came up with an American football, which the champ took and tossed back and forth with us for several minutes.

Eventually, though, the TWA crew came out and told us to re-board. I don't know what our parting words were to the champion boxer, but I do know he gave several of us his autograph (which I have subsequently lost). He went back to his seat in the first-class cabin and we returned to ours in coach.

***

So much has happened in the intervening half century since that chance meeting.

Later that year, Clay converted to the Muslim faith and changed his name to Muhammad Ali. He went on to fight and win in several more championship matches, only to eventually lose as age and too many blows to his head began to take their toll.

His outspoken opposition to the Vietnam War and refusal to serve in the military drew the ire of millions of Americans.

Although it was not his intention, he contributed to a nation that for a while became as divided as it is now. It was a time when symbolic gestures like the wearing of an American flag lapel pin or accepting Clay's name change to Ali marked you as a "patriot" or not - as did a bumper sticker with the catch phrase "America: Love it or Leave It."

Ali was diagnosed at age 42 with Parkinson's disease, a condition that he struggled with until his death a few years ago. While his fame and fortune were built on his prowess in the boxing ring, Ali would also go to his grave noted for his many acts of kindness and philanthropy later in life.

My cousin Bill eventually took over his parent's business, did well with it, but sadly died at age 65 a few years ago. I went on to a career as a historian, only to be afflicted, like Ali, with Parkinson's disease.

When asked one time how he coped with the condition, he compared his struggle with Parkinson's to being in the ring: "Don't quit. Suffer now but live the rest of your life as a champion."

These are words I have tried to abide by myself.

_____

Richmond *Times-Dispatch*, July 1, 2018

3

AMERICA'S NOT SO WELCOMING PAST

The issue of immigration has become a major topic of debate in the upcoming midterm election. The Trump administration's hard-nose immigration policy has appealed to his base of supporters who argue that the country is awash with aliens, mainly from Latin America.

Opponents of Trump's course of action contend that it runs counter to the immigration principles that have guided the United States as expressed in Emma Lazarus' quote on the Statue of Liberty: "Give me your tired, your poor, Your huddled masses yearning to breathe free, The wretched refuse of your teeming shore."

The issue is nothing new.

***

Americans have rarely greeted immigrants with open arms. Controversy surrounding immigration has long troubled Americans, and at times it has led to extreme actions and policies that run counter to the nation's founding principles.

No better example of this can be found than the reaction of the American people to the flood of desperate Irish immigrants in the mid-19th century.

The Irish people relied on potatoes as the mainstay of their diet and their financial well-being. The tuber, which originated in Peru and made its way to Europe in the late 1600s, was about the only crop that flourished in Irish soil. Packed with nutrients and easy to grow, potatoes were consumed by the Irish people in staggering amounts.

Then the bottom dropped out. In the 1840s, a blight that caused potatoes to rot in the ground began to spread throughout Europe. No part of Europe was harder hit than Ireland. Already impoverished because of a neglectful ruling British government, the Irish could ill afford the cruel blow directed at them now.

Pleas for relief fell on deaf ears. British officials were so thoroughly tied to laissez-faire capitalism that they refused to provide government aid to relieve a colossal humanitarian crisis. They argued that it would interfere with the natural course of free markets.

During the next seven years, Ireland's population plummeted by 50 percent. Nearly 1 million died of starvation and disease, while another 2 million moved away altogether, most to the United States. They poured through a leaky border into a country ill-prepared to handle the sheer numbers.

After a difficult 3,000-mile passage, Irish immigrants arrived with several strikes against them. For one, they were poorer than most other immigrants. Without the financial resources to move inland, they tended to congregate in cities along the northeastern and Atlantic seaboard, crowding into slums.

Most had made their living on farms in Ireland, and therefore lacked the skills required to work in an increasingly industrial economy. Yet they were accused of taking jobs away from Americans.

Despite newspaper classified ads proclaiming "No Irish Need Apply" for many positions, they usually performed the least desirable and most dangerous jobs for low pay. They slaved in textile mills. They dug ditches and tunnels, laid railroad and streetcar tracks, and installed water and sewer pipes. They cleaned stables, homes, and offices. By providing cheap labor, they played a key role in America's transition from an agricultural to an industrial-based economy.

***

Their religion was another concern. Virtually all of the new Irish immigrants were Catholics settling in a nation that was predominantly Protestant. They were charged with practicing an alien faith that was personally directed by the pope in Rome.

Opposition to the Irish grew to such an extent that many of its adherents established the Know Nothings, a political organization that became America's first legitimate third party. Founded in New York in 1853 initially as a secret society called the American party, the Know Nothing party got its name from the response its members gave when asked anything by outsiders: "I know nothing."

Most members were of Anglo-Saxon ancestry, Protestant, and anti-Catholic. Among other things, they advocated mandatory Bible readings (King James version) in schools; a 21-year naturalization period for immigrants to gain citizenship; the removal of Catholics from public office; the deportation of immigrant beggars and criminals; and restrictions on the purchase and consumption of alcohol.

Irish immigrants became the chief target of the Know Nothings, who accused the newcomers of being lazy, spreading crime and disease, and committing rape.

In the meantime, the Know Nothing party flourished for several years, filling a void left by the dying Whig party that was being torn asunder over the issue of slavery.

Bolstered by the battle cry "Americans must rule America!" the Know Nothings gained enough strength to win more than 100 congressional seats and eight governorships, control six state legislatures, and claim the mayor's office in Boston, Philadelphia, and Chicago.

They nominated former President Millard Fillmore to head the party ticket in the 1856 presidential election. Although Democrat James Buchanan defeated Republican John C. Fremont and Fillmore, the latter gained more than 20 percent of the vote.

Despite this relatively strong showing, the Know Nothing party declined rapidly as the even more divisive issue of slavery and its spread to the western territories overshadowed the immigration issue. Despite residual prejudice, Irish-Americans began to assimilate into the mainstream of the country. Some even displayed the same bigotry toward newcomers that they had experienced.

* * *

But prejudice against immigrants has never fully left the American psyche. While Irish immigrants were the principle targets of discrimination on the East Coast, Asians experienced similar treatment on the West Coast. And even though antipathy toward Irish immigrants diminished with the end of the potato famine in the 1850s and a concurrent decline in their numbers, a wave of new settlers, mainly from eastern and southern Europe, more than made up for the decline in Irish newcomers. Mostly Jewish or Catholic in their religion, these newcomers were subjected to many of the same prejudices as the Irish had been.

The similarities of the experiences of these various waves of immigrants are striking. Most of today's immigrants, both legal and illegal, are trying to escape from poverty, corrupt governments, violence, and hunger to live in a country that has long been what Abraham Lincoln proclaimed as "the last best hope on Earth."

Is our country now turning into a gated community writ large that will shut out those "huddled masses yearning to breathe free?"

Richmond *Times-Dispatch*, July 29, 2018

4

SURRENDERING TO TEMPTATION: SCANDALS AND EVANGELICALS

Recently I reread Sinclair Lewis' classic 20th-century novel *Elmer Gantry*, a story about a flawed man who was a hypocrite. The narrative is based on interviews Lewis conducted with various evangelical preachers and his own experience of growing up in an evangelical church.

The book's protagonist, Elmer Gantry, was an evangelical minister who secretly was attracted to alcohol, gambling and loose women despite condemning such sinful practices from the pulpit.

Elmer Gantry created a public furor when it first was released in 1927. Banned in some cities and denounced from pulpits throughout the country, the book nevertheless became a number one bestseller. Evangelist Billy Sunday accused Lewis of being "Satan's cohort."

One character in Lewis' book is Sharon Falconer, an itinerant evangelist who becomes Gantry's lover. Lewis loosely based Falconer on one of the most influential and popular evangelists of the 1920s and 1930s - Aimee Semple McPherson.

Endowed with good looks, stylish clothing and a dynamic personality that instinctively charmed large crowds, she was in the forefront of American evangelism in her time. Known as "Sister Aimee," she pioneered the use of the radio in services broadcast nationally from her Angelus Temple in Los Angeles.

Her services regularly featured faith healing and "speaking in tongues." Her temple in some ways resembled today's "megachurches" that often are centered on a "cult of personality" preacher who is an "innovative spiritual leader with considerable persuasive powers," as described by professor Scott Thumma, director of the Hartford Institute for Religion Research.

Using her carefully honed preaching skills from the pulpit and over the radio, she developed a magnetic image of herself that helped her develop a vast national audience and considerable wealth.

Married three times (once widowed and twice divorced), she was dogged with allegations of extramarital affairs as she reached the zenith of her ministry. At one point, someone threatened to release nude moving pictures of her and a friend unless she paid a $10,000 bribe.

She denied that such a film existed and refused to pay the blackmailer. Although no evidence is thought to exist of her infidelity, rumors of various assignations followed her until her death from an overdose of sleeping pills in 1944.

Over the past several decades, we have witnessed other major scandals involving dynamic church leaders. In the late 1980s, prominent television televangelist Jimmy Swaggart tearfully confessed publicly to multiple affairs with prostitutes.

At the same time, evangelist Jim Bakker and his wife, Tammy Faye, used their daily television program to promote Heritage Village in South Carolina that they described as a "Christian Disneyland." It was a scam from the beginning. In addition to using donations to support a lavish lifestyle, Bakker kept a double set of books to hide a $250,000 bribe he paid his former secretary with whom he had an affair.

After a while it all eventually unraveled. Bakker was convicted of fraud, embezzlement and tax evasion, for which he was sentenced to 45 years in federal prison but was released after only five years. When Bakker found himself in financial trouble, he asked Jerry Falwell Sr. to assist him in hopes that his television ministry could be salvaged.

The two never got along, and the partnership fell apart with Falwell calling Bakker a liar, embezzler, sexual deviant and "the greatest scab and cancer on the face of Christianity in 2,000 years."

Falwell Sr., who died in 2007, more than likely would have been appalled by the scandal created by his own son a decade later. Indeed, in the last several months, we have witnessed an Elmer Gantry-like scandal of our own in Virginia.

The news coming out of Lynchburg, Virginia's Liberty University, the country's largest evangelical Christian educational institution, has raised eyebrows almost everywhere.

Its president, Jerry Falwell Jr., admitted that his wife, Becki, had a six-year affair with Giancarlo Granda, pool boy-turned business associate. Granda said Falwell participated in some of the liaison as a voyeur, *The Associated Press* reported, which Falwell has denied.

Apparently when Granda threatened to extort the Falwells by releasing lurid photographs of the affair to the public, the couple called on Michael Cohen, the personal attorney of their friend Donald Trump, to help them. An expert in cleaning up messes, Cohen was able to keep the photographs from the public eye.

Ironically, sometime during all of this, Liberty conferred an honorary doctoral degree on Trump, and Falwell became the first high-profile evangelical to endorse Trump's candidacy for the presidency in 2016. In August, Falwell resigned as president and chancellor of Liberty, the school founded by his father.

Falwell has sued Liberty University, alleging the school damaged his reputation.

The word "hypocrisy" has been bandied about a lot as we wrap up a brutal presidential election. Now we tend to accept hypocrisy as just part of the political game. "So what? That's just politics," we say. Likewise, should we say: "So what? That's just religion." Somehow we as a people should not be willing to accept either form of hypocrisy as the norm.

Richmond *Times-Dispatch*, November 1, 2020

Charles F. Bryan, the author's father, researched the folk music of Appalachia and incorporated it into his symphonic compositions, leaving an important legacy of musical interpretation of American folklore and culture

5

REMEMBERING MY THREE FATHERS

Today we honor fathers, a celebration that began in the early 20th century to complement Mother's Day. For me, it is a day to remember my real father, but also two men who played a vital role in my life, each in his own way.

For a while Father's Day was a painful experience for me. Only until I reached my teens did it no longer bring back searing memories of witnessing my 43-year-old father's sudden death of a massive heart attack when I was a young boy.

My father has been described as "one of Tennessee's greatest musicians, composers, and prolific collectors of folk music." He studied composition at Yale under the brilliant German musician Paul Hindemith. One of his works premiered at Carnegie Hall. His death merited an obituary in the *New York Times*. Several colleges and universities had tried to persuade him to join their faculties.

I have often wondered what my life would have been like had he lived to old age. I am certain that it would have been profoundly different. Would I have followed his example as a musician? I love music, but after his death, that love did not turn into talent. My mother insisted that I take piano lessons. After four years, however, she finally gave up and let me play football instead. To this day, I cannot read music.

Had my father lived longer, would I have felt overshadowed by his relative fame and success? Many sons simply do not try or are unable to compete with fathers who were highly successful in their given endeavors. One of my commanding officers in the Army was Maj. Gen. George S. Patton IV. He came

across as tough, impatient, and driven much like his father of
World War II fame. But one couldn't help but sense that he always
stood in his father's shadow.

Before my father's death, I spent little time with him because of his absence from home as he frequently traveled the country giving recitals and lectures. But his love of history and folklore,
which permeated his music, and a passion for sharing it with the
public, must have rubbed off on me. Although I did not become a
musician, my career as a historian had many similarities to his in
the performing arts.

***

Because of my young age when my father died, I feel
cheated in not getting to know him better or eventually developing
an adult relationship with him. That came later with two other men.

One was my grandfather, who probably influenced me
more than any other man. Indeed, because of him my love of history blossomed at home, not at school. After my father's death, my
mother moved our family back to the small Tennessee town where
she and my father had grown up. We moved in with my grandfather, who was a widower.

From the beginning, he told me stories about the past and
our family. He told me tales about how his father and his family
survived the trauma of the Civil War; of the first automobile he
ever saw; of taking his first train ride; of the great flu pandemic of
1918; and scores of other stories of what life was like before my
time.

His tales about the past captured my imagination. They
excited and awed me, and they were true stories, not fiction. They
connected me in time to the world in which I was being raised.
They gave me a process - the act of imagining history. I was fortunate to grow up with someone who made the past come alive by
one of the oldest ways of relating history: storytelling.

I also learned from him that I should be proud of my family
and myself, but to never think we were better than anyone else. He
insisted that I look at the good in people and not judge them by the

color of their skin, and to never use the "N" word. He also taught me the things that most boys learn from their fathers - how to tie a necktie, shine my shoes, shave, and how to drive.

The concept of "men's work" and "women's work" overlapped with him. At his insistence, he and I cleaned up and washed the dishes after dinner every evening. He did the laundry for my mother, who worked full-time as a teacher.

Charles F. Bryan, Jr. in 1958 with C. J. Bryan, the grandfather who helped raise him.

Finally, he served as a perfect role model for me as a father and now a grandfather. When I'm with my grandchildren, I often think about my grandfather and hope I am having the same positive influence on them that he had on me.

When he died in 1970, I was devastated. But another person came along to assume the mantle of fatherhood for me. How that happened is serendipity at its best.

***

I earned my college degree from the Virginia Military Institute. Even though I was a history major, all cadets were required to take heavy doses of math and sciences courses. Math and chemistry were my downfall.

Between my general incompetence in those subjects and two demanding professors, I failed both and had to attend summer school at VMI.

It was there that I met and started dating Cammy Martin, a cute, petite blond with an infectious smile, who attended Mary Baldwin College in Staunton - and was the daughter of a VMI professor. He wasn't just any professor. It was his math course I had failed, forcing me to spend my summer at VMI!

Cammy and I started dating and before long I was in love. By my third year at the Institute, the feelings were mutual. We became engaged my last year at VMI, and we were married a month after my graduation.

Despite my less-than-stellar performance in his class, my father-in-law and I developed a friendship that lasted until his death. We both were born and raised in small Tennessee towns. We shared a common love of hot biscuits slathered with butter and sorghum molasses blended together. And even though he taught math, he loved history.

I admired him for his determination to stay in top physical shape until illness slowed him down near the end of his life. After he turned 50, he participated in dozens of senior track meets, winning medal after medal, and even holding the record for his age group in many events. He inspired me to stay in shape, and until his last few years he could run circles around me.

What drew me closer to him over the years, however, was learning about his World War II service. As a historian, I became fascinated with his war experiences, which he could remember in remarkable detail.

As a proud member of the Third Infantry Division, he saw action in North Africa, Sicily, Italy, France, and finally Germany, ending the war at Hitler's mountain hideaway at Berchtesgaden. Awarded a Silver Star, two Bronze Stars for valor, and

First Lt. (later Captain) Joseph E. Martin in Italy in the winter of 1943-44. Within a matter of months after this photo was taken, Martin would be wounded twice and awarded a Silver Star for gallantry as an infantry officer.

two Purple Hearts for wounds he suffered in Italy, he was the most decorated veteran on the VMI faculty. Yet he never boasted about his record. That was Joe Martin, a true gentleman, but also a gentle man who was a pillar of Lexington Presbyterian Church, assistant track coach at VMI, faithful husband, good father, proud grandfather, and intimidating math professor.

We grew to love each other like father and son. I was proud of him and much to his embarrassment I boasted to other people about his impressive war record. But much to my embarrassment, he bragged about me, taking great pride in my rise in the history profession.

Sadly, he developed incurable cancer. With his time on Earth limited, I persuaded him to write his war memoir before he left us. He spent day after day telling his saga in a neat handwritten narrative. As the days passed away, the words became harder for him to find and the writing difficult. But like a soldier on a long, grueling march, he plodded on despite the pain and fatigue. He completed his Iliad only a few weeks before his death in February 2003.

In his last days, he wanted his wife, his daughter, and me by his side. He was an American soldier to the end, one of millions of that war's veterans who are no longer with us. But in the words of the late author Stephen Ambrose: "So they fought, and won, and all of us living and yet to be born, must be forever profoundly grateful."

I will be forever grateful for the three men who helped shape my life - one a brilliant musician, one a kind grandfather, and one a brave soldier. Each in his own way was my father.

Richmond *Times-Dispatch*, June 19, 2016

PART II

THE HARDEST OF SCHOOLS

Few colleges and universities have alumni as loyal as that of the Virginia Military Institute (VMI). Most of us who attended it, griped the four years we were there and could not wait to get out. But in time with that experience behind us, we begin to see the school in a different light. It shaped us in ways that we did not realize when we were cadets. In a perverse way, it seems to have served us well. While the majority of us who went to VMI are better for it, we should not be considered better than graduates of other colleges. Our experience was simply different as the following four essays may help explain.

6

REFLECTIONS ON A REUNION: THE VMI CLASS OF 1969

Recently I attended my 50th class reunion at the Virginia Military Institute in Lexington. Of course, my classmates and I did the usual reunion activities of golf, tennis, banquets, sipping bourbon and telling tall tales. Some activities, however, gave us an opportunity to reflect on our time at VMI and the events swirling around us half a century ago. They also reminded us of four classmates in particular who were not there.

Although every VMI class develops its own unique personality, the class of 1969 stood out in several ways. For one, it attracted more applications and had the lowest acceptance rate (about 38%) of any previous class, a record that would remain unbroken for some three decades. The then-director of admissions noted that large numbers of young men who would have been accepted in previous years were rejected. Among those selected were the grandson of Gen. George S. Patton and the son of Martha Mitchell, the flamboyant wife of U.S. Attorney General John Mitchell.

Why so many applicants? Our being in the first wave of the baby boom generation explains it in part, but the most important reason was the absence of a major armed American conflict when we applied. Statistics bear this out. Our class had nearly 1,600 applicants, but by the time we were seniors, the number had plummeted. Only 811 young men applied to the class of 1972, of which nearly 75% were accepted.

This precipitous decline was closely tied to the war in Vietnam and a growing anti-military sentiment among young Americans. Nationwide, from 1968 to 1972, ROTC enrollment on college campuses dropped 75%. The service academies experienced significant drops in applications as well.

But those of us already at VMI seemed to buck that trend. A straw poll of the corps taken in May 1968 revealed that 96% supported the war effort. A headline in the weekly cadet newspaper proclaiming "VMI Gung Ho on War" reflected this sentiment.

Every military and air science class we took reminded us that combat was a distinct possibility in our futures. Our field training exercises involved mock ambushes, long-range patrolling, cover and concealment, coordinating close air support, and a number of other activities that assumed most of us would end up in the jungles of Vietnam.

The most sobering reminder of the war, however, came when we learned of the deaths of VMI alumni. With the corps fully assembled in the mess hall for dinner, the cadet adjutant would announce the names of those who had been killed in combat.

By our junior year, the war became much more personal when these announcements came more frequently, the names belonging to people we knew in the corps only a few years earlier. Indeed, the class of 1966 lost 11 men, the most of any class.

When we graduated in May 1969, however, the war was taking a different turn. Newly elected President Richard Nixon began to shift more responsibility for fighting the war over to the South Vietnamese military while the American presence gradually diminished. The Pentagon also announced that fewer officers were needed, and deferments of up to three years could be granted to those wanting to earn graduate degrees or take temporary jobs in the civilian sector before going on active duty as reserve officers.

A large percentage of our class took that option, and by the time they reported for service, many were required only a two-year obligation, and in some cases six months for active-duty training only. Eventually our class produced a record number of physicians, dentists, other medical professionals, attorneys, judges and Ph.Ds. Two among us became generals, including the chief of the Corps of Engineers. Of the 261 who graduated, 80% served in the military, with more than 50 going to Vietnam. Four classmates paid the ultimate price there.

It was those four we honored again after having dedicated space in Preston Library in their memory at our 25th reunion. We gathered in the Class of 1969 Memorial Room, a quiet haven for cadets wanting to study and escape the chaos of barracks. As we entered the room we saw on the far wall portraits of our four classmates ' all young and vibrant.

Tom Blair was a serious, driven cadet who didn't suffer fools gladly. He was posthumously awarded the Silver Star for gallantry in action on May 29, 1971, repeatedly exposing himself to enemy fire although seriously wounded.

Lee Galloway, who was killed while leading his platoon in an attack on enemy forces on March 27, 1971, bucked the VMI system from day one. Known equally for his keen sense of humor and his caustic tongue, Galloway was a prodigious reader who was described by one of his VMI roommates as a "true renaissance man."

Jack Kennedy seemed to have it all - good looks, brains, star athlete and an all-round good guy. A pilot, he flew an O-2 Cessna 337 Skymaster as a forward air controller (FAC), one of the most dangerous assignments in the Air Force. On Aug. 16, 1971, his plane disappeared and crashed into triple canopy jungle. Some 25 years later his remains were found and confirmed by DNA testing. In 1996, Kennedy was laid to rest in Arlington National Cemetery with 90 of his VMI classmates in attendance.

Frank Webb did not graduate with us, but after dropping out of VMI, he earned an Army commission from Officer Candidate School, and was highly regarded by his soldiers when he was killed on May 5, 1968.

As we honored those four classmates, I, along with many of my classmates, wondered why those four and not us. I could not help but remember lines from World War I poet Laurence Binyon:

They shall grow not old, as we that are left to grow old
Age shall not weary them, nor the years condemn
At the going down of the sun and in the morning
We will remember them.

Richmond *Times-Dispatch*, June 23, 2010

7

THE VMI RING

Next to a diploma, graduates of the Virginia Military Institute (VMI) hold their class rings as the most important symbol of their association with the college. Presented to cadets in November of their second class (junior) year, it represents a milestone event during their time at VMI.

By this stage in their cadetship, they have survived the rigors of the Rat Line, have taken on some of the responsibility of running the Corps of Cadets, have forged lifelong friendships and seriously are thinking about what they will do following graduation.

Class rings first were presented at graduation in 1848, but their distribution varied from one class to another until the early 20th century. In 1927, however, every class from then on began to design its own ring, which over the years has grown larger and more extravagant. Each class had an elaborate and symbolic design with iconic images worked into the ring's side.

These iconic symbols clearly demonstrate just how much the school embraced the so-called Cult of the Lost Cause. The majority have petite images carved in them of the Stonewall Jackson statue, and any number of other symbols such as the Confederate battle flag and a portrayal of Robert E. Lee astride his war horse, Traveller.

Why such an obsession with the Confederacy and the Civil War? Both were central to VMI's heritage. Referred to as "The Confederacy's Cradle of Command" by one historian, the institute played a crucial role in the Southern war effort. When I attended

VMI, more than two-thirds of corps came from states of the former Confederacy.

More than 90% of its alumni, including a dozen generals, served in the Confederate army. Crucial to the war's narrative was the Battle of New Market, when the entire cadet corps turned an almost certain Confederate defeat of Union forces into a stunning victory in 1864.

After many years of resisting, the school eventually integrated in 1968, and when the first five African Americans became members of the Class of 1972, their class ring prominently featured a large image of the Stonewall Jackson statue and the words "tradition" and "change" on it. Stonewall Jackson and other Confederate symbols were featured on class rings until recent years, when celebrating the Lost Cause increasingly became controversial.

Jackson had an important but relatively brief association with the school. A graduate of West Point, he served as an unpopular and not so effective professor of physics for nearly 10 years. Cadets made fun of him behind his back, calling him "Tom Fool." Nevertheless, he is regarded as one of the Civil War's greatest tacticians.

Had there been no Civil War, however, he, much like Ulysses S. Grant, probably would have died in obscurity. Finally, Jackson fought for a cause founded on the defense of slavery, and we all can be thankful that the Union prevailed in the most costly of American wars.

The time has come for VMI to look at other iconic figures that all cadets can admire.

As VMI looks to the future, I suggest that it embrace two graduates who can serve as models for every cadet, regardless of race or gender - George Catlett Marshall and Jonathan Daniels.

In addition to being graduates of the institute (where Marshall served as regimental commander and Daniels as his class's valedictorian), both exemplified a key principle inculcated in every VMI alumnus - service above self.

Marshall went on to a career that would make him one of the most significant figures of the 20th century.

Serving as chief of staff of the Army during World War II, he bore the responsibility for organizing, training and deploying American troops throughout the globe. He was principal adviser to President Franklin D. Roosevelt in the prosecution of the war.

With the war's end, he was appointed secretary of state, where he led the reconstruction of Europe and Japan through the Marshall Plan. After stepping down from the U.S. State Department, President Harry Truman tapped him to lead the Department of Defense. In 1953, he was awarded the Nobel Peace Prize - the only career soldier to receive that signal honor. Winston Churchill described him as "the architect of victory."

Jonathan Myrick Daniels, VMI Class of 1961, was a civil rights activist who was murdered in 1965 by a special county deputy in Haynesville, Alabama, while shielding a Black protester, 16-year-old Ruby Sales, from a shotgun blast.

Both were working to desegregate public spaces and to register Black voters following passage of the Voting Rights Act by Congress earlier in the year. The death of Daniels generated further support for the civil rights movement.

Daniels eventually was designated as a martyr in the Episcopal Church, along with the Rev. Martin Luther King Jr.

In 1997, VMI established the Jonathan Daniels Humanitarian Award to recognize individuals for extraordinary service to humanity.

The latest Daniels Award was bestowed on the late John Lewis, member of the U.S. House of Representatives from Georgia and civil rights activist. In addition, VMI created an arch into the barracks and adjoining courtyard in memory of Daniels.

VMI has much to be proud of. Proclaiming that "the measure of a college lies in the quality and performance of its graduates and their contributions to society," the school's record of alumni who have distinguished themselves in a wide variety of endeavors can be matched by few colleges its size.

Former Secretary of Defense and retired Marine Corps General James Mattis addressed this in 2019 when he spoke to the corps: "I have had [VMI] graduates serve around me, above me, under me and there is a debt this country owes you that goes back many decades for a school that develops this sense of service before self, of putting others first."

From now on, let the rings the cadets wear represent men and women who can be admired for what they did to best serve the United States of America and contributed to its greatness.

Richmond *Times-Dispatch*, November 15, 2020

8

VMI's Civil Rights Hero

When I attended VMI in the late 1960s, the school was very much a Southern institution. About three-fourths of the all-white corps of cadets came from former Confederate states. The Civil War was central to the Institute's heritage.

Referred to by one historian as the "Confederacy's Cradle of Command," VMI played a crucial role in the Southern war effort. More than 90 percent of its alumni, including a dozen generals, served in the Confederate army.

Every May 15, the corps performed a solemn ceremony honoring the ten cadets who died in battle, with "Dixie" playing in the background by the VMI band.

Even after the landmark 1954 Supreme Court decision outlawing segregation, VMI remained an all-white school for another 15 years, except for a handful of cadets from Asia. The school finally integrated in 1968, making it the last state-supported college in Virginia, and one of the last in the country, to do so.

So how is it that this bastion of the South became the alma mater of a person who would be recognized as one of 15 martyrs by the Episcopal Church in England's Canterbury Cathedral for his work as a civil rights activist? Jonathan M. Daniels certainly did not fit the image of the typical "VMI type."

***

A native of New Hampshire, Daniels could have attended any number of excellent colleges in New England. Instead, he

chose the Virginia Military Institute, later described by novelist Pat
Conroy as "an austere grotto of Spartan military life."

A cadet private during his four years at VMI, he
nevertheless excelled in academics as an English major. Chosen as
valedictorian of the class of 1961, he addressed his classmates with
these prophetic words: "We have spent four years in preparation
for something. What that something is or who we are, we do not
know." Few would have guessed what that "something" would
have been for Daniels.

He received a prestigious Danforth Fellowship for post-
graduate study in English literature at Harvard, where he enrolled
the following fall. During an Easter service the following year,
however, he said he felt called to follow God in the ministry. He
then left Harvard and enrolled in the Episcopal Theological School,
in Cambridge, Massachusetts.

Although engrossed in his seminary studies, in the spring of
1965 Daniels responded to a call from the Rev. Martin Luther King
Jr. for fellow clergy to come to Alabama and join in the civil rights
movement.

With several other fellow seminarians, Daniels was granted
permission to spend the rest of the semester in Alabama working
on voter registration and marching in demonstrations.

After several months in the South, he returned to the
seminary to take his semester examinations, only to go back to
Alabama a few weeks later. He lived in Selma with an African-
American family and worked long hours to provide assistance to
black families in need, tutor young people, and tirelessly register
black voters.

***

In August, Daniels and twenty-nine protesters were arrested
in Fort Deposit, Alabama, for demonstrating in front of whites-only
stores. Transported in a garbage truck to the jail in nearby Hayne-

ville most of the demonstrators were detained for six days in stifling cells without air-conditioning.

Finally released without explanation and with no transportation back to Fort Deposit, Daniels, Catholic priest Richard Morrisroe, and two teenagers, Joyce Bailey and Ruby Sales, took off on foot.

Parched by the blazing Alabama sun, the four stopped at a nearby general store to buy soft drinks. As they approached the door, they were confronted by an angry Tom Coleman holding a shotgun.

Coleman, a former deputy sheriff, pointed the weapon at Sales, and shouted, "Leave or I'll blow your damn brains out!" Daniels shoved the teenager out of the way, just as Coleman's gun discharged, hitting the seminarian full blast in the stomach. He died instantly. Morrisroe was wounded by a second shot, but survived.

Coleman left the scene and turned himself in to local authorities. Months later, a grand jury indicted him for manslaughter rather than murder based in part on his claim of self-defense, with the assertion that Daniels had pulled a knife on him. An all-white jury then declared him innocent.

***

Other than a brief obituary in the *Alumni Review* in the fall of 1965, VMI did not formally recognize Daniels for his act of extraordinary courage for another 32 years.

But in 1997, the board of visitors voted to establish the Jonathan M. Daniels '61 Humanitarian Award to recognize people who have made "significant sacrifices to protect or improve the lives of others."

It also named one of the four archways in the VMI barracks and a memorial courtyard for Daniels. While the other three entrances honor men who achieved fame in the military - George Washington, Stonewall Jackson, and George C. Marshall - the Daniels Arch honors a hero of a different sort.

Although VMI was late in recognizing Daniels, I am proud of my alma mater and its effort to honor what Dr. King said was "one of the most heroic Christian deeds of which I have heard in my entire ministry."

Richmond *Times-Dispatch*, February 17, 2019

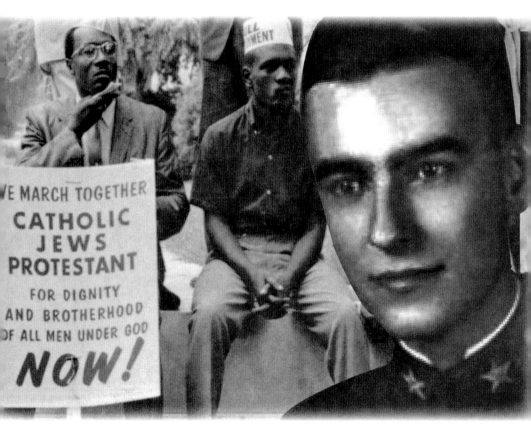

Jonathan M. Daniels

9

The button: a symbol of perseverance

When I talk to young people who say they are interested in going to the Virginia Military Institute (VMI) or a federal service academy, I always ask them: Are you sure you want this? I remind them that there are plenty of easier ways to earn a college degree, but if that's what they want, go for it.

With that in mind, imagine the reaction my wife and I had when we were sitting around the dinner table one evening in 1988 talking with our teenage daughter about where she might want to attend college.

Because she had strong academic and extracurricular activity records, not to mention high SAT scores, she could think about applying to some highly competitive colleges. That's when she dropped a bombshell on us by saying, "I think I might be interested in the Air Force Academy."

After picking ourselves up off of the floor, her mother and I asked why she was interested in the U.S. Air Force Academy. She mentioned the appeal of the challenge it offered, the desire to do something different and the prospect of learning to fly.

No doubt, some of her interest came from family. One of her grandfathers was a decorated World War II veteran and had been a professor at VMI. I had graduated from VMI. Her mother grew up on the VMI post. Both of her uncles and two of her first cousins were institute alumni.

Left - The Bryan family (Cammy, Charles, Alethea, and Charlie) in front of the statue of Tecumseh at the U.S. Naval Academy, November 1991.

You therefore would think she would be interested in VMI. But the school still was all-male then and would not open its doors for women until 1997, after being ordered to do so by the U.S. Supreme Court the previous year.

By her junior year of high school, she was ready to begin the arduous process of applying to the Air Force Academy, in addition to the University of Virginia and Duke University. It soon became evident that getting into a service academy takes hard work and patience.

In addition to having high SAT scores and an outstanding academic record, she needed to demonstrate leadership skills, and participation in some form of athletics. She had to be in top physical condition. And finally, she had to receive an appointment from either our congressional representative or one of Virginia's U.S. senators.

In the beginning, the Air Force Academy was her first choice, but when we mentioned this to a family friend, he asked our daughter if she had considered the U.S. Naval Academy in Annapolis, Maryland. His sister worked there and was happy to arrange a visit. At first our daughter was reluctant to go, saying she preferred the Air Force, but we persuaded her to at least look at the Naval Academy.

So, in April of her junior year, we drove up to Annapolis to see what it had to offer. On a beautiful spring day, with flowers and forsythia in full bloom, the admissions office arranged a full tour of the grounds led by a sharp female midshipman.

Late that afternoon, we headed back to Richmond with our daughter now interested in the school. When she received her letter of admission from the Naval Academy later in the fall before hearing from any other school, she immediately accepted and began preparing to become a member of the brigade of midshipmen.

Fast forward to July 9, 1991, Induction or "I Day" at the Naval Academy. The four of us, including our son, drove to

Annapolis the day before our daughter was to report. Having gone through the Rat Line at VMI, I had some sense of the difficulty she would be facing as a plebe, and it concerned me.

If she was like I was when I was 18 years old, at times, she would be tempted to drop out and transfer to a college less demanding. She was beginning the greatest challenge of her young life. One has to experience it to fully comprehend its difficulty.

I had been trying to think of something she could carry with her to help give her strength in the coming months - a good luck talisman of some sort. Then it came to me: one of the brass buttons from my full-dress VMI uniform.

So, just as we got ready to leave for Annapolis, I quietly slipped up to our attic and snipped a button off of my full-dress uniform ("coatee") and put it in my pocket.

That evening the four of us went to dinner in Annapolis, which took on the atmosphere of a prisoner's last meal. As we waited for our dessert, I pulled the VMI button out and handed it to my daughter, saying, "This button went through four difficult years with me at VMI, and I'm giving it to you to help see you through your next four years."

As she took it, tears welled up in my eyes, and before long all four of us had tears rolling down our cheeks.

After a fitful night's sleep, we drove over to the academy, where our daughter spent most of the day getting registered, vaccinated, issued uniforms, a haircut and seemingly a million other things.

In the meantime, the three of us nervously waited until 5 o'clock that evening when the entire plebe class was marched into "T Court" in front of massive Bancroft Hall where they were sworn into the Navy.

After raising her right hand and saying, "I solemnly swear that I will support and defend the Constitution of the Unites States against all enemies, foreign and domestic ...," our daughter now belonged to Uncle Sam and no longer to us.

She and her 1,100 classmates were ordered to fall out and were given 10 minutes to say goodbye to their families. Amid many tears and hugs, we parted ways as she walked through the giant doorway into Bancroft Hall, her life never to be the same.

Four years later, we watched with immense pride as she walked across the stage to receive her diploma, graduating with distinction and ranking in the top 10% of her class. Following the ceremony, we greeted each other warmly.

As I hugged my daughter, she reached into her pocket and pulled out her VMI button. She then told me that it not only brought her good luck, it helped several of her classmates. When word got around that she had a "magic button," they would borrow it for good luck while taking a difficult exam.

Alethea Bryan at her 1995 graduation parade from the Naval Academy, where she served as 4th Company Executive Officer her senior year.

The story does not end there. Two years later, when our son prepared to enter VMI, our daughter passed the button on to him, but this time with a brass button from one of her Naval Academy uniforms tied to it. He then carried those buttons with him for the next four years until he graduated with high honors in 2000.

Eight years later at a dinner in my honor when I retired early from the Virginia Historical Society because of Parkinson's disease, my children were asked to make remarks about their dad.

They said some nice thing about me and their mom, and as they ended their remarks, my son reached into his pocket, saying he wanted to give me something that would help me in the battle I had ahead of me. He then handed me three buttons, now including one from his VMI uniform.

Since then, I have given buttons to certain young men and women as they prepared to enter VMI. So far it has brought good luck to each recipient.

Not long ago, I ran into a young man whom I had helped get into VMI. Without my asking, he pulled out his wallet and reached in to show me the button I gave him 12 years before. He said it continued to bring him good luck.

Magic? No, but I think it serves as a reminder to never quit and as a result, you will never regret the decision to stay the course.

Where are they now?

After graduating from the Naval Academy, Alethea Bryan spent seven years of active duty in the Navy, including two tours in the Persian Gulf on a guided missile cruiser and an aircraft carrier. She spent her last two years of service at the Office of Naval Intelligence in Suitland, Maryland.

While stationed in Norfolk, she met her husband, Glenn Gerding, who graduated from the University of North Carolina Phi Beta Kappa, a Judge Advocate General (JAG) officer, now a captain in the Navy Reserve, and an appellate defender for the state of North Carolina. Alethea is the managing editor of three scientific and medical journals. The couple has two boys, Graham and Jackson, and lives in Chapel Hill, North Carolina.

Charles Bryan III graduated from VMI in 2000 with a degree in computer science with high honors. Unable to qualify for a commission in the armed services because of asthma, he, nevertheless, installed computer systems on Navy warships at Dahlgren.

While at VMI, he met Angela Roman, a student at neighboring Washington & Lee University, where she graduated with high honors. She earned her doctorate of medicine from Virginia Commonwealth University School of Medicine. She holds the rank of lieutenant colonel and is a pediatric rheumatologist at Fort Lewis, Washington.

Charles is a senior lecturer in computer science at the University of Washington-Tacoma. They have a daughter, Olivia.

Richmond *Times-Dispatch*, June 6, 2021

VMI Cadet Charles F. Bryan, III

Left - We looked sharp as we marched past the reviewing stand.

10

MEMORIES OF AN INAUGURATION

Fifty-two years ago I experienced the coldest day of my life. It was January 20, 1969, and as a first-classman (senior) at the Virginia Military Institute, I, along with some 250 of my classmates had been invited to represent the Commonwealth of Virginia in the inaugural parade honoring the recently elected 37th President Richard M. Nixon.

Were we excited about this opportunity to participate in a historic event that would place VMI in the national limelight? Hardly. It wasn't because of Nixon, who had overwhelmingly won a presidential straw poll of the corps the previous fall. It was the fact that we had just returned from Christmas furlough to the bleak, cold VMI barracks, and we were in no mood to march in any parade. But when word came down from Governor Mills Godwin's office in Richmond that we, along with Virginia Tech's "Highty Tighty" military marching band, would represent Virginia in the parade, we could grumble all we wanted to no avail. We had to march in the parade whether we wanted to or not.

Ensuring that we would represent VMI well, we practiced nearly every day leading up to the big parade. Of course, many of us continued to grouse about having to participate, but the closer we got to January 20, dread turned to acceptance. We would appear on national TV, and a few of us thought this was something we could tell our grandchildren.

In the wee morning hours of January 20 we were roused from a deep sleep, quietly marched down to the mess hall in the frigid dark for breakfast, and returned to barracks to pick up our M-1 rifles or sabers for cadet officers. Loaded on to a dozen buses, we arrived four hours later at Bolling Air Force base where we groggily stepped off of the stuffy buses and were greeted by numbing cold. We changed into our overcoats with their brilliant red capes pulled open and white cross web belts put on. Despite our initial reluctance to be in the parade, we were determined to look and march better than any other unit. Even the grubbiest cadet private looked sharp with all leather and brass shined to a high gleam.

We reboarded our buses and headed to the assembly area in downtown Washington near the Mall. Although we had been warned that temperatures would hover in the teens, most of us were ill-prepared to stand around in our wool overcoats in the assembly area for nearly two hours. The old adage of military life of "hurry up and wait" took on a whole new meaning as a breeze picked up. Soon most of us were shivering and our feet began to feel like blocks of ice.

Then all of sudden we were surrounded by a large group of scruffy looking anti-war protestors shouting, "Baby killers!" None of us were exactly sure how to respond. The regular Army officers who accompanied us warned us not to confront these "hippies" unless we were physically attacked. Thankfully the discipline that had been instilled in us during our time at VMI held, and violence was avoided. For that matter, an always courteous classmate said to one protester: "Hey, man, we're no baby killers. These rifles don't even have firing pins in them." The protester looked blankly back at him, not sure how to respond.

After about an hour the demonstrators were unable to get us to respond to their taunts and left us to confront another group in the parade. Nevertheless, they had delayed us nearly an hour.

Finally, the order was given, and forming up behind the Highty Tighty marching band, we stepped off in a battalion mass formation with our cadet first captain, Chris L'Orange, and his regimental staff in the lead. As one newspaper reported, we marched "flawlessly" and that we were treated to an unexpected compliment when President Nixon turned to his family and pointed out the VMI unit. His daughter, Tricia, then blew kisses at us as we marched by.

After another half hour of marching, we finally ended the parade near George Washington University just as it was getting dark. We were once again confronted by screaming demonstrators who were held back by the D.C. police. Cold and exhausted, we climbed back on our buses to return to Lexington, where we arrived at around 11:00 that evening.

Many of us felt that our time would have been better spent staying at VMI, but when we heard from parents who had watched the parade with pride as the corps passed in review on national TV, the unpleasant memories began to fade. A full-page cover photograph of parading cadets in LIFE magazine a week later further countered the grumbling.

It's a shame that recent events have made it impossible to hold a proper inauguration of a new administration, which, every four years is a celebration of America no less so than the Fourth of July.

As the years slip by, the bone chilling cold I experienced on January 20, 1969, has long faded to a warm memory of my youth during troubled yet hopeful times.

Richmond *Times-Dispatch*, January 21, 2021

We practiced on the parade ground every day leading up to the 1969 inaugural parade. It paid off. The day after the parade, one newspaper reported that the VMI unit marched "flawlessly."

11

IS VMI BEING PICKED ON?

My alma mater, the Virginia Military Institute, has been the subject of considerable media attention this year, much of it negative. Extensive exposes in TIME magazine, the Washington *Post,* and a variety of electronic media have painted a picture of a college where racial insults are regularly directed at Black cadets; where female cadets are subjected to unwanted sexual advances; where the school's vaunted honor system has been unfairly singled out Black cadets for violations of the code; and where the school's long-standing embrace of its Confederate heritage seems out of step in today's highly charged political atmosphere.

Like most alums, I was disturbed when this information came out. VMI is better than that, or at least it should be.

On the one hand I am concerned that such conduct could be allowed to go on at the school or any college for that matter. On the other hand, I wondered about the accuracy of these news accounts. I have a son and a nephew who graduated respectively in 2000 and 2017, who assured me that they had never witnessed or heard of any such thing during their four years as cadets. I will be even more disturbed, however, if the information contained in the media stories turns out to be true.

There is no question that for decades, VMI has only reluctantly faced the issues relating to race and gender. From as early as 1953, for example, African Americans contacted the school about applying for admission. All such inquiries were politely rejected with no explanation given. Even after the 1954 Supreme Court decision outlawing segregation in public schools, VMI would not open its doors to Blacks for another fourteen years, my first class or senior year.

On the other hand, in 1953, Virginia Tech admitted its first Black who joined the school's cadet corps, making it the first public college in Virginia to integrate. VMI would be the last to do so.

While the federal service academies enrolled their first women in 1976, females had to wait until 1997 to apply and be admitted to VMI.

VMI did not make these changes willingly or easily. They were one of two American colleges that did so under a ruling from the U.S. Supreme Court. As a matter of fact, when I graduated from VMI in 1969, there were 214 all male colleges in the United States. All but three of those schools made the move to coeducation voluntarily and in response to fundamental changes in a society that was becoming increasingly inclusive and diverse in its make-up.

Despite its reluctance to change, VMI is held to a higher standard than other colleges. It should be.

VMI has been taken to task by the media, members of the General Assembly, and Governor Ralph Northam, a VMI alumnus, for its lack of diversity. The Institute has responded in part by appointing its first Black superintendent, Major General Cedric Wins (VMI '85); Kasey Meredith as the first woman to serve as its regimental commander; and Colonel Jamica Love as director of diversity, who is charged with ensuring that the make-up of the corps represents the increasing diversity of the people of Virginia.

Under the leadership of former superintendent General J. H. Binford Peay, the school has reached new levels of academic exellence and has become one of the nation's premier ROTC programs.

Recently, the issue of diversity has overshadowed those positive aspects of VMI. In addition, the Institute reports that despite the impression of lack of diversity, the number of Blacks in the corps of cadets is already in line with other Virginia colleges. With 7 percent of the corps Black, that number equals William & Mary's student body which stands at 7 percent. It compares favorably with other Virginia colleges such as the University of Virginia with a Black enrollment of 6.2 percent and Virginia Tech which stands at only 4 percent. VMI's next door neighbor, Washington & Lee University, which is private, trails all of the colleges I surveyed with only 3.8 percent.   If one counts online students as part of its total, Lynchburg's Liberty University claims a black enrollment of 14.6 percent. VCU, however, stands out with the most diverse student body among Virginia colleges with a 17.5 percent Black student enrollment. The statistical information given above and below was gleaned from the websites of each school.

How does VMI compare with other military colleges -- the federal service academies and the so-called "senior military colleges" that offer a more concentrated ROTC program than others? While West Point stands out with a 12 percent Black presence, VMI has a larger percentage of Blacks than the Naval Academy (6.9 percent), Air Force Academy (6.6 percent) and Coast Guard Academy (4.9 percent). It, however, trails The Citadel, South Carolina's state military college, with its 7.9 percent.

With a female enrollment of 14 percent, VMI lags behind most of the other military schools. The brigade of midshipmen at the Naval Academy, for example, now is 27 percent female, while the Coast Guard Academy is 38 percent women. West Point and the Air Force Academy each have approximately 22 percent women enrolled. The Citadel reports that 13 percent of its corps is composed of women.

Regardless of statistics, the question of how Blacks and women are treated at VMI frankly is more important. Are females at VMI at greater risk of sexual assault than at other colleges? Do women in leadership positions within the corps receive the same respect as their white counterparts? Are Blacks unfairly targeted for honor violations, and banished from VMI with little hope of ever being reinstated in the corps? Do white cadets, particularly males, receive preferential treatment over their non-white counterparts?

If VMI can provide meaningful and effective responses to those questions and more, it will not only survive the current crisis, it will thrive as it has many times in its long history.

PART III
HISTORY: MYTH AND REALITY

The late southern writer John Egerton argued that there are essentially three kinds of history: "what actually happened; what we are told happened; and what we finally believe happened." He contended that the third of those forms of history "is the ultimate shaper of our individual and collective understanding, belief, and identity." He might have added that our views of the past can change over time and that history is not just an agreed upon list of facts, dates, and events. By using that approach, history becomes a deadly boring method by which many of us were taught history in the 1950's and 60's. The following essays show how given the same set of facts, dates, and events, people can and do interpret the past in different ways.

12

HOW HISTORY CHANGES OVER THE YEARS

One of the most valuable courses I took when I earned my Ph.D. in history was a graduate seminar on historiography, the study of how history is researched and interpreted over time. We learned that the same set of facts presented to one historian may be interpreted in different ways by another, according to his perception of those facts and how they are presented.

I was reminded of this recently when I discovered a box of books in our attic that were at one time part of my personal library when I was growing up. Included in the stash were a dozen or so Landmark Books.

I loved Landmark Books because the subject matter in them was all history. The series, which was published from 1951 to 1970, consisted of nearly 200 books, mostly on U.S. history and all geared to middle school readers.

Among the Landmarks Books in my collection were *Thirty Seconds Over Tokyo*, *Robert E. Lee and the Road to Glory*, and *Daniel Boone and the Opening of the Frontier*.

Another item in the box was *The Golden Play Book of American History Stamps*, originally published in 1952 by Simon & Schuster.

With forty-eight color picture stamps of historical events and written narratives for each, you affixed the square 2.5 inch by 2.5 inch stamps to the appropriate page. I don't know when I acquired the stamp book, but it probably was the first overview of American history I ever read.

At the bottom of the box I found a high school textbook on American history published in the late 1940s that my older sister had apparently used. In its preface, co-authors Gertrude and John Southworth promised teachers that their volume was more comprehensive than other textbooks in use then.

***

As I thumbed through all of these books, reading certain passages and looking at the pictures, I began to realize that I have had an abiding love of history since the earliest days of my youth. But when I examined them more closely, I began to understand how incomplete and one-sided they were, something I was truly blind to when I read them nearly sixty years ago.

The history they presented reflected attitudes and opinions relating to race and gender in the 1950s.

Take, for example, my *Golden Play Book of Stamps*. I was struck by how incomplete the story of America it was. The stamps were dominated by dozens of illustrations of white men - except for one with a woman holding a baby standing behind Daniel Boone, another with Sacajawea, and one - if you count statuary - with the Statue of Liberty.

The African-American experience was confined to a brief passage on the hostility between North and South over the issue of the spread of slavery into the West before the Civil War.

But it was the textbook that caught my attention the most, as it conjured up images worthy of *Gone With the Wind*. Margaret Mitchell could have written its description of the antebellum South, as is evident in the following excerpt:

"Plantation life in the South was very pleasant. The master of the house spent his time in overseeing the labor of the slaves, in hunting, in taking long rides through the country on his fine, thoroughbred horse, or entertaining at his home. ... The women spent their time in sewing ... and in entertaining at the great balls which were frequently given in their grand plantation houses."

For those held in bondage, the account went this way:

"The slaves usually led a happy life. ... They had good food and warm clothing. When their daily work was done they were allowed to go to their cabins. ... There they could sing and dance, and enjoy themselves in other ways. ... Except that they received no pay, their lot was much like that any other servants."

Its description of Reconstruction was standard fare for the history curriculum in the 1950s. In a section titled "Negro Rule," the authors observed:

"The rule of the Negroes, the carpetbaggers, and the scalawags was a terrible period for all of the southern states. ... Negroes swaggered through the streets, and neither the life nor the property of any white man was safe."

But because "white men knew that Negroes as a class are superstitious," they formed the Ku Klux Klan, who dressed in white robes to look like ghosts. With the rise of the Klan, "unscrupulous scalawags and Negroes who were abusing their power were driven from their places, and white men regained the balance of power."

***

Reading passages like those reinforced something that I learned in my historiography seminar: Our views of the past are shaped by the present. When those books were published half a century ago, America, particularly the South, was a segregated society. Legal separation of the races was prevalent throughout the former states of the Confederacy, and was practiced in many other sections of the country.

Career opportunities for women outside of the home were limited mainly to teaching, nursing, and secretarial work. Jokes making fun of certain ethnic groups and races were commonly told. The thought of a person of color or someone with a Hispanic name serving as a federal judge or a member of Congress was almost inconceivable.

When I hear someone lamenting how unfortunate it is that history is not taught like it was, I'm tempted to say, "Thank God." The history being taught today (particularly in Virginia) is richer, fuller, and frankly more interesting than what I was taught half a century ago.

The American population is changing and diversifying rapidly. Over the next five decades, the majority of population growth will be linked to Hispanic and Asian immigration. With this trend, the history that was written in the mid-20th century will become even more anachronistic than it is today. I wonder how anachronistic the history being written today will be?

Richmond *Times-Dispatch*, December 4, 2016

13

DON'T KNOW MUCH ABOUT HISTORY?

Several influential commentators have argued that we face a crisis of historical amnesia in America. Lynne Cheney, wife of the former vice president, has declared "a refusal to remember the past is a primary characteristic of our nation."

Pulitzer Prize-winning historian David McCullough has warned, "We, in our time, are raising a new generation of Americans, who, to an alarming degree, are historically illiterate."

A former president of the American Historical Association lamented that "the public ignorance of our cultural heritage has alarming implications for the future of our nation."

I have questioned the assertions that historical illiteracy is a new problem. I am not convinced that previous generations of Americans were more knowledgeable about history. But it seems that a basic understanding of American history should be an important requisite for certain people, particularly anyone holding the nation's top elected office.

Most of our presidents have had a least some knowledge of history, and several actually were good, albeit amateur, historians. Harry Truman was a voracious reader of history, and probably knew the subject better than any president. U.S. Grant's memoir is regarded by many scholars as the most insightful and best-written autobiography of any president.

Theodore Roosevelt published several highly regarded books on American history. Woodrow Wilson came to the presidency with a Ph.D. and with an impressive record of scholarly publications in history and American government.

***

How about our current president? His recent gaffes over Frederick Douglass, Andrew Jackson, the Civil War, and American diplomatic history concern me. As columnist George Will recently observed: "What is most alarming (and mortifying to the University of Pennsylvania, from which he graduated) is not that Trump has entered his eighth decade unscathed by even elementary knowledge about the nation's history. Rather, the dangerous thing is that he does not know what it is to know something."

President Trump has made immigration reform a major part of his agenda, arguing that people seeking citizenship should receive "extreme vetting" before being allowed to join the American family.

One could argue that candidates seeking the presidency should also receive "extreme vetting" to demonstrate their qualifications for the job. Therefore we should expect our president to have at least a basic understanding of American history.

With that in mind, I suggest that any person seeking the presidency be required to pass the same test given to immigrants seeking U.S. citizenship. The current one requires immigrants to answer numerous questions covering American history and civics.

***

Here are some sample questions based on the examination given by the U.S. Citizenship and Immigration Service that we could ask presidential candidates:

1. Who was the principal author of the U.S. Constitution?

2. Who did the U.S. fight in World War II?

3. During the Cold War, what was the main concern of the United States?

4. Name one war fought by the United States in the 1800s.

5. Who is the author of the Declaration of Independence?

6. Name one American Indian tribe.

7. What was Martin Luther King Jr.'s role in American history?

8. The Federalist Papers supported the passage of the U.S. Constitution. Name one of its authors.

9. Name a reason immigrants came to the American colonies.

10. What did Susan B. Anthony do?

11. What territory did the U.S. buy from France in 1803?

12. Who was president when that purchase from France was made?

13. Who was president during World War I?

14. In what war was the U.S. capital captured and burned?

15. What did the Emancipation Proclamation do?

16. Name one issue that led to the Civil War.

17. What are two rights described in the Declaration of Independence?

18. The idea of self-government is in the first three words of the Constitution. What are they?

19. How many amendments does the Constitution have?

20. What are two rights everyone living in the U.S. is guaranteed?

(Answers at bottom of page)

***

I wonder how the current president would fare on this examination. From what he has demonstrated so far, I doubt that he would do well unless he spent more nights boning up on the subject rather than Tweeting.

In an interview, David McCullough noted that in Trump "we have put someone in the pilot seat who has never flown a plane before; who doesn't know how government works; who has no interest in the history of the country and said so on more than one occasion; who (until recently) has never read a book about the presidency or a biography of a president and claims ... that he doesn't need to read books because he knows so much intuitively."

In oft-cited quote of Thomas Jefferson's somehow seems appropriate now: "If a nation expects to be ignorant and free in a state of civilization, it expects what never was and never will be."

Answers to Bryan questions

1. James Madison

2. Germany, Japan, and Italy

3. The spread of Communism

4. War of 1812, Mexican-American War, Civil War, Indian Wars, Spanish-American War

5. Thomas Jefferson

6. Cheyenne, Mohegan, Lakota, Teton, Cherokee, Chippewa, Apache, Blackfeet, Arawak, Huron, Seminole, Hopi, Navajo, Choctaw, Iroquois, Shawnee, Oneida, Crow, Inuit, Sioux, Pueblo, Creek

7. Civil Rights

8. Alexander Hamilton, James Madison, John Jay

9. To escape tyranny, for religious freedom, for economic freedom, to enrich themselves

10. Fought for women's rights

11. Louisiana

12. Thomas Jefferson

13. Woodrow Wilson

14. War of 1812

15. It freed the slaves

16. Slavery, tariffs, states rights

17. Life, liberty, and the pursuit of happiness

18. "We the People"

19. Twenty-seven

20. Freedom of speech, freedom of assembly, freedom to petition the government, freedom of religion, the right to bear arms

---

Richmond *Times-Dispatch*, June 4, 2017

14

CONSPIRACY THEORIES AND "FAKE HISTORY"

L ast Fourth of July, my wife and I attended a brass band concert of toe-tapping patriotic music, including my favorite, John Philip Sousa's "Liberty Bell March" and ending with his always popular "Stars and Stripes Forever."

We enjoyed the concert, but throughout it, I kept thinking about the assertion a man made as he handed out copies of the U.S. Constitution to all concertgoers. With each copy he distributed, he opined, "Be sure to read this because it's not being taught in school anymore."

Really?

I wondered if that assertion could be true. So when I returned home, I went online and randomly selected half a dozen states scattered throughout the country and looked at their public school's learning standards as they related to the teaching of the U.S. Constitution.

Lo and behold, I found that all of these states did, indeed, teach the Constitution, although some went into greater depth than others.

Also, last year I was a speaker at a patriotic society dinner at which one of the other speakers observed with a straight face that: "George Washington isn't even mentioned in history textbooks anymore," to which a seemingly knowledgeable audience nodded in agreement.

Again, to check the accuracy of that assertion, I later examined several college and high school American history textbooks currently in use, and every one gave our country's first president his due.

Some people contend that there is a conspiracy by educators to emphasize the negative aspects of our past and drop mentioning anything that frames the United States positively. Why do we have to teach our students certain disturbing aspects of our nation's history such as the lynching of African Americans or how we mistreated Indians? That concerns me.

Manipulating or fabricating the facts of history to suit one's argument is unethical according to the principles of scholarship proclaimed by the American Historical Association. These standards are notably similar to those prescribed to journalists. It was one of the first things we learned in graduate school, along with several other ethical canons. These include:

Do not plagiarize. Do not ignore contradictory evidence. Reveal any biases you might have. "Tell it like it was" based on solid factual evidence. Do not intentionally distort evidence to prove a point.

Indeed, we historians stress the importance of basing our arguments upon correct information, and we strive to practice what we preach. There is a term referred to as "historical denialism," which means a misrepresentation of the historical record to reinforce one's argument. Examples of this kind of distortion of the past include denying the Holocaust, the Armenian genocide and Japanese war crimes.

A textbook used in Virginia public schools as late as 2010 posited that thousands of African Americans fought in the Confederate army, including two black battalions under the command of Stonewall Jackson, an assertion that was not made until the last quarter of the 20th century and lacks solid evidence to support it.

George Orwell portrayed denialism in his novel *1984*. In addition to practicing the deliberate distortion of current events, Orwell's fictional nation of Oceania is ruled by The Party that employs the Thought Police to eliminate independent thinking and individuality. The novel is set in a time when the government relies on intentional misrepresentation of the facts, secret surveillance and the blatant manipulation of historical evidence to substantiate its arguments. An independent free press has been eliminated, thereby allowing only state-sponsored information to be used to inform the public.

We can find real examples of Orwell's portrayal of the deliberate manipulation of information about the past during the last century by a central authority in Nazi Germany, the Soviet Union, Communist China and North Korea.

There is another, almost opposing form of denialism, however, that in its use has become influential today - social media. Whether it is current events or history related, information coming out of social media often is unfiltered and unedited for its accuracy.

Conspiracy theories are nothing new, but abound now on social media such as the so-called "birther movement" that denied the legitimacy of the Obama administration under the claim that he was not born in the United States. Nation of Islam's leader Louis Farrakhan has contended that the federal government deliberately created AIDS in an attempt to decrease the nation's African American population. Both sides of the current impeachment debate have resorted to conspiracy theories in an attempt to reveal the treachery of their political opponents.

On the surface these theories seem outlandish. Most reasoned people do not accept these reported conspiracies as legitimate, although the current president seems all too frequently swayed by them. He and others who depend on the social media as legitimate sources of information would do us all a favor if they did some simple background investigation rather than accepting them at face value.

Richmond *Times-Dispatch*, December 8, 2019

15

WHAT SHOULD BE DONE WITH THE STATUES?

UNITING, NOT DIVIDING

Images of the shocking death of George Floyd by a police officer in Minneapolis have led to a violent reaction that has spanned the globe. Cities and towns throughout the United States and beyond have seen peaceful demonstrations turn into bloody confrontations between law enforcement officers and protesters.

Richmond has not been immune from this violence that has been caused in part by Floyd's death, but also another issue that has festered in this city for years - what to do with its Confederate heritage.

Two weekends ago, the citizens of Richmond woke up to the news that all of the Confederate statues on Monument Avenue had been spray-painted with profanity-laced demands for their removal. Several days later, Governor Ralph Northam announced that the Robert E. Lee statue, which is state property, would be removed and put in storage until its fate can be determined. Richmond Mayor Levar Stoney then proclaimed the removal of other Confederate statues.

Across the city, people of all backgrounds celebrated the decision. But not everybody was happy as some expressed disappointment and even outrage over the decision.

Cries for Northam's impeachment are being bandied about. Homeowners on Monument Avenue worry that property values will drop without its iconic statues. A former Richmond Chamber of Commerce official predicts a significant drop in tourism and its associated revenue. Confederate heritage groups contend the city is erasing its past and is ignoring their pleas to keep the statues in place. Frankly, either way the city went on this issue, hurt feelings, anger and possibly violence would have resulted.

How can we move forward from this dilemma? For one, we must recognize that naming public spaces or erecting statues of people runs the risk of falling out of favor when societal values change.

Never has the losing side of a civil war been treated with such leniency as the American South. None of its leaders was executed, nor was their property confiscated. And although slaves were freed as a result of the war, they were relegated to second-class citizenship. In the late 19th century, Southern state legislatures began passing Jim Crow laws that denied blacks the basic rights of American citizenship.

They were denied the right to vote or hold public office. They attended inferior segregated schools and had limited economic opportunity. They had little voice in the affairs of the city, including erecting statues of prominent Confederate figures. Richmond was anything but an inclusive city.

For most of the following century, Richmonders, both white and black, accepted these statues and Confederate flags as part of the city's cultural landscape. Even if African Americans objected to public displays of Confederate symbols, there was little they could do to stop or change them. By the 1960s, however, the civil rights movement began to run counter to Confederate glorification.

Iconic symbols, such as the Confederate battle flag, increasingly appeared at white pride rallies, in some cases with Nazi banners and on bumper stickers with slogans such as "The South Shall Rise Again" or "Forget Hell!" The argument that the South fought because of a disagreement with the federal government over states' rights began to be crushed under a mountain of evidence and subsequent scholarship that without the issue of slavery, there would have been no Civil War.

By the mid-20th century, African Americans little by little began to gain a foothold in Richmond.

Despite strong opposition from the white community, Richmond schools became integrated. Public transportation was no longer segregated. An increasing number of blacks were elected to public office, with L. Douglas Wilder becoming the nation's first black governor since Reconstruction.

As the number of descendants of slaves gained more power and influence in Richmond, vestiges of the Confederacy increasingly became anachronistic.

I must admit that part of me regrets the removal of the statues. Each has a story to tell and provides us with lessons from the past. What persuaded these men to break their oaths to protect and defend the U.S. Constitution? Did they own slaves? If so, how did they treat them? How did it feel to own another person? How would history have turned out had the cause for which they fought succeeded?

These questions will have to be asked somewhere other than Monument Avenue. Perhaps the statues of the Confederate generals could go to the Chancellorsville battlefield, where all four played a significant role in that overwhelming Confederate victory. And what about the empty circles where the statues stood as sentinels for so long? Other statues of famous people leave the door open for more disagreement and divisions within the community.

Instead, envision a grand fountain in Lee Circle and smaller fountains at the other circles. Lighted at night, these fountains could bring the community together rather than dividing it. They are something of which we could be proud.

It is regrettable that it has taken so long and the tragic death of someone 1,200 miles away to gain some form of resolution to a long simmering issue. I am reminded of the words of William Faulkner:

"We speak now against the day when our Southern people who will resist to the last these inevitable changes in social relations, will, when they have been forced to accept what they at one time might have accepted with dignity and goodwill, will say, Why didn't someone tell us this before? Tell us this in time?"

Richmond *Times-Dispatch*, June 14, 2020

16

Is the "End of Times" Near?
Reversing Growing Threats

When I was in high school, I worked with a couple of Jehovah's Witnesses who earnestly proclaimed the approaching "end of times." I have since heard these dire warnings many times during my 73 years, all of which I have readily dismissed.

Then came the COVID-19 pandemic that recently has made my imagination run wild at times. Life on Earth can't last forever, so why not now? This message of Earth's demise made me think of an influential prognosticator of the globe's fate - Thomas Malthus.

Malthus was an English cleric, scholar and economist who devoted most of his career to writing and lecturing on the living and the dead. His influential book, *An Essay on the Principle of Population*, published in 1798, and followed by numerous revisions, posited that world population would continue to surge until disease, famine, war or natural disaster reversed that trend.

Most philosophers of the 18th and early 19th centuries contended that progress was inevitable and that the human population would keep growing, eventually reaching a high standard of living or even utopia. Malthus, on the other hand, argued that available land for the production of food for humans was finite and that over time we would be unable to sustain ourselves.

"The power of population is indefinitely greater than the power to produce subsistence for man," he argued.

Furthermore, every effort to increase food production only can lead to a population increase that would more than cancel out the food supply, a state of affairs that became known as the "Malthusian Trap."

Achieving utopia was impossible, wrote Malthus. Humanity is doomed, and forever is at the edge of starvation. He also contended that charity only serves to slow the plight of the poor. As anthropological writer Charles Mann observes of Malthus, "No matter how big the banquet table grows, he believed that there will always be too many hungry people wanting a seat at the table."

The story of the human species is a continuing cycle of expansion and retraction.

Have his theories relating to the survival of the human race been proven valid? Take Malthus' premise that the world's population could double within 25 years barring natural disasters, pandemics, famines or major wars. In the 20th century, at least 50 million victims were claimed by the worldwide flu pandemic of 1918-19.

Add to that the death of nearly 80 million soldiers and civilians in the two world wars, and you would think that Malthus had it figured out. Despite those horrific numbers, the globe actually experienced a population explosion in the 20th century.

Although the number of years required exceeded Malthus's calculation, the peopling of the earth required just 40 years after 1950 to more than double from 2.5 billion to 6 billion. At the current rate it could reach more than 12 billion by the end of the century.

Where had Malthus gone wrong? Most important was that his calculation did not take any scientific developments into account. In his lifetime, germs, viruses and bacterial infections were unheard of. A lack of understanding about basic sanitation, personal hygiene, the importance of clean drinking water and a healthy diet meant that people lived short, dirty and often miserable lives.

The practice of medicine was no more sophisticated in 1798 than it had been for centuries. Physicians relied on concoctions of their own making that might have killed as many people as they cured. Bleeding of patients was common.

With no knowledge of their causes and how they spread, typhoid fever, malaria, measles and cholera periodically swept through towns and cities, leaving thousands of dead in their wake. When Malthus published his essay, the average life expectancy of a human only was about 25 years with infant mortality rates of 400 deaths per 1,000 live births.

Not until the late 19th century did doctors truly begin to embrace science in the practice of medicine. The germ theory gained acceptance, as did the importance of sanitation in treating patients. The education and licensing of physicians became standard.

Pharmaceuticals became strictly regulated by government authority and more effective in their application to patients. The public began to understand the importance of exercise and diet.

The development of public health systems was just as significant. Modern clinics and hospitals, staffed by trained medical personnel, spread throughout most developed countries. Government and private funding for medical research led to cures and improved treatment of numerous diseases. Mass inoculations for polio, smallpox, influenza and mumps have saved countless lives. Infant mortality rates have plunged to only about seven per 1,000 live births.

Scientific farming also has played a significant role in the population explosion. Take the United States, for example. Despite Malthus' prediction that population growth would result in less land for food production and eventual starvation, just the opposite has occurred. In 1870, about half of the American population lived on farms and produced enough food to feed the country's 38.5 million people.

According to the latest census, only 2% of the American population produces enough to feed 330 million people and to export to millions more abroad.

So is the "end of times" near? It could be if you believe Cambridge astronomer Martin Rees, who has been called the Malthus of our age. In his sobering book *Our Final Hour*, Rees calculates that we humans "are more at risk than at any phase in history" and have only a 50% chance of living until 2100.

The threat of our planet colliding with an asteroid is not new, nor is the increasing awareness of ever-growing population and global warming. But, Rees observes, the power that science now gives a small number of people endangers our species unlike anything before. One person's mistake or irrational decision could doom us all. In addition to threats from biological and nuclear weapons, developments such as genetic engineering could create new forms of life that uncontrollably consume or destroy vital materials in the environment.

Would the world's major powers come together to resist any of these threats? If the response to the global pandemic is any example, we should be concerned. In that case, let's hope that Rees' predictions for the future are as wrong as those of Malthus.

Richmond *Times-Dispatch*, August 9, 2020

17

A CONFESSION
WHOM SHOULD WE HONOR?

I have been torn by the removal of the statues from Monument Avenue. Part of me wishes they could have remained in place and interpreted as Civil War icons of men who were heroes to some people but villains to others. Regardless, they were symbols of a dark time in our nation's history.

I grew up in a small Middle Tennessee town that overwhelmingly voted for secession in 1861 and whose citizens joined the Confederate army in large numbers, paying a huge price as a result. The town square features an obelisk with hundreds of names inscribed on it of those who died for the South, including one of my great-great-grandfathers.

In my youth I became fascinated with the Civil War, of course, from a Southern white perspective. I fantasized about a great victory by Robert E. Lee at Gettysburg and ultimate Southern independence. A picture of Lee hung on the wall in my room. I cheered for our City High School Rebels and, along with my all-white fellow students, waved Confederate flags and sang "Dixie" at athletic events.

The Civil War heritage of VMI in part drew me to it as my college of choice. An image of Stonewall Jackson appears on my VMI class ring and a Confederate battle flag is a prominent component of our class crest.

I cannot ignore that part of my life, but over the years my assumptions and beliefs about the war have changed. As I studied that war and its causes from different perspectives, I found it harder to side with the South in the nation's bloodiest clash of arms.

Also, the evolution of my thinking coincided with the civil rights movement of the 1960s. For the first time, my eyes were opened to the injustices that whites had imposed on Blacks in the century following the Civil War.

I no longer could ignore the fact that the Confederacy largely was founded for the defense of slavery. As Confederate Vice President Alexander Stephens asserted in 1861, "Our new government is founded upon ... the great truth that slavery ... is [the Negro's] natural and normal state."

In 1861, a commissioner to the Texas secession convention voted for his state to secede from the Union proclaiming, "The people of the slaveholding states are bound together by the same necessity and determination to preserve African slavery."

Even though I might not have thought of it this way, the men represented by those statues tacitly had been agents of a government founded on perpetuating human bondage. As noble as those men might have been portrayed by their artists and admired by whites, including me at one time, they chose to fight for the wrong side in this most tragic of American wars.

The other reason for my change of heart is best answered with a question: What if the South had won the war? I shudder to think of the consequences. Not only would we have had two countries to begin with, I suspect that more nations would have been carved out of the remaining states and territories similar to the seven countries that make up Central America.

They might have had a common language and similar cultural traits, but a Balkanized continent with periodic border disputes and conflicts among the various nations more than likely would have resulted. Other questions rise assuming Southern victory.

What about the fate of slavery? Scholars contend that it probably would have lingered for decades more, perhaps not dying out until the turn of the 20th century, following Brazil, the last country to free its slaves.

Some historians speculate that the Confederacy would have attempted to annex Cuba either by negotiation or war with

Spain. Would the U.S. government have stood idle and prevented that from happening, or would it have intervened by invoking the Monroe Doctrine?

What would the consequences have been in the 20th century? Had the South won the Civil War, the U.S. probably would not have become the mighty "Arsenal of Democracy" that helped lead to Allied victory in World War I, and played a crucial role in defeating Nazi Germany and Imperial Japan in World War II. More than likely, it would not have been able to oppose Soviet hegemony and eventually see its collapse in the face of American might.

Instead of those alternatives, the nation that emerged from the Civil War grew into the greatest in history within a matter of years, far from perfect, but one that became a beacon of freedom and opportunity, or in the words of Abraham Lincoln, "the last best hope on earth."

Whom then should we honor for their roles in the Civil War? Two native Virginians come to mind. Both clearly helped save the Union. One was General Winfield Scott, born and raised near Petersburg, and the other was General George H. Thomas from Southampton County. When it came time for them to decide whether to resign their commissions in the federal army and join the Confederacy, both remained loyal to the Union.

Early in the war, Scott developed the winning strategy that eventually led to federal victory - the Anaconda Plan.

Thomas became one of the Union's greatest generals, winning every battle he fought and implementing many modern innovations with the armies he commanded.

They, along with 16 other native Virginians, who remained loyal to the country and went on to become generals, are my real heroes of the Civil War. At long last, they deserve recognition for their service under the Stars and Stripes rather than the stars and bars.

PART IV

OUR SADDEST LEGACY: THE CIVIL WAR

In volume I of Imperfect Past, *I devoted more space to the Civil War than any other topic, nearly twenty percent for that matter. Yet this volume has only three essays on the subject. Why such a disparity? Most of it has to do with timing. The essays I wrote between 2011 and 2015 appeared during the 150th anniversary of the Civil War, and it was only natural that I would devote considerable attention to America's most costly war. By the time the Sesquicentennial commemoration ended, however, most of the public, including me, were ready to move on to something else—the American presidency.*

18

BATTLEFIELD VIRGINIA:
A CENTURY OF CONSEQUENCES

A few years ago, I sat next to a European businessman on a long domestic flight. Our conversation turned to the world wars and how Europe suffered unfathomable casualties and vast physical destruction. He then proclaimed that we Americans have been fortunate not to experience such horrors.

Protected by two wide ocean barriers east and west, the United States was spared the physical devastation inflicted on other countries during the world wars. The sinking of ships by U-boats in the early years of the war was the closest Americans came to combat in their midst.

But to say that this country has not suffered first-hand from hard war is a mistake. On at least three occasions - the American Revolution, the War of 1812, and the Civil War - armed conflict has scarred our nation's landscape. For that matter, the last of those three conflicts resembled the experience of some European countries in the 20th century.

This was especially true in Virginia, where the violence reached a scale equivalent to anything found in Europe during World War I. The Old Dominion endured being the major battleground of the bloodiest war in American history. The first major clash of armies occurred on Virginia soil, as did many of the war's other most significant battles.

***

As the northernmost state of the Confederacy, Virginia was threatened with attacks from federal forces within days of its withdrawal from the Union. Unlike other states, with the exception of Tennessee, it experienced almost unrelenting combat until the end of the war.

Some of the largest armies ever gathered desperately fought each other for nearly four years, one trying to capture the Confederate capital of Richmond, the other trying to defend it. In addition to being the seat of government, the city was the industrial heart of the South, the world's largest flour producer, and a leading transportation center.

With the move of the Confederate national government from Montgomery, Alabama, to Richmond in 1861, never in the history of modern warfare had two enemy capitals been so close to each other. As a result, the land between and around the Richmond and Washington became the most heavily fought over in the Western Hemisphere. In terms of death and destruction, it resembled the Western Front of France during World War I.

Most of the military action occurred in central Virginia, but the rest of the commonwealth was not spared. Union and Confederate armies trudged up and down the Shenandoah Valley, stopping frequently to clash in small but costly battles. The town of Winchester changed hands dozens of times.

Tidewater, with its extensive east-west river systems, and coastal Virginia experienced some of the earliest military and naval action of the war. Hampton Roads was the site of the world's first armed confrontation between ironclad ships.

Even remote Southwest Virginia could not escape the conflict. Its rich mineral deposits and natural resources became a target of Union forces. Vicious guerrilla warfare plagued those counties, as it did many other areas of the commonwealth. Small units engaged in countless skirmishes for nearly four years.

***

By war's end, more than a half million men on both sides had been killed, wounded, declared missing, or captured in Virginia. Untold numbers of civilians died from disease spread by the armies or were killed, victims caught in the middle.

One out of every five soldiers who joined the Southern army never returned home, casting many white families into remorse and a hatred for things Northern for decades to come.

The physical destruction wrought by the war set the South back for almost a century. Some 4 million slaves gained their freedom, but because they were the region's No. 1 source of capital, its financial underpinnings were wiped out. Within a decade, the former Confederate states began passing oppressive laws that made the former slaves little more than second-class citizens.

Unlike post-World War II Europe, there was no Marshall Plan to rebuild the South and to get its people back on their feet. The country's highest poverty levels settled on the South, affecting white and black citizens alike. Not until World War II, did the former Confederacy begin to recover.

Many people who have moved to the South are puzzled why the region is so hung up on something that happened 150 years ago. As historian John Esten Cooke, a Confederate veteran, wrote after the war: "It was in every point of view the most tragic, unprecedented and anomalous of conflicts." Something as catastrophic as the Civil War is difficult to forget, especially if it occurred in one's own backyard.

Richmond *Times-Dispatch*, April 19, 2015

19

WHY ARE SO MANY ARMY POSTS NAMED FOR LOUSY CONFEDERATE GENERALS?

A movement to change the names of public buildings and remove statues has gained momentum in recent years. The figures being honored are heroes to some people, yet symbols of hate and division to others. Recently the question of names has come up with military bases, particularly Army posts. It's something I wondered about when I served in the Army fifty years ago.

A majority of Army posts have been located in the South. Of the 36 Army forts listed on that service's website, 19 are in former Confederate states. Why so many in the South? With milder winters than most other states, posts in the South can train troops year-round.

But powerful U.S. senators and congressmen from southern states greatly influenced the location of military installations in the 1930s. Senators such as Virginia's Harry Byrd, Georgia's Richard Russell, Mississippi's John Stennis, and others - including John Nance Garner of Texas, who served as speaker of the House and vice president - skillfully worked the political system to secure military installations in their respective states.

That may also explain why of the 36 Army forts, 15 are named for Civil War generals, 10 of whom served in the Confederate army. Why? Is it because they were great commanders, and their deeds on the battlefield made them stand out? That is hardly the case.

***

Of the list of fort namesakes, only Lee (as in Robert E.) and maybe A.P. Hill, all of whom were Confederates, rate recognition for their solid war records. On the Union side, only Fort Meade (as in George), named for the victor at Gettysburg, and commander of the Army of the Potomac, rates as a good, but not a great general. Justification for many of the other forts puzzles me. (Forts Lee and Hill aren't far from Richmond.)

Fort Bragg, North Carolina, for example, bears the name of a Confederate general who was despised by the soldiers who served under him, and at one point the generals under his command petitioned for his removal, arguing that he was incompetent.

An iron-fisted disciplinarian with a distinguished pre-war army career, Braxton Bragg excelled at training troops, but failed to use them well in battle. He suffered the ignominy of having his army routed by U.S. Grant in battle near Chattanooga in 1863. He hardly represents his native North Carolina well.

Fort Hood, Texas, is named for John Bell Hood, who was an effective combat soldier suited well for subordinate command but not for the top job. He fought with great dash and valor under Robert E. Lee in the eastern theater and under Joseph E. Johnston in the Atlanta campaign.

When promoted to army command in the fall of 1864, however, he suffered one defeat after another, and ultimately saw his army virtually destroyed at the battle of Nashville, ending his military career in crushing defeat.

***

George Pickett, who graduated last in his class at West Point, participated in one of the Civil War's worst tactical blunders - Pickett's Charge - a hopeless attack on a strong Union line the third day of Gettysburg.

Although he was following the orders of Robert E. Lee, the hapless Pickett has suffered the fate of having his name associated with the disastrous charge. The rest of his war record was less than distinguished. Fort Pickett is near Blackstone, Virginia.

Fort Polk, Louisiana, carries the name of another Confederate general whose war record was mediocre at best. A graduate of West Point, Leonidas Polk left the Army after a relatively short career, became an ordained Episcopal priest, and was elevated to bishop before the Civil War.

Once his native Louisiana joined the Confederacy, he offered his services to the new nation. Within a relatively short period, he became a corps commander, a position he held with little distinction until being killed by an enemy artillery shell in Georgia in 1864.

Fort Benning, Georgia, received its name from Henry Lewis Benning, a rabid secessionist, and an outspoken critic of abolition. He argued that if blacks were no longer enslaved, "the white race will be completely exterminated" and America "would go back to a wilderness and become another Africa." A competent but not great brigade commander in Lee's army, far more famous and successful military commanders can be found to name one of the Army's largest and most important posts.

***

In fairness, one Army fort is named for a less-than-successful Union general - George B. McClellan. Like Braxton Bragg, "Little Mac" did a superb job of training troops, but was reluctant to commit them to battle.

He kept up a running feud with President Lincoln, who eventually sacked him for insubordination and numerous failures to defeat the enemy even when the odds heavily favored him. Ironically Fort McClellan is located in Alabama.

In a recent article in the *Washington Post*, Jason Dempsey, a writer and retired Army officer, questions the justification for keeping the names of men who he contends were traitors attached to Army posts - especially considering that some 30 percent of soldiers are African-American now.

When asked about this, an Army official replied that the forts are "named for soldiers who hold a place in our military history. Accordingly, these names represent individuals not causes or ideologies." I find that hard to swallow, considering the war records of many of those whose names are attached to army installations.

It doesn't take much imagination to come up with other soldiers who deserve more recognition: George Washington, Winfield Scott, U.S. Grant, William Tecumseh Sherman, George H. Thomas, John J. Pershing, Dwight D. Eisenhower, George C. Marshall, Omar Bradley, George S. Patton, and even Douglas MacArthur would be more suitable names for Army posts.

Let's face it: reconstruction of the American South after the Civil War was relatively easy when compared to what happened to the losing side in other countries. None of its principal leaders was executed. No one had his land confiscated. The denial of basic political rights for the defeated white population was relatively brief.

Within years, many of the people who led the South to secession in 1861, and who played important roles in the Confederate war effort, held prominent positions in the postwar years. Some even had Army forts named for them. Only in America.

Richmond *Times-Dispatch*, November 27, 2016

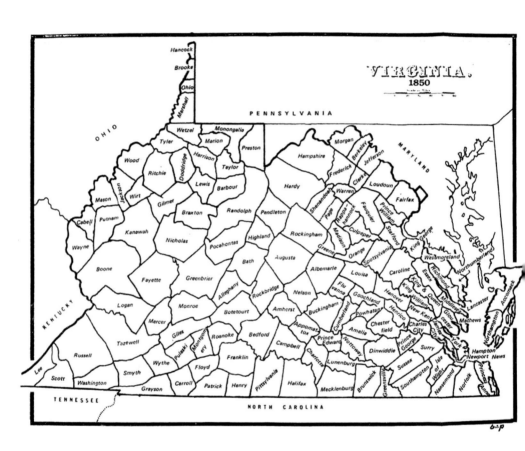

20

How East Tennessee Almost Became the Next West Virginia

One question left unanswered by the Constitution until the Civil War was: Can a state secede from the Union? But another question arose about whether local governments, such as counties, can leave their mother state. The answer came, at least in part, in 1861 when a large portion of Virginia - 38 western counties - declared that the state government's decision to leave the Union and join the Confederacy was "null and void."

Officials in Richmond rushed troops to the western counties to force their return. For months, Confederate and Union forces struggled for control of the region, including a futile campaign by Robert E. Lee. By 1862, superior numbers of federal troops prevailed and remained in control for the rest of the war. President Lincoln signed a statehood bill - and West Virginia was admitted as the 35th state in the Union in 1863.

***

The actions of Virginia's western counties could have been repeated in one of the commonwealth's neighboring states - Tennessee. Indeed, by the mid-19th century, the 31 counties of East Tennessee, much like western Virginia, had evolved into a unique region.

Possessed of a society and economy far less dependent on slavery than most of the South and the rest of the state, the majority of East Tennesseans saw little future in joining the Confederacy, in which they had little at stake and much to lose.

When citizens from the middle and western regions of the state voted overwhelmingly for Tennessee to secede in June of

1861, East Tennesseans cast their votes against it by more than two to one.

A few days later, delegates from throughout the region met in a convention to consider separation from Tennessee. After considerable debate, the delegates petitioned the General Assembly to allow East Tennessee to become a separate state. Gov. Isham Harris, with the backing of the legislature, refused to consider the request, declaring supporters of the petition "Tories."

Almost immediately, East Tennessee became a thorn in the side of the Confederacy. Confederate authorities were deeply concerned over the safety of the East Tennessee & Virginia Railroad, a vital supply line from the Deep South to the Old Dominion. They not only feared a potential invasion by a federal army from Kentucky, but even more a mass uprising of East Tennessee Unionists.

In response to these threats, Confederate President Jefferson Davis ordered nearly 20,000 troops to be posted throughout the region. The increased military presence only emboldened the East Tennessee Unionists.

***

Late one night in November 1861, saboteurs destroyed six crucial railroad bridges in East Tennessee, convincing Confederate officials that the region would have to be ruled with an iron fist. Davis declared martial law and instituted conscription, targeting suspected Unionists.

Over the next two years, a series of Confederate commanders of the Department of East Tennessee arrested large numbers of Unionists with little or no reason. They required county government officials to swear a loyalty oath to the Confederacy and then collect arms, arrest deserters, and enforce conscription. East Tennessee became the only region, North or South, to undergo long-term Confederate military occupation.

As a result, thousands of East Tennessee Unionists fled to Kentucky to escape what they perceived as tyranny. An estimated 35,000 East Tennesseans joined the Union army, more than all the other Confederate states combined and more than five Northern states.

Finally, relief came to the Unionists of East Tennessee when a federal army under Ambrose Burnside advanced unopposed into the region in late August of 1863.

Burnside's men were greeted as an army of deliverance and made a triumphal entry into Knoxville.

A soldier wrote home that he saw a group of old men, women, and children wildly clapping and cheering as the troops marched by. In the middle stood an old woman with "tears running down her withered cheeks in torents [sic]." At first she was speechless, but then she finally burst out, "Thank the Lord at last you have released us. At last we are saved. God bless the Yankees."

Although most East Tennesseans sympathized with the Union, a sufficient number supported the Confederacy to create a civil war within a civil war. In the remaining two years of the war, both sides seemed bent on destroying those who refused to conform to the appropriate cause.

Neighbors, former schoolmates, family members, and even fellow worshipers at local churches became fierce enemies. As a result, whether under Confederate or Union occupation, life for East Tennesseans became one of almost constant fear and distrust, not to mention violence.

Unfortunately, the end of the war in 1865 did not bring peace to the people of East Tennessee. Relief organizations attempted to alleviate the material suffering of the populace, but they could not eliminate the hatred engendered by four years of civil war. At war's end, for example, many churches had split into Unionist and Rebel factions, congregational divisions that remained for decades.

The strong Unionism that emerged in East Tennessee was remarkable for its strength and endurance. With the exception of West Virginia, no other major region of the South demonstrated such devotion to the American flag during the Civil War. And while the former Confederate states coalesced to become the Solid South, a bastion of the Democratic Party for more than a hundred years, East Tennessee became a stalwart of the party of Lincoln.

It has voted Republican in every presidential election since 1868, something that even West Virginia cannot match.

Richmond *Times-Dispatch*, August 12, 2018

21

SAVING AMERICA'S BATTLEFIELDS

Having lived in Richmond nearly 35 years, I cannot tell you how many times I have flown in and out of the city's airport. On incoming flights, as we prepare to land, I sometimes glance out my window trying to imagine what the landscape must have looked like a century and a half ago.

It was here that Confederate and Union forces clashed for two days of desperate fighting in the late spring of 1862. Known either as the battle of Fair Oaks or Seven Pines, the combined losses totaled nearly 14,000, making it the highest casualty count in the Eastern theater of the Civil War to date.

The bloody clash ended in a draw, but Union commander George B. McClellan's large army still threatened Richmond. Although the public could not know it at the time, the battle would prove to be a turning point in the war.

Soon after Seven Pines, Confederate President Jefferson Davis replaced the wounded Confederate army commander Joseph E. Johnston with his chief military adviser, Robert E. Lee. As a result, the war's course dramatically changed.

Three weeks later, Lee launched a major offensive that drove the federals from Richmond in the Seven Days Battles. With Lee at the helm, the federal army lost the initiative, and did not come close to the Confederate capital for another two years at a cost of hundreds of thousands of lives.

Why has Seven Pines received relatively little attention compared to other battles? In large part because most of the land upon which it was fought fell victim to commercial and residential development.

Ironically, another war led to the initial destruction of that battlefield. With America's entry into World War I in 1917, demand for gunpowder dramatically increased. As a result, scores of sites in rural areas across America with railroad access to them became prime locations for gunpowder plants.

With a rail line running through a quiet corner in eastern Henrico County, federal agents thought the Seven Pines area was perfect for a large munitions plant. Work began in late 1917 and was completed by July 1918. Within four months, however, the war ended with the plant humming at full production levels.

In the meantime, more than 400 homes, along with stores, a school and a library, were built for the plant's workers. Named for one of its developers, the town of Sandston occupies what had been the staging area for the Confederate attack on May 31, 1862.

Then in 1927, officials broke ground close by to build a commercial airport. As the airport's footprint expanded over the next several decades, more of the battlefield was built on and paved over. In the 1970s, the completion of Interstate 64 through the most heavily fought-over part of the battle administered the coup de grace.

Today the nearby Seven Pines National Cemetery, a few cannons, some barely visible earthworks and a handful of historical markers are the only reminders of one of the Civil War's crucial turning points.

Seven Pines is not alone in its fate. Not every battlefield could be preserved. Many of the battlefield sites such as Fredericksburg, Chattanooga, Atlanta and Nashville, among others, long have been built over and destroyed. The same holds true for many Revolutionary War and War of 1812 battle sites.

On the other hand, a movement to preserve American battlefields has been underway for nearly 175 years. In the mid-19th century, portions of Revolutionary War battle sites such as Bunker Hill and Yorktown were set aside to remember those who died in the cause of American independence. Civil War veterans from both sides began placing memorials to their units and fallen comrades at battlefields almost immediately at war's end.

By the turn of the 20th century, five battlefields (none in Virginia) were declared as national parks under the auspices of what then was the War Department, which regarded them as "outdoor classrooms" to teach strategy and tactics to Army officers.

Others gradually were added to the War Department inventory, all of which eventually were turned over to the National Park Service in 1933. An increase in public interest during the Civil War centennial in the 1960s led to numerous additions to the list.

At the same time, an explosion of urban and suburban development threatened scores of battlefields. Small local preservation groups simply did not have enough clout to prevent the destruction.

In 1987, however, a group men and women, fed up with all of the damage done, convened in Fredericksburg determined to develop a strategy to halt or significantly slow the uncontrolled sprawl. Out of that gathering grew the organization now known as the American Battlefield Trust, which protects land associated with the Revolutionary War, the War of 1812 and the Civil War.

Although it struggled at first, under the leadership of recently retired president, James Lighthizer, and his successor, David Duncan, the American Battlefield Trust has done a remarkable job of fulfilling its mission. It raised almost $500 million that it leveraged with federal government matching grants and state programs that, in turn, have led to saving some 53,000 acres in 24 states.

Thanks to the trust's efforts, Richmond greatly has benefited from this endeavor. By combining private dollars raised with federal matching funds, it has poured some $40 million into the area to purchase nearly 4,300 acres of land, including the Seven Days battles of 1862 and U.S. Grant's Overland Campaign of 1864.

Earlier this month, the trust announced that it paid $260,000 to purchase land at New Market Heights, where Black soldiers distinguished themselves in securing a portion of the Confederate line in September 1864.

We as a people have attempted to preserve those things that help us understand the lessons the past offers. The Library of Congress, the National Archives, the Smithsonian Institution, the thousands of archives and museums around the country, and historic sites such as Jamestown, Mount Vernon, Monticello and Hyde Park all safeguard the nation's collective memory in one form or another. So do America's battlegrounds.

Likewise, battlegrounds are significant community assets as an educational resource, a financial enhancement through heritage tourism and as valuable green space. Most of all, they serve as memorials to the hundreds of thousands of Americans who paid the ultimate price for helping liberate 4 million enslaved people.

Try to remember that the next time you fly out of Richmond, you are treading on hallowed ground.

Richmond Times-Dispatch, February 21, 2021

PART V

RUNNING A COUNTRY FOR BETTER AND FOR WORSE

Finding a topic to fill that gap with my columns was not difficult. A year after the end of the Civil War Sesquicentennial, Americans voted in one of the most controversial presidential elections in our history. It pitted former First Lady and Secretary of State Hillary Rodham Clinton against New York real estate mogul and television reality show host Donald J. Trump.

Trump, who had never held elected office and who was not given much of a chance to win, ran a brilliant campaign based on the simple message that the United States was in dire straits and that he would "make America great again." His message struck a responsive chord with enough citizens to win the presidency in the Electoral College, although he fell short by some three million popular votes.

The next four years turned out to be even more tumultuous than anyone could have imagined. Using a slash and burn strategy in reversing programs and initiatives launched by previous administration of Barrack Obama, Trump will be remembered as the first president to be impeached twice. He fed the myth that his reelection was stolen from him. He also cultivated a sense of mistrust toward the government and the media among the American public.

He began to dismantle America's global leadership and to direct it with more inward-looking policies, from which the extent of the damage to the country's international reputation remains to be seen. Only the passage of time will tell if Trump's legacy will be positive or negative, but his two impeachments and his failure to win re-election do not bode well for him.

22

IS THE UNITED STATES NO LONGER A GREAT NATION?

American democracy has produced a remarkably stable form of government, one that has lasted nearly 250 years.

Donald Trump has pledged to "return America to greatness" if he is elected as our next president. When asked what he means by "return to greatness," his response provides few specifics.

Great nations have existed for thousands of years. Studies of the ancient Egyptians, Persians, Greeks, and Romans reveal mighty nations that spread their power, wealth, and influence well beyond their own borders. Each left its mark on the world and shaped the course of history for centuries to come.

After the Middle Ages, the emergence of nation-states in Europe turned tiny countries such as Portugal and Holland into economic powers that shaped their times in the 16th and 17th centuries more than did many larger countries.

Spain, France, and Great Britain evolved into the superpowers of their time, but were superseded by the United States and the Soviet Union in the 20th century. Germany and Japan threatened the balance of power for a while, only to be crushed by combined American and Soviet military might and the industrial juggernaut of the United States.

The U.S. and Soviet Union came out of World War II as the two most powerful countries - and as bitter rivals. Locked in a Cold War that lasted a half-century, America emerged as the sole great power in the world when the autocratic Soviet Union, burdened with a flawed governing concept and corrupt economic system, collapsed in the early 1990s.

***

Although the U.S. has its share of problems, one can argue that it has become the greatest nation in history. It has enormous wealth. It fields military forces superior to any other on Earth. The language it inherited from England is used universally. Its natural resources make it almost self-sufficient.

The country is one of the earth's leaders in the field of technology. Its people live in better housing than most, are blessed with good health, are better educated, and enjoy a degree of financial security that would have been unthinkable two or three generations before them. For better or worse, its popular culture has weaved its way into the lives of people on every continent. It is taking a lead role in helping save the environment.

Why has this country been elevated to such a lofty position? Dozens of reasons can be given, including a democratic governing system that allows a majority of its citizens to participate and have a voice. It has been a remarkably stable form of government, one that has lasted nearly 250 years. The system is far from perfect, but in the words of Winston Churchill: "Democracy is the worst form of government, except for all the others."

The U.S. economy has operated under the free enterprise system, which has its share of flaws, but it is the most successful wealth-creating economic form in history, and has made America and its people the most prosperous ever.

***

As important as those factors are, another is arguably the most important of all - location, location, location.

In his latest book, *Prisoners of Geography*, British author Timothy Marshall argues that too little attention is paid to geography in explaining the strengths and vulnerabilities of nations. According to Marshall, no country has benefited more from its geography than the U.S.

"Geography has determined that if a [country] could get to and then control the land 'from sea to shining sea,' it would be a great power, the greatest history has known." When the U.S. developed a large blue-water navy at the turn of the 20th-century, it was well on its way to becoming the world's greatest power.

With most of its border protected by large oceans, and with barriers of "the great Canadian Shield" to the north and a desert environment to the south, the U.S. has achieved, according to Marshall, the "rare geographical position of near invulnerability from conventional attack." It is little wonder that only three of the 13 wars and major conflicts America has fought have been on U.S. soil.

America's location on the globe arguably is the best of any nation. In addition to having an advantageous strategic position, its climate is varied enough from one region to another to produce a cornucopia of agricultural products. It is blessed with mineral resources - gold, silver, copper, lead, coal, uranium, oil, and natural gas - that have helped make it wealthy and more self-sufficient than most other nations.

For three decades now, some politicians and pundits have warned that the sky is falling on the United States. I have trouble believing their message of doom and gloom. As Tim Marshall observes, "The planet's most successful country is about to become self-sufficient in energy, it remains the preeminent economic power, and it spends more on research and development for its military than the military budgets of all the other NATO countries combined."

Furthermore, the American population is not aging as it is in Europe and in many parts of Asia.

If countries could sell stock shares, which ones of the following would I keep in my portfolio? Which ones would I buy or sell?

China: keep what I have but buy no more anytime soon;

Russia - sell;

India - sell;

Japan - keep but maybe buy;

The European Union- sell;

The United States - buy!

Despite the challenges facing the U.S., it is still a blue chip stock, and will be for a long time

---

Richmond *Times-Dispatch*, March 6, 2016

23

WHAT MAKES A PRESIDENT GREAT?

Fifty years ago historian Thomas A. Bailey of Stanford University published one of my favorite books. In *Presidential Greatness*, Bailey used dozens of markers to analyze each American president's record. He then rated all presidents up to Lyndon Johnson as great, near great, average, below average, or a failure.

Although the book was published in 1966, and is out of print, Bailey's attributes to determine presidential greatness are as valid now as they were then. Several stand out.

First was that successful presidents have been skilled and experienced politicians. He noted, "Few men have reached the White House without a strenuous political apprenticeship." Those who had not run the political gauntlet included war heroes Zachary Taylor, U.S. Grant, and Dwight Eisenhower.

Herbert Hoover, an engineer by profession who helped save much of the European population from starvation after World War I, was also a political novice. In addition, Bailey pointed out that William Howard Taft had served only in appointed offices, except for an early election to a judgeship.

None of the five had formed strong political loyalties, had gone through the process of political initiation, or had been involved in active political campaigning. They, therefore, had little or no experience in the give and take aspects of governing, of knowing how to win over a seemingly uncompromising opponent, or understanding how to work effectively behind the scenes to get what they wanted.

Former President Harry Truman observed that one of Hoover's problems was "that in a political way he started at the top instead of the bottom. It would be like my starting an engineering career without knowing anything about engineering."

For decades, experts on the American presidency have given this quintet of political neophytes low marks for their time in office, although Eisenhower's stock has risen in recent years and Grant's presidency has not been judged as harshly as it was when Bailey published his book.

Nevertheless, Bailey argues that most successful presidents have assumed the role of politician-in-chief and used it to their benefit. Abraham Lincoln and the two Roosevelts were masters of the political game and understood the art of dealing with people. They knew how to persuade others to their ways of thinking. Franklin Roosevelt, for example, did not badger or bully his opponents, but he beguiled them.

***

Another of Bailey's measures is the test of character.

"The first requisites of a President of the United States are intellectual honesty and sincerity," wrote Herbert Hoover several years following his less-than-successful tenure in the White House. Although Hoover is regarded at best as a mediocre president, his argument on the importance of character and the American presidency are particularly valid today.

As Bailey notes, many politicians rely on half-truths and sometimes outright lies to win office.

"If he is a dedicated politician, he has presumably convinced himself that (he) is the repository of all virtues, and that there is no rectitude in the opposition camp," Bailey observes. "The one is infallible; the other is insufferable."

Once in office, however, prevarication or the perception of it can end a presidency as it did Richard Nixon's. Surrounded by men who were willing to outright lie to the American public, Nixon's assertion that "I am not a crook" made a mockery of him and the office he held, forcing him to be the only president to resign.

Bill Clinton's second term in office never fully recovered from his statement, "I did not have sex with that woman" when it was later revealed to be less than truthful.

***

The third trait that has proven important with our presidents is temperament. Few people are willing to run the gauntlet of an election for perhaps the most difficult job in the world. Do they do it because they are consumed with ambition, or does it relate to a genuine desire to serve the public?

Is it both?

As Bailey points out, the ablest presidents had a "deep rooted love of country." This in part makes clear the extreme sacrifices that many have made in assuming the crushing burdens the job entails.

Whether ambition or a sense of duty drives someone to the presidency, the job requires the ability to form sound judgments and then act or not act on them.

Common sense is an essential component of judgment, something that served Abraham Lincoln well as he led his nation through its most traumatic experience.

On the other hand, his successor, Andrew Johnson, had a paucity of common sense yet an abundance of stubbornness that caused his presidency to founder during the troubled days of Reconstruction.

In addition to common sense, Bailey argued that the greatest presidents not only did big and bold things during their terms in office, they also had a sense of moderation.

"They were men of restraint who realized that problems will often be resolved more quickly if one does not rush at it with both arms flailing. They realized that ... high-level politics called statesmanship is the art of the possible, of the attainable, often of the next best," wrote Bailey.

I wish that Bailey's book were still in print. With a presidential election looming that features two candidates with their share of flaws, voters would benefit immensely from reading about what makes great presidents great before deciding which candidate should be elected.

Even better would be for the candidates to read Bailey and take to heart the lessons to be learned from this unique and informed treatment of the presidency.

Richmond *Times-Dispatch*, July 10, 2016

24

The Politics of Wealth

The United States experienced breathtaking changes as it entered the 20th century. The emergence of a new, industrial order made the country an economic power to be reckoned with; but it created a multitude of new issues and challenges that increasingly demanded attention.

In the years following the Civil War, rapidly growing cities became industrial centers that spawned deplorable living conditions for millions of recently arrived immigrants from Southern and Eastern Europe. In rural America, farmers grew increasingly angry as the prices for agricultural products plummeted.

A mounting income gap between the wealthy, who benefited from the new economic order, and millions of low-paid factory workers and poor farmers created a dynamic tension that neared the boiling point.

The South, left impoverished by the Civil War and its white citizens embittered by defeat, imposed a series of state laws that formally established apartheid between the races and ensured that African-Americans would be treated as second-class citizens for years to come.

And one by one the main drivers of the American economy - the steel, oil, and railroad industries, and high finance - began to merge, passing from competition to consolidation. By 1900 a few large corporations controlled almost all of the major facilities of production and distribution in the country.

***

Despite these troublesome matters, political leaders, Republican and Democrat alike, mostly ignored the issues in the second half of the 19th century. Indeed, they seemed more interested in traditional concerns such as tariff and freight rates, civil service reform, and whether the currency should be expanded or reduced - all of which were abstract and unintelligible to most American citizens.

The nation's political leadership seemed unprepared and unwilling to face the new problems created by an industrial giant. As British historian James Bryce observed in 1888: "In America the highest positions in the land are seldom won by men of brilliant gifts."

Most American leaders in the post-Civil War decades came from backgrounds that made them ill-suited to face the new reality. Of the seven presidents who served between 1865 and 1900, all came from small-town or rural backgrounds.

Most seemed more comfortable with a pre-industrial mindset and had little direct personal contact with the crucial new realities of a changed America. They began their careers in professions such a law, small business, the ministry, or teaching.

In the judgement of almost every presidential ranking by historians, the men who occupied the White House during this period were mediocre, at best. Among seven who served between 1865 and 1900, two ranked as barely above average (Grover Cleveland and William McKinley), two as average (Rutherford Hayes and Chester Alan Arthur), two as below average (U.S. Grant and Benjamin Harrison), and one as a failure (Andrew Johnson).

(James Garfield was assassinated just a few months after taking office in 1881, so did not serve long enough to be ranked.)

***

The people who appeared to control the country's destiny were the captains of industry and finance - Andrew Carnegie, John D. Rockefeller, J.P. Morgan, and a number of other wealthy businessmen. They poured millions of dollars into presidential elections, supporting candidates who were committed to pro-business policies.

Even more important than presidential contests was the growing importance of senators who represented large corporate interests. By 1900, a third of the U.S. Senate had direct connections to large corporate interests. Fifteen senators were heavily involved in railroads; fifteen in minerals, oil, and lumber; nine in banking and finance; six in commerce; and three in manufacturing.

These men were not puppets of big business, but on issues affecting the national economy, their policies favored corporate and moneyed interests rather than those of farmers, factory workers, and the poor.

Their growing political influence led to policies that resulted in the implementation of a regressive tax system and laws that limited the rights of laborers, as well as blocked attempts by reform-minded politicians to implement child-labor laws and basic safety standards in factories and mines.

This is a period in American history that became known the Gilded Age, derived from Mark Twain's 1873 novel *The Gilded Age: a Tale of Today* - a satirical account of an era of serious social problems masked by a thin layer of gold gilding.

But the gilding began to wear thin by the 1890s as more and more Americans who occupied the lower rungs of the social and economic ladder began to foment for change and reform.

Disturbed by the inequity, corruption, and injustices of the era, reform-minded citizens argued that change must be implemented at all levels of government and that unregulated business needed to be reined in. Calling themselves Progressives, they ushered in a whole new era that would define the role of government in the lives of the American people, for better and for worse, for nearly a century to come.

25

A MOVE TO REFORM

Many progressives supported women's suffrage, arguing that women were inherently more honest than men, and would clean up the nasty business of politics.

Writers Thomas Gordon and John Trenchard profoundly influenced political thinking in 18th-century Great Britain. Arguing that governments operate under an ongoing struggle between liberty and power, their views were read widely in America and played a role in transforming 13 separate colonies into an independent nation.

They also helped influence the American Constitution. A government based on a system of checks and balances is one of that document's key elements.

The liberty versus power struggle also can apply to how a nation operates its economy - hands-on, hands-off, or a compromise between the two. Known as laissez-faire or free enterprise, a hands-off system is marked by limited government involvement in economic affairs, with minimum controls and regulations. Its proponents argue that laissez-faire policies have turned the United States into an economic powerhouse.

Critics of the system, however, contend that while laissez-faire policies worked well as long as the nation's economy was primarily agriculturally based, the new industrial order demanded tighter controls. Under the new paradigm, for example, a relatively few people can take advantage of an unfettered system to enrich themselves at the expense of the many. Deregulation often results in corruption on a large scale.

***

No better example of this can be found than in late 19th-century America during the Gilded Age. With few restrictions on their actions, and by eliminating competition, men such as John D. Rockefeller, J.P. Morgan, Andrew Carnegie, and Henry Frick amassed huge fortunes that seemed unimaginable in earlier years.

By the end of the 19th century, however, more and more Americans began to speak out against the growing inequity between the very wealthy and those on the lower rungs on the economic ladder. Increasingly these critics became convinced that those who gained great wealth did it by exploiting the poor and vulnerable.

They objected to the mistreatment of children in the labor force; to factories and mines that frequently left workers permanently disabled or dead because of little or no safety standards; to ghastly slum conditions in almost every American city; and to crooked elected officials on all levels who colluded with equally corrupt business interests to line their pockets.

The ideas these activists presented to solve problems that were created by the new economic order varied.

On the left were the socialists, many of whom were immigrants who developed their political philosophy before coming to America. They believed that ownership and control of business and industry should be shared by the people at large.

Inspired by writers such as Henry George, Edward Bellamy, and Henry Lloyd, they attacked corrupt business practices and argued that government should control enterprise to ensure economic equity and honesty.

Uppermost in the minds of these reformers was the notion that if conditions did not improve quickly and dramatically, the United States would explode into class warfare. Surely, they reasoned, abused workers and impoverished slum dwellers would not tolerate their condition indefinitely - and a social catastrophe was close at hand.

Indeed, the evidence seemed to mount that social chaos had begun already. Attempts by workers to organize unions to stand up for their rights were vehemently opposed by the business tycoons of the time, who saw unionism as an infringement of their authority.

A series of violent strikes at the Homestead Steel plant in Pittsburgh, the Pullman railroad car factory near Chicago, Cripple Creek Mine in Colorado, and numerous other places throughout the country were ruthlessly shut down by management, backed by federal troops or state militias to restore order.

***

On the other side of the reform movement were mostly middle-class Americans who argued that the future political and social health of the country did not require radical change, but rather a series of basic reforms.

Calling themselves progressives, most believed that a decent society for all Americans could be created by gradual reform. They argued that poverty is destructive, wasteful, and demoralizing, but preventable. Furthermore, poverty is immoral and unacceptable in the midst of a nation as wealthy as the United States. Most progressives were a part of the American political mainstream, spanning both the Democratic and Republican parties.

The movement initially took on political machines and their bosses and sought regulation of monopolies. It also embraced other significant reforms. Many progressives advocated prohibition in part to destroy the power of the local political bosses who operated out of saloons.

Other progressives supported women's suffrage, arguing that women were inherently more honest than men, and would clean up the nasty business of politics. Many progressives embraced a movement to identify inefficiency and corruption in almost every sector of life. They advocated reforms in local government, public education, insurance, medicine, finance, industry, railroads, and numerous other areas of life in America.

For any reform movement on a national level to succeed requires strong leadership and inspirational advocates, usually coming from the White House. The presidents American voters elected in the last quarter of the 19th century were unwilling or unable to embrace reform.

Beginning in 1901 and lasting for nearly another 20 years, three American presidents embraced progressivism and oversaw intense social and political changes in American society.

Richmond *Times-Dispatch*, April 30, 2017

26

PROGRESSIVES IN THE WHITE HOUSE

One of the keys in the early 20th century was that reform and progressive thinking crossed party lines. Two of the three progressive presidents were Republicans.

On Sept. 14, 1901, President William McKinley died from a gunshot wound delivered by a crazed assassin two weeks earlier. Republican Party leaders were stunned by the recent string of events. Vice President Theodore Roosevelt, former Republican governor of New York and hero of the recent Spanish-American War, would now occupy the White House, something the party bosses viewed with grave concern.

They had put the popular Roosevelt on the ticket to help ensure McKinley's re-election in 1900, despite the fact that many of them thought he was a reckless maverick.

Everything went according to plan after the election with a safe, traditional Republican in the White House. The assassin's bullet, however, changed everything. While McKinley fit the profile of the non-activist presidents who had held office previous half-century, Roosevelt was almost the opposite.

At age 42, he was the youngest man to hold the office, and unlike most of his predecessors, Roosevelt was anything but a hands-off president. The worst fears of traditional Republicans became reality when Roosevelt began using his office as a "bully pulpit" to promote an activist government to serve the interests of most Americans over those of the few masters of big business.

He called for a "Square Deal" for all Americans - businessmen, laborers, farmers, and consumers. He implemented stronger federal control of corporations by attacking the large trusts and monopolies that had squelched competition; by giving more authority to the Interstate Commerce Commission; and by protecting the country's natural resources.

He received congressional support for the Pure Food and Drug Act, and the Meat Inspection Act to protect consumers from hucksters and unscrupulous food producers. More than any previous president, he took bold steps to protect some 230 million acres of the country's wilderness from unchecked development.

***

The Progressive Movement clearly had an ally in President Roosevelt, and it did not end when he completed his next term, which he had won in a landslide. Clearly, his activist presidency resonated well with the American public. For that matter his popularity helped ensure the election of his handpicked Republican successor, William Howard Taft, in 1908.

Although Taft continued breaking up monopolies and trusts, he seemed unable to control the Republican conservatives, who tried to reverse many of Roosevelt's initiatives. He himself was more conservative than Roosevelt, and he took issue with many of the reformers and their demands for immediate action. A lawyer and judge by profession, he preferred a slower and more deliberate pace for reform legislation.

Taft's less-than-vigorous pursuit of reform raised the ire of his predecessor to such an extent that it led to a civil war within the Republican Party. The conflict grew so intense that Roosevelt challenged Taft for the Republican nomination in 1912, splitting the party wide open.

Frustrated that the incumbent Taft had his re-nomination locked up, Roosevelt and his supporters walked out of the Republican convention and launched a third party, the Progressive Party, better known as the Bull Moose Party. Their platform advocated expanding the powers of the federal government to bring about more reform and regulations.

With the Republicans torn asunder, the Democratic Party, which had elected only one man as president since 1860, saw victory within its grasp. The native Virginian and strong reform governor of New Jersey, Woodrow Wilson, received the nomination and won the election by taking only 42 percent of the popular vote, but receiving 435 electoral votes to Roosevelt's 88 and Taft's paltry 8.

**

Once in office, Wilson pursued an aggressive reform agenda. He created the Federal Reserve, giving the country a regulated currency. He pushed legislation that established the Federal Trade Commission to prohibit unfair business practices. He supported the ratification of the 16th Amendment that resulted in a graduated income tax, requiring wealthy Americans to pay a higher percentage on their earnings. And he addressed a number of social issues, such as greatly restricting child labor and limiting the hours of railroad workers.

Despite these many reforms, some of his policies were backward-looking. Following the example of his native South, he implemented formal segregation in the federal government. For example, government buildings in Washington were required to have white and "colored" bathrooms. Appointments to federal jobs through civil service became increasingly difficult for African-Americans to obtain.

Perhaps the most controversial piece of legislation coming from Wilson's administration was prohibition. Approval in 1919 of the 18th Amendment, which banned the manufacture, sale, and transport of intoxicating spirits, has been described as the greatest failure of a social experiment in American history. The amendment resulted in a huge illicit liquor enterprise and an explosion of organized crime. Within 14 years, it became the only amendment to be repealed in its entirety.

World War I and its aftermath dominated Wilson's second term, as did a nearly fatal stroke, taking his attention away from continued domestic reforms.

The United States emerged from the war as the most powerful nation on Earth economically, but the American public had grown weary of Wilson's activist government and reform in general.

A severe postwar recession contributed to a landslide victory in 1920 for Republican presidential candidate Warren G. Harding, who ran on a ticket pledging a "Return to Normalcy" and a repudiation of the progressive agenda of political and social reform.

There would be no "bully pulpit" presidents for another 12 years, when Franklin D. Roosevelt was elected in a landslide in the depths of the Great Depression.

***

What can we learn from the Gilded Age and the Progressive Era? Some critics contend that we are experiencing a new Gilded Age. They argue that during the past few decades, corporations and elected officials (many representing safe gerrymandered districts) have rolled back many of the gains made by working and middle-class people during the Progressive Era.

They point out that despite its great wealth, the country now has the highest level of income inequality in 90 years. Most disturbing to these critics is that federal and state tax cuts benefited the wealthy at the expense of the poor and many in the middle class.

Advocates on the other side of the political spectrum, however, argue that government has become more intrusive than ever, thereby stifling the economic potential of the nation and interfering with our individual freedoms.

In his run for the White House, candidate Donald Trump pledged "to return America to greatness" by slashing regulations, easing government controls, and reforming the tax code, among other things. Once elected to office, much like Theodore Roosevelt, the president has used his own bully pulpit to implement his campaign pledges.

But a hundred-plus days into his presidency, little of his agenda has been carried out, despite having Republican majorities in both houses of Congress. Why? Is it his political inexperience? Is it his confrontational style? No doubt those are factors, but I think it is something more fundamental.

A century ago, conditions in the country were as problematic, if not more so, than they are today; yet three successive presidents were able to bring about major reforms to address the issues. One of the keys then was that reform and progressive thinking crossed party lines. Two of the three progressive presidents were Republicans.

Through compromise, cooperation, and effective persuasion, they were able to work with Congress to bring about needed reform. They found viable solutions to the problems created by the painful transition from the 19th century to modern America.

Today, anyone who cooperates with members of the opposing party is an anathema. Cooperation within both parties also has become more difficult. The rhetoric has become increasingly confrontational. Fealty to party or faction within a party appear more important than loyalty to country. It is unfortunate that today's monumental challenges are not being met by either side of the political spectrum.

Perhaps the time has come for introducing fundamental change in the way we govern ourselve,s much as the American people did a century ago.

Richmond *Times-Dispatch*, May 21, 2017

27

THE BIG LIE

In his early 16th-century essay "The Prince," Italian diplomat Niccolo Machiavelli argued that to successfully govern a nation, rulers needed to learn the art of subtle lying.

"Occasionally words must serve to veil the facts," he observed.

Unfortunately, lying by our "rulers" has been anything but subtle or an art form. It seems that in some instances, the bigger the lie, the more some people buy into it, despite strong evidence to the contrary.

Referred to as "the big lie," the Oxford standard dictionary defines it as "a gross distortion or misrepresentation of the facts, especially when used as a propaganda device by a politician or official body."

Nazi propaganda minister Joseph Goebbels supposedly said: "If you tell a lie big enough and keep repeating it, people will eventually come to believe it … It becomes vitally important for the State to use all its powers to repress dissent, for the truth is the mortal enemy of the lie, and ... the truth is the greatest enemy of the State."

The 2020 presidential election and the January 6 violent insurrection in Washington are good examples of how the big lie still lives. Claiming that the election was stolen from former President Donald Trump through massive voting fraud, many of his supporters threatened to overturn the election results and eventually install their man as the legitimate president. They did this despite overwhelming evidence to the contrary.

Much like the disputed election, some Trump Republicans say the January 6 insurrection actually was a nonviolent event led by "peaceful patriots" who were taking a "normal tourist visit" of the U.S. Capitol. One only has to watch the news footage of the display of violence and destruction that went on at the Capitol to think there was anything peaceful about that day's events.

Cases of the big lie are nothing new. For example, Goebbels used it to tap into long-standing German antisemitism. He perpetuated the myth that "international Jewry" ultimately were responsible for Germany's defeat in World War I.

Long before that use of the big lie, a nativist political party and movement in the 1850s in the U.S. effectively used the big lie to its advantage. Calling themselves the Know Nothings, its xenophobic supporters were anti-Catholic, anti-Irish and anti-immigrant. Members also spread a big lie that a "Romanist" or "Papist" conspiracy to establish an official state religion (Catholic) was undermining religious and civil liberty in America.

The Know Nothings briefly emerged as a major political party in the 1856 presidential election, garnering nearly 22% of the popular vote. Despite this surprisingly strong showing, the party's existence was short-lived and it collapsed within a few years, riven over the issue of slavery.

A more significant and longer-lasting lie was the myth of the Lost Cause, consisting of a set of arguments describing slavery as a benign institution that had nothing to do with causing the Civil War.

Instead, advocates argued that a clash of cultures and Northern efforts to deprive the South of its unspecified states' rights led to an internecine conflict. The South, they contended, eventually lost the Civil War because of the overwhelming odds it faced in a mighty, industrialized North.

Named after Edward Pollard's book *The Lost Cause* (1866), the movement advocated white supremacy, the relegation of African Americans to second-class citizenship and portrayed the period of Reconstruction as a nightmare for Southern whites.

To Lost Cause advocates, the Confederacy had nothing to do with slavery, but was instead a noble endeavor, led by gallant men who sought to defend their homeland from Northern aggression.

Overwhelming documentary evidence, however, undermines the argument of those who claim the Civil War was not about slavery. The Confederacy was a nation based on laws and constitutional authority protecting slavery and the right of its citizens to own their fellow human beings. The Lost Cause myth held forth in the South for well more than a century, much to the detriment of its Black population.

The big lie also can be attributed to presidents who were less than truthful as the country edged toward war.

Both Presidents Woodrow Wilson and Franklin D. Roosevelt ran for re-election with the pledge to maintain neutrality as wars were raging in Europe. Using the slogan "He kept us out of war" helped Wilson gain re-election in a very close race but, within seven months, he asked and received a declaration of war on Germany.

Likewise, Roosevelt watched war break out in Europe in 1939, convinced that the U.S. eventually would be drawn into the conflict. Knowing that public opinion overwhelmingly was against involvement in the war, he used executive authority to quietly arm the nation in case it did.

Like Wilson in 1916, FDR ran for re-election in 1940 under a promise to keep the U.S. neutral, saying: "I've said it once and I shall say it again, and again, and again. Your boys are not going to be sent to any foreign wars."

He won re-election, but by the end of the next year, after the Japanese attack on Pearl Harbor, American boys would be in combat in almost every corner of the globe for the next four years.

In the cases both of Wilson and of Roosevelt, we can speculate that their less-than-truthful promises to the public were what they genuinely believed at the time and that we can be thankful that the country was better prepared to fight had the two presidents not done otherwise.

No better example of the big lie can be found than with U.S. Sen. Joe McCarthy of Wisconsin. In 1950, this little-known, first-time senator jumped onto the national stage by accusing his colleagues of ignoring the large number of communists who had infiltrated various federal departments and who sought to undermine the government.

The senator intuitively knew how to stir the emotions of the public by staging melodramatic congressional hearings where he and his staff grilled people they accused of being "communist stooges."

The exposure gained him a huge following, most of whom tuned into daily television broadcasts of the hearings. This went on for nearly four years, but after a while, when he failed to identify any foreign agents, the McCarthy witch hunt began to stand down.

Little by little, opposition to the senator grew. Even his Republican colleagues began to see him as a liability. His once-high positive numbers in the Gallup poll plummeted, and when the Senate overwhelmingly voted to censure him, his political career virtually was over. Already a heavy drinker, he imbibed even more and died at the age of 48.

Other examples of presidential actions could be regarded as the big lie - the Gulf of Tonkin Resolution and America's entry into the Vietnam War led by President Lyndon B. Johnson, and President George W. Bush's decision to go to war in 2004 under the dubious assertion that Iraq held a stockpile of weapons of mass destruction.

Does the big lie work? If most of the examples given above are any indication, the big lie might work in the short term but inevitably fails the test of time.

Richmond *Times-Dispatch*, May 23, 2021

28

THE LONG HISTORY OF MEN
BEHAVING VERY BADLY

T he recent cascade of the news of women accusing men of inappropriate sexual advances, and in some cases, outright rape, has been disturbing. In most cases, these accusations are directed toward men in positions of power, and have come from any number of sources- including the halls of Congress, the White House, Hollywood, Fox News, NPR, CBS, NBC, corporate boardrooms, the world of sports, and the military. The impending U.S. Senate election in Alabama has been consumed with charges of sexual misbehavior by candidate Roy Moore.

Women are beginning to rally as never before against a form of behavior that is as ancient as the Bible. The Old Testament relates that while King David strolled on the roof of his palace one spring morning, he observed a married woman, Bathsheba, taking a bath. He was immediately aroused.

David sent her a message, and then according to the scriptures "she came to him, and he slept with her," resulting in her pregnancy. He then had the audacity to order Bathsheba's husband serve in the front rank in battle, where he was killed so that the king could carry on his affair.

England's King Henry VIII gained notoriety for his six wives and his many dalliances. Two of his wives lost their heads for their failure to produce a male heir, one of whom was accused to having sex with someone other than her husband.

Improper conduct regarding sex in the past was not limited to Europe. One only has to look at colonial America to find an extensive record of sexual offenses. Take early New England, for example. It is generally assumed that the Puritans were prudes and squeamish about the facts of life; but in reality they regarded sex as a normal human necessity as long as it was within the proper bonds of marriage.

Despite laws that could punish adultery and rape with death, and proscribed public whipping for fornication, the Puritans frankly became inured of sexual offenses because there were so many. The records of the 17th-century New England courts reveal that illicit sexual activity was common.

The large number of criminal cases involving fornication and adultery may seem as a surprise today, but as historian Edmund S. Morgan observed, the reason "was the large number of men in the colonies who were unable to gratify their sexual desires in marriage."

Many of the early settlers were men who had left their wives in England, expecting to bring them later when they were able. Their sexual appetites, however, did not remain in England. As a result, female indentured servants became easy prey. Most servants lived in homes with their masters and were at their mercy. Servant women, however, rarely reported rape, knowing that the odds of conviction of the accused were almost insurmountable.

Given the widespread violation of the sexual codes of the time, the Puritans rarely imposed the severe penalties prescribed by their laws. They understood that humans could not possibly live up to these codes because of human frailty.

Rather than sentencing someone to death for adultery, the penalty usually was a public whipping, a fine, or branding, or a combination of the three. Rape was punished in the same way as adultery. Sodomy, on the other hand, was regarded as an unpardonable sin and on at least three occasions resulted in the death penalty.

***

While illicit sex in colonial New England occurred mostly between white people, interracial relations were common in the colonial and antebellum South. Much like servant women in the northeast, slave women were at the mercy of their masters and virtually any white man.

Civil War diarist Mary Boykin Chesnut of South Carolina recorded, "Our men seem to think of themselves as models of husbands and fathers. But in reality, like the patriarchs of old they live all in one house with their wives and their concubines and the mulattoes one sees in every family exactly resemble the white children."

Initially, mulatto children in colonial America were allowed to follow the race of their father, as was the case in the colonies of France, Holland, Portugal, and Spain. In 1662, however, the Virginia House of Burgesses passed legislation that required babies born as a result of interracial coupling to follow the condition of their mother, which usually meant they became slaves the moment they were born.

Were sexual relations between a white man and a black woman consensual or forced? It is impossible to determine in most cases. White overseers and planters often received sexual favors from female slaves in return for gifts or for time off from work in the field. Some women submitted to advances out of fear of being flogged or assigned exceptionally hard labor.

***

How does this account of sexual misconduct apply to us? Until recently, women have been virtually powerless to fight off the unwanted advances of men. Perhaps Oscar Wilde was on to something when he said, "Everything in the world is about sex except sex. Sex is about power."

As American women have gained power, wealth, and influence in almost all aspects of society, they have been emboldened to say, "Enough is enough!"

If Wilde was right, we are witnessing a significant paradigm shift of sexual relations. Men will still prey on women, but perhaps at long last most will learn there is a line that simply should not be crossed.

Richmond *Times-Dispatch*, July 9, 2017

29

FDR: War Leader Extraordinaire

As my wife and I prepare to move into a retirement community, we have been downsizing. For me that has meant culling books from my large history collection that I have accumulated for more than half a century. I have been donating them to the Virginia Historical Society for its annual fall book sale.

I acquired some of these books from my graduate school courses, and much to my wife's displeasure, I find myself stopping to re-read from a few of the volumes.

One is a collection of essays titled *World War II on the Homefront*, edited by Phyllis Emert. It reminded me of how the United States pulled off one of the most incredible feats in human history.

When it was attacked by Japan at Pearl Harbor on December 7, 1941, the U.S. was still struggling from the effects of the Great Depression and possessed a small and weak military force. Germany and Japan were the world's two leading military powers.

Yet it took only two years for the U.S. to exceed the combined industrial capacities of Germany, Japan, Great Britain, and the Soviet Union and to become the globe's mightiest military force. With the full weight of American might committed to the war, the once powerful Axis coalition collapsed in less than four years.

How did America pull off this remarkable feat? Many factors contributed to it, but as Professor Emert argued, one key was the extraordinary presidential leadership of Franklin D. Roosevelt.

***

Even before the U.S. entered the war in 1941, Roosevelt believed it would eventually be drawn into the conflict. Despite widespread political opposition to American involvement, he turned his attention from domestic matters to prepare the country for war.

He began to strengthen the country's armed forces by instituting the country's first peacetime draft. He replaced old and tired military leadership with energetic new senior officers. Once the U.S. joined the fray, he took a number of steps that in retrospect were essential to victory.

Under FDR, the U.S. mobilized some 12 million people into military service, nearly as many as the Soviet Union, which had a population 40 percent larger.

Wartime manufacturing growth was astounding. America produced more airplanes than all of the world's major powers combined. With some 6,000 ships in its fleet, the U.S. Navy became the largest in history.

Despite being labeled a socialist by some critics, Roosevelt used the free enterprise system to work within the framework of wartime regulations to create a powerful combination of economic forces unlike that of any other nation.

With large numbers of men going into the armed forces, American industry expanded as its workforce experienced a pronounced increase in women and minority laborers. By the end of 1942, virtually the entire country and its people were mobilized for war.

***

Roosevelt took advantage of the country not having to rely on other nations for the resources to wage war. Because it was blessed with an abundance of natural resources of its own, the U.S. could fill its own needs in military vehicles, munitions, weaponry, and foodstuff, but also provide huge quantities of weapons and materiel to its allies Great Britain and the Soviet Union.

Roosevelt inherently understood that he would have to be forthright with the American people about the task ahead. He candidly told them to expect a long and hard war, but he inspired them by declaring that the U.S. represented good versus an enemy aligned "against the whole human race."

He was a savvy and experienced politician who knew that he needed to work with the Republican opposition to get things done. Therefore, he appointed Republicans to a number of key positions - realizing that the good of the country outweighed political partisanship if the Republicans brought certain skills and experience to the job.

While FDR concentrated his efforts on broad strategic matters, he put together a first-class team of military leaders, headed by General George C. Marshall, to conduct the war. He then delegated most responsibilities to his generals and admirals. Yet he was self-assured in his own decisions and opinions, and was not reluctant to countermand his military leaders if needed.

He had enough confidence in himself that he did not feel threatened by or jealous of the successes of his subordinates.

Roosevelt was not a perfect person or president. He could be duplicitous. He could be secretive to a fault. He could be reluctant to admit mistakes. He stayed in office too long, allowing himself to run for a fourth term despite his declining health, which led to his eventual death only months after his re-election.

When I compare FDR's leadership to that of the current president, however, I cannot think of a greater contrast.

One had considerable experience in public service going into the job, and had the skills to effectively pull the levers of government. He had the temperament and experience to lead the nation during hard times and its largest war. His ability to inspire people with his words and reassuring voice were perhaps the best of any president. His messages aroused hope, not fear. As a result, even during the darkest days of the war, his approval rating neared 70 percent.

The current president, on the other hand, was and still is ill-prepared for the job. With an approval rating of less than 40 percent in the latest polls, it will be difficult for Donald Trump to recover from the lowest numbers ever accorded a new president.

Some of his defenders argue that we need to give him time to learn and to grow in the position. Others say that his in-your-face style and unpredictable actions reflect the will of the people who elected him. Supporters also contend that he has surrounded himself with competent advisors. Unfortunately, he tends to ignore or contradict them regularly.

You can excuse a person's amateurish blunders only so many times. The stakes are too high for the nation and the world to have an apprentice at the helm. Franklin Roosevelt was a statesman of the first order, the architect of victory. Whether they agree with Donald Trump's policies or not, the American people should realize by now that he does not have the background nor the temperament to lead the nation. I shudder to think of what would have happened if someone like him had been president in 1939 when war broke out in Europe.

Richmond *Times-Dispatch*, September 3, 2017

30

WILD MAN IN THE WHITE HOUSE

He skillfully used the press to directly woo public support, bypassing the Republican Party establishment.

He was born into wealth and had a privileged upbringing in New York City. He graduated from an Ivy League college. He first became known nationally for his best-selling books. He had a bigger-than-life personality that appealed to many people, but offended others.

He had an overweening ego and was easily offended by criticism. He was a brash self-promoter who tapped into the public's anger over politics as usual. He assumed the presidency as a Republican but was regarded as an outsider by many in his own party because his views did not match theirs on many key issues. The policies he implemented were a significant change in direction for the nation.

Whom am I describing? Donald Trump? Or Theodore Roosevelt? Though the two men share certain similarities, the dissimilarities are far more striking.

While they both came from wealthy families, Roosevelt devoted the majority of his career to public service, whereas Trump entered the rough-and-tumble world of the New York real estate business, where he achieved enormous wealth and international fame. At the same time, he gained notoriety as a television personality.

Roosevelt entered politics as a young man, and eventually became the youngest president to be sworn into office. Nevertheless, he was arguably the best prepared of any person to assume the presidency.

In addition to volunteering and participating in combat during the Spanish-American War, he served as a member of the New York legislature, the U.S. Civil Service Commission, president of the New York City Police Board, assistant secretary of the Navy, governor of New York, vice president of the United States, and eventually as president upon the assassination of President William McKinley.

Although he built a business empire, Trump is arguably the least prepared president in U.S. history, never having been elected or appointed to public office. As a candidate for the White House, Trump touted his lack of political experience as a virtue. Thomas A. Bailey, however, observed in his classic book, *Presidential Greatness* (1966), that the "most successful presidents have been skilled and experienced politicians."

***

Once in the White House, Roosevelt put his experience to work. Considered by many scholars to be the first modern president, he greatly expanded the power and influence of the executive branch.

He launched a program he labeled the Square Deal that was designed to protect citizens from unscrupulous business practices; regulate corporations from becoming monopolies; and conserve the country's natural resources. He challenged the concept of individualism and limited government. He used the federal government to achieve social and economic justice.

In terms of race relations, Roosevelt was a moderate for his era. He believed that equality for African-Americans would eventually come with the passage of one generation to another, possibly two.

He drew the ire of many Southern politicians, one of whom condemned Roosevelt for "mingling and mongrelizing" the races, especially when he had the audacity to invite Booker T. Washington to dinner in the White House, a hugely symbolic gesture for the time.

More so than any previous president, he signed an unprecedented number of executive orders to carry out his agenda, particularly relating to conservation and the environment.

He conducted an especially aggressive foreign policy and was awarded the Nobel Peace prize for negotiating a peace agreement between Russia and Japan.

The majority of the public adored him, and he easily won the 1904 presidential election to secure his own term. He skillfully used the press to directly woo public support, bypassing the Republican Party establishment.

**

On the other hand, Trump is the oldest person elected to the presidency, but his lack of political experience has hindered him.

Trump has hired and fired members of his own administration with such regularity that continuity of purpose has been difficult to detect. His main thrust appears to be policies of dismantling rather building, except a promise to construct a wall on the U.S./Mexican border to keep illegal immigrants out of the country.

He seems almost consumed with the idea of overturning the policies of his predecessor Barack Obama and, in some cases, those of George W. Bush.

Despite having Republican majorities in both houses of Congress, until the last-minute passage of a comprehensive tax reform bill, his legislative achievements have been modest.

Unlike most presidents who enjoy relatively high poll numbers during their first year in office - and despite a strong economic forecast for the nation - Trump's approval record has been the lowest of any president at this stage in his administration, rating as little as 35 percent.

Candidate Trump ran on a pledge to "Make America Great Again." Nearly two-thirds of the American public now doubts the current president is capable of achieving that goal, and more than half of voters question his assertion that the nation no longer is great.

***

Only one year into the Trump presidency, is there enough time for him to turn things around? What happens if in this fall's election, Democrats take one or both houses of Congress? Has he gained enough of the factor that historian Bailey argues is the key to success in office - experience?

Maybe comparing him to that other brash New Yorker is unfair at this stage of the game. Other men, such as Harry Truman and Ronald Reagan, have had rough starts to their presidencies, but finished their terms on a high note or have been judged kindly by history. They were able to adapt to the challenges of running a country, relying on their previous experience in politics and government to guide them.

From what I have observed so far, however, President Trump is too far behind on the learning curve to turn things around to rescue his presidency.

Richmond *Times-Dispatch*, February 18, 2018

31

AMERICAN PRESIDENTS AND CRISES

How presidents react to crises often determines the success or failure of their time in office. "One of the first requisites of a presidential leader is the ability to form sound judgments and then act on them, or not act on them," observed diplomatic historian Thomas A. Bailey.

In some instances restraint is called for, while in others audacious action is required. Going either way can have serious consequences. Here are three examples of how presidents faced crises.

The first major crisis a president faced came in the nation's infancy in 1794. Known as the Whiskey Rebellion, Pennsylvania farmers refused to pay a recently imposed federal tax on the whiskey they produced. Based on a policy developed and implemented by Secretary of the Treasury Alexander Hamilton, revenue from the tax was earmarked to pay down the national debt and to prevent future financial burdens on the country. Hamilton believed that if a nation was to prosper, especially a young one like the United States, it must possess solid financial underpinnings and demonstrate sound fiscal management.

In this case, however, the tax was a failure as large numbers of outraged farmers refused to pay it. They resorted to mob violence, tarring and feathering tax collectors, destroying property, and eventually forming a 7,000-man armed force to protect their interests. Attempts to negotiate a settlement failed, leaving President George Washington with no option other than armed confrontation.

Using the Militias Act of 1792, he assembled a 12,000-man army from other state militias to force compliance from the Pennsylvanians. This well-armed provisional army marched into western Pennsylvania with Washington at its head and a uniformed Hamilton at his side, ready for action. Although Washington's army was greeted with jeers and minor resistance, the farmers eventually caved in when confronted by such an overwhelming force.

Washington could have had the rebellion's ringleaders executed after their arrest, but he magnanimously pardoned them to the chagrin of Hamilton and other members of Washington's Federalist party.

Washington's low-key but firm actions in forcing the rebels to end the dispute revealed that constraint and then forgiveness in this case were in the end the best way to end this crisis by working out a peace agreement with the rebellious farmers. The tax was never fully enforced and was dropped several years later. Washington, however, proved that the new government had the will and ability to confront resistance to its laws.

Other presidents perhaps would not have reacted with such restraint. Washington's vice president and eventual successor, John Adams, for example, was obstinate, opinionated, vain and impatient. In foreign affairs he was decidedly anti-French and pro-British, an issue that became the most divisive of its time. Adams was easily offended by those who opposed his policies, particularly when he strongly enforced the Alien and Sedition Act that restricted freedom of speech and political dissent.

Adams ordered newspaper editors who disagreed with him tried, convicted, fined and jailed. He welcomed new laws developed by his own Federalist party that allowed a president to deport new immigrants and deny certain ones the right to vote. His presidency lasted only one term, despite his best efforts to tamp down his opposition. Most Americans then remembered having rid themselves of one oppressive government, and they did not want to impose another on the people. Adams never held public office again.

Two centuries later, the nation faced another crisis, one that could have resulted in nuclear warfare. John F. Kennedy, the youngest person elected president and with no executive experience, had been in office a little more than a year when American intelligence sources revealed that the Soviet Union was installing missiles armed with nuclear warheads in Cuba, only 90 miles from American soil.

Kennedy faced a fateful decision with three basic options: (1) do nothing and live with the consequences; (2) declare a blockade to disrupt all shipping into Cuba: and (3) take military action, by attacking and destroying limited targets in Cuba or launching a large-scale invasion.

After intense debate among his inner circle, Kennedy finally decided to overrule his military advisers and go with the second option, calling it a "quarantine" rather than a more provocative term of "blockade."

Kennedy's gambit exerted maximum pressure on Soviet Premier Nikita Khrushchev. After a week of tense negotiations following the imposition of a blockade, Khrushchev quietly agreed to remove all missiles from Cuba in exchange for an American promise that it would not invade Cuba. Kennedy's deft handling of the situation had prevented a possible nuclear conflict, the consequences of which are almost too frightening to consider.

In a study of modern presidents and crises, author Michael Bohn notes that few presidents can "realistically accomplish what the public expects in a crisis. Everyone demands bold and decisive action to right wrongs." But as Bohn observes, presidents who have taken aggressive steps often have failed to accomplish what they set out to do. When, for example, Great Britain took several actions that harmed American commerce and trade in 1807, President Thomas Jefferson imposed a self-destructive tariff in response. According to U.S. Congressman John Randolph of Virginia, it was like cutting off a toe to cure it from corns. Indeed, the tariff nearly ruined the American economy and proved to be a disastrous failure.

How would the current occupant of the White House perform during a crisis?

As Bailey argued, "the test of top-drawer [presidential] leadership is firmness and coolness of the incumbent in handling crises." With potential emergencies with North Korea, China and Iran facing the nation today, we can only hope President Donald Trump would carefully study how some of his predecessors let restraint outweigh action.

The American people should expect no less.

Richmond *Times-Dispatch*, May 26, 2019

32

A MODERN-DAY OLD HICKORY?

Forty years ago, I started my first job as a professional historian. Upon finishing my Ph.D., I took a position as assistant editor of the Andrew Jackson Papers, a documentary editing project located at The Hermitage, Jackson's home near Nashville. I spent more than three years there transcribing and editing the seventh president's voluminous correspondence, which was published eventually by the University of Tennessee Press.

At that time, scholars rated Jackson in the top tier of chief executives, as a "great" or "near great" president. Like most historians then, I agreed. His rags-to-riches life story was compelling. He was a national military hero and an iconic public figure who left the White House with even more popular approval than when he entered it. He claimed the mantle of championing the common man. As president, he took decisive action in resisting the secession of South Carolina in 1831, thereby perhaps preventing civil war. In many ways, he was bigger than life.

Over the years, however, my perspective, along with those of many other historians, began to change. Almost from the beginning, Jackson's administration was beset with controversy, most of it of his own doing. Branded by his political enemies as dictatorial and capricious, he maintained that he was the only elected official of all the people and that he should uphold their interests against a sectionalized, incompetent Congress, a body that he confronted frequently.

He was the first president to use the veto for reasons of expediency rather than on constitutional grounds, tipping the balance of power toward the executive branch. For that matter, he issued more vetoes in his term as president than all of his predecessors combined.

Furthermore, he appointed loyal men to his cabinet with whom he rarely consulted, relying instead on an unofficial "kitchen cabinet" that provided him mostly with managed news reported to him by "yes men."

He attempted to make himself co-equal with the judicial branch in determining the constitutionality of legislation. He defied the Supreme Court on several issues, knowing that it had no real authority to ensure compliance with its rulings. In one case, he was reported to have said about the chief justice of the United States, "Mr. Marshall has made his decision, now let him enforce it."

Two issues in particular stand out as examples of Jackson's misguided policies. The first involved Indian lands in North Carolina, Tennessee and Georgia. As the commander of an American army in the War of 1812, Jackson waged hard war against the Creek Indians, who had allied themselves with the British.

Upon his election as president, he brought a deep-seated resentment against Indians with him to office. In his 1829 inaugural address, Jackson called for the relocation of all Eastern Indians to beyond the Mississippi River. This was a popular idea among white settlers, particularly when gold was discovered on Indian lands in Georgia. The president's wish became federal law when he lobbied Congress to pass the Indian Removal Act in 1830.

After several years of legal wrangling, and Jackson's refusal to respond to pleas from the Indians, he forced the removal of some 14,000 Cherokee from their native lands to the current state of Oklahoma. Escorted by soldiers, the group lacked adequate clothing and food, and was poorly prepared for the deplorable weather they experienced, an estimated 4,000 men, women and children died before reaching their final destination.

Long relegated to brief references in American history textbooks, the Trail of Tears now has been brought to the forefront by scholars as one of the most tragic chapters in the American experience.

Another misguided Jackson policy that would have long-standing consequences centered on the economy. For years, Jackson had a deep distrust of banks in general, but especially the Bank of the United States, which had been the brainchild of Secretary of the Treasury Alexander Hamilton during George Washington's presidency. Designed to provide enduring economic stability to the nation, the bank, Jackson argued, was controlled by a few wealthy men who lined their pockets at public expense. When the bank charter came up for renewal in 1836, Jackson refused to sign it, and for all intents and purposes the institution went out of business, with its assets distributed among several state banks.

This action, combined with a shortsighted policy of demanding only gold or silver to pay for the purchase of public lands, led directly to a financial panic in 1837. Had he simply curbed some of the central bank's practices rather than crush it altogether, he could have saved the nation from weakened finances that brought untold misery to hundreds of thousands of people for many years to come.

Ironically, Jackson made the presidency so strong during his two terms in office that most of his successors were weak leaders who were unable to effectively lead the country through a series of crises that eventually led to civil war.

It is perhaps not surprising that Donald Trump has embraced Jackson as his hero. Soon after his inauguration, the president hung Old Hickory's portrait in the Oval Office and called him "an amazing figure in American history."

One can go too far in comparing the two men, as there is as much dissimilarity between them as there is similarity. Nevertheless, even though the times and circumstances are different, for better and for worse, we seem to have a modern-day Old Hickory in the White House now.

Richmond *Times-Dispatch*, August 11, 2019

33

THE UNINSPIRING PRESIDENCY OF HERBERT HOOVER

N early a century ago, the United States was in the throes of the Great Depression. With the stock market crash in October 1929, followed by a downward spiral in the economy, the American people were stunned by the turn of events that resulted. Businesses across the country began shutting down while the ranks of the unemployed soared, eventually rising to more than a staggering 30%.

The crisis had widespread implications and created a ripple effect. The automobile industry, for example, had become one of the most important sectors of the American economy. With the financial collapse, car sales plummeted, which in turn led to dramatically reduced production and sales in the steel, rubber, glass and oil industries.

The situation demanded strong and inspirational leadership from the White House to grapple with the challenges the nation faced. That leader was Herbert Hoover. Elected in 1928 as the third Republican president in succession, Hoover never had served in an elected office nor was he an astute politician.

Though a brilliant engineer by profession, he lacked warmth and color. He was especially thin-skinned, and he seemed incapable of accepting blame for even the smallest of mistakes he made.

He came across as shy, standoffish and uninspiring. He gave the American people the distinct impression that he didn't care about their needs and wants, something that eventually came back to haunt him.

Hoover believed that the economy would return to prosperity sooner than the pundits predicted. He consistently discounted estimates provided by his advisers on the number of unemployed American workers. He urged business leaders to be optimistic, to buy raw materials while prices were down, to maintain the level of employment and wages and then count on sales to rise.

In May 1930, despite the warnings of many economists, Hoover signed into law the Smoot-Hawley Tariff Act that so drastically raised duties on more than 900 items that it resulted in a sharp decline in international trade, and only made the situation worse.

Hoover then directed his messages to the general public, urging Americans to have faith in business and to buy rather than hoard. Like his campaigns to spur on business, his public endeavor accomplished little.

Ironically, he did more to address the nation's financial problems than any previous president who faced an economic crisis. He accelerated federal construction projects, urged state and local governments to speed up spending, and attained promises from the railroad and utility companies to increase capital expenditures.

He took other measures that foreshadowed the deficit spending relief program implemented by his successor, Franklin D. Roosevelt.

But as presidential historian Thomas A. Bailey noted, "Hoover offered active leadership but not effective leadership... He was not so much a do-nothing President as he was one who apparently did nothing that worked to stem the tidal wave of depression."

In 1933, Hoover left the White House a bitter man after losing in a landslide election to Roosevelt, who promised a "New Deal" for the American people.

It took Roosevelt nearly eight years and a global war to end the Depression, but he had certain skills and a temperament that served him well as president. He inspired the American people and led them in recapturing faith in themselves and their government. Unlike the glum Hoover, Roosevelt led with a self-assured buoyancy and contagious optimism that united the country.

Historian Bailey noted that the most highly ranked presidents - George Washington, Abraham Lincoln, Roosevelt - exhibited "the firmness and coolness incumbent in handling emergencies."

But as the late *USA Today* columnist Michael Medved observed, "All presidents at one time or another face dire, unexpected crises in which success or failure depends on the way they process challenges more than on their philosophical outlook."

President Donald Trump's philosophical outlook is difficult to pin down, but his abilities as a leader of the nation have come under question, especially lately. He often is called to task for his unabashed disregard of the truth, whether that be the size of the crowd at his presidential inaugural or the availability of test kits for the coronavirus.

With a presidential election in the offing, Trump will put his performance as our nation's chief executive to a vote by the American people. If his initial response to the current pandemic and economic crisis seems no better than Hoover's to the Great Depression, chances are likely that he will be a one-term president.

Richmond *Times-Dispatch*, July 19, 2020

34

CONTROVERSIAL ELECTIONS
ARE NOTHING NEW

W ith only a matter of weeks to go before the 2020 presidential election, the American public anxiously awaits its outcome. Although many presidential elections have been contentious, this year's version seems unusually combative.

Many political experts contend that its final results might not be determined until well after the Nov. 3 election date. President Donald Trump repeatedly has argued that if he loses, the election is rigged and a hoax. To date, he has not said that the results are bogus if he wins.

Regardless of the final tally, it could be one of many controversial presidential elections in American history. Here are some examples of others:

1800

Exactly 200 years ago, Americans experienced their first disputed presidential election. Anyone who has seen the hit Broadway musical "Hamilton" knows the story.

The process of electing presidents differed then because each Electoral College member had two votes that did not differentiate between the presidency and the vice presidency. The man who received the most votes assumed the presidency, while the runner-up became vice president.

In this case, Thomas Jefferson was presumed to be pitted against the incumbent John Adams for the presidency. But under the existing system, Jefferson's 73 electoral votes were tied by 73 for Aaron Burr, a presumptive vice presidential candidate from New York. Adams garnered 67 votes. Because of the tie, the election went to the House of Representatives for resolution.

Burr was an anathema to many people, especially Treasury Secretary Alexander Hamilton, who openly lobbied against him. Even though Hamilton had no love for Jefferson, he considered him a better choice than Burr whom he said, "loves nothing but himself" and "thinks of nothing but his own aggrandizement."

Nevertheless, Jefferson became president and relunctantly had to accept Burr as his vice president. Three years later, Vice President Burr killed Hamilton in a duel over accusations of marital infidelity. Wanting to avoid future situations when the president and vice president were political opponents, Congress approved the 12th Amendment to the Constitution that required electors to vote for the country's two highest offices separately.

1824 and 1828

Twenty-four years later, Americans experienced another controversial presidential election. By 1824, the death of an infant two-party system led to chaos with four candidates vying for the presidency. Andrew Jackson, hero of the Battle of New Orleans in 1815, ran against John Quincy Adams, son of the former president; House Speaker Henry Clay; and Treasury Secretary William H. Crawford.

Jackson won the popular vote by 40,000 and landed 99 electoral votes, followed by Adams with 84 electoral votes, then Crawford and Clay. With no candidate earning a clear majority of electoral votes, the election once again went to the House of Representatives under the leadership of Speaker Clay.

House members went into secret negotiations for a month and finally emerged with a winner - Adams. Soon afterward, Adams announced his cabinet, awarding the prestigious secretary of state position to Clay.

Suspecting collusion, a livid Jackson denounced the appointment as a "corrupt bargain" and declared that he again would run against Adams in 1828. As the new head of the Democratic Party, he kept his word in one of the most mean-spirited elections in American history. Adams supporters argued that Jackson's mother had been a prostitute and his wife was an adulterer.

Jacksonians responded by accusing Adams of being a pimp for the czar when he served as ambassador to Russia. Of course, none of these allegations was proven true, but the accusation of an illicit scheme haunted the incumbent throughout his term and ultimately led to a crushing political defeat rendered by Jackson in 1828.

1948

The outcome of this election stunned the nation as no other and turned out to be one of the greatest upsets of all presidential contests.

Harry S. Truman was a relatively unknown senator when President Franklin D. Roosevelt asked him to be his running mate in the 1944 election. Roosevelt was elected to an unprecedented fourth term in a close race but a few months later, he died.

Roosevelt had kept Truman in the dark regarding most policy issues and security matters, including the existence of an atomic bomb. Nevertheless, as president, Truman made some of the most significant decisions in American history, including dropping two atomic bombs on Japan, thereby ending World War II; implementation of the Marshall Plan to restore war-torn Western Europe; and the racial integration of the armed forces.

Energetic, outspoken and self-confident, he proved to be a strong president. Yet few presidents have had a worse working record with Congress, even within his own party. His stands on civil rights and labor split the Democratic Party into three factions in 1948.

Given little chance of being elected in his own right, he nevertheless was nominated by the party to run against Republican Gov. Thomas E. Dewey of New York. Most polls and political experts gave Truman little chance of victory, but he took his case directly to the public on a whistle-stop train tour of the nation.

Using the "do-nothing" Congress as his primary target, Truman's message gained resonance with a growing number of Americans. On Election Day, Truman pulled out a victory in what has been described as a political miracle. Although he had a low public approval rating when he left office in 1953, today he is ranked as a near-great president by most historians.

Other controversial contests provide additional insights into our process of electing presidents. The elections of 1860, 1876, 1912 and 2000 demonstrate that the current way of choosing presidents is not perfect, yet it has worked reasonably well for two centuries.

It would be a shame if careless talk about the upcoming election being riddled with fraud and a hoax undermined one of the most important rights American citizens possess.

Richmond *Times-Dispatch*, September 27, 2020

35

BEWARE OF SEDITION LAWS
THE ROAD TO TYRANNY

John Adams undoubtedly belongs among the pantheon of the Founding Fathers, along with George Washington, Thomas Jefferson, James Madison and Benjamin Franklin.

Yet as the nation's second president, Adams was not successful. He was obstinate, opinionated, vain, impatient and he lacked good judgment. He was a poor administrator. Furthermore, he was thin-skinned and intolerant even of mild criticism directed at him and his Federalist Party, especially when it came from his political opponents under the influence of Republican Thomas Jefferson.

The struggle between the two factions revolved around monetary policy, state versus federal authority and foreign affairs. Adams and his fellow Federalists favored Great Britain in its seemingly endless conflict with France, while Jefferson's followers were Francophiles.

The clamor against Adams was relentless, with much of it coming from recent immigrants. Included among them were French aristocrats who had fled their country's bloody revolution, anti-Royalist English radicals and Irish nationalists. Most of these newcomers were Anglophobic and staunch backers of the Jeffersonian Republicans.

While we tend to think that the rhetoric invoked by politicians and their respective media today such as Fox News and MSNBC are partisan and sharp-edged, it almost seems tame compared to the invective used at the turn of the 19th century.

Both factions engaged in a bitter war of words, pulling no punches. Each side outright owned newspapers that trumpeted their respective party lines, and regularly peddled dubious stories of corruption and scandal about its opponents.

Federalists in Congress decided that it was time to muzzle the critics of Adams. In the summer of 1798, Congress passed four highly restrictive measures collectively known as the Alien and Sedition Acts.

The first, a new Naturalization Act, increased the length of residence in the U.S. necessary to attain citizenship from five to 14 years. It also required all aliens to register and to give five years' notice of their intention to become citizens.

Next came the Alien Act, which permitted the president to expel any immigrant whom he deemed "dangerous to the peace and safety of United States." If the alien refused to obey, the president could have him jailed for up to three years.

The third, the Alien Enemies Act, empowered the president to imprison or banish any alien who was a subject of an enemy nation.

Last came the most controversial measure - the Sedition Act. Clearly aimed at rival Republicans, it imposed large monetary fines and imprisonment of up to two years for anyone who should "write, print, or utter any false, scandalous and malicious writing ... against the government of the United States."

The act also included punishment for anyone who criticized or defamed members of Congress or the president. If that wasn't enough, the accused person could be fined for as much as $5,000 (more than $100,000 today) and given a jail sentence of up to five years. The entire concept of freedom of speech and the press guaranteed in the Bill of Rights seemed in jeopardy.

The Jeffersonian Republicans denounced the Sedition Act as despotic, an alarming assault on free speech and unconstitutional. On the other hand, with Adams' approval, the Federalists argued that they were essential in light of the threat posed by civil unrest fomented by recent immigrants.

With the power to suppress almost any form of dissent, the Federalists went into action. Citing the Sedition Act, Federal authorities arrested 24 Republican newspaper editors, including Benjamin Franklin's grandson. James Callender, editor of the Richmond Examiner, was sentenced to nine months in prison. Many of the sedition trials were blatant parodies of justice.

Congressman Matthew Lyon, an Irish immigrant, was convicted on three counts of libel and sent to jail in Vermont for a letter he had published questioning Adams' sanity.

Jefferson was determined to have these laws overturned. Today, resolving the constitutionality of legislation is decided by a process known as "judicial review," whereby the Supreme Court justices rule on a law's legitimacy based on their interpretation of the Constitution.

The concept of the court's role and authority as one of three equal branches of government, however, did not come until later. As a result, Jefferson and James Madison attacked the new laws by secretly going through the Virginia and Kentucky legislatures. The Virginia and Kentucky Resolutions, written by Madison and Jefferson, declared the Alien and Sedition Acts as unconstitutional and that in such cases, "states are duty bound to interpose."

The acts remained on the books for another decade, but they no longer were enforced, and eventually were repealed or allowed to lapse.

They, however, left a permanent stain on the reputation of John Adams. His Federalist Party was disrupted and demoralized, never to regain control of the national administration. Since then, the few times that sedition legislation has been imposed, it has created more discord than ever was intended.

Recently, U.S. Attorney General Bill Barr urged federal prosecutors to consider filing sedition charges against protesters in several American cities. Although reserved for those who have posed an immediate threat to government authority, such measures usually are a violation of the First Amendment of the Constitution and are rescinded by the courts.

Silencing free speech is one of the first steps on the road to tyranny. Jefferson vehemently opposed any measure that curtailed the ability of citizens to speak their minds. The threat posed by a president and government with too much power is well worth remaining vigilant against today.

Richmond *Times-Dispatch*, October 12, 2020

36

Presidential Winners and Losers

The recent presidential election is being wrapped up amid controversy. Initially, it almost reminded me of a comedic Gilbert and Sullivan musical.

Unfortunately, the potential consequences are real and anything but funny. While President Donald Trump has limited his ventures outside the White House since the election mainly to play golf, the COVID-19 pandemic has re-emerged as a national health crisis. At the same time, Trump's reluctance to ensure a smooth transition to a new administration reflects a level of irresponsibility rarely seen in presidential history.

Although his actions have been odd, this is not the first time there has been a less-than-smooth transfer of presidential power.

Indeed, presidential transitions can be awkward, especially if the incumbent president has lost the recent election to his successor. The period between election and inauguration also can lead to serious consequences for the country as it did in 1932.

Incumbent Republican President Herbert Hoover had a deep dislike of his opponent, Democrat Franklin D. Roosevelt, whom he accused of dishonesty and "for dealing from the bottom of the deck." Furthermore, Hoover charged Roosevelt with being a socialist who would lead the country on a "march to Moscow."

At the same time, Roosevelt had little respect for Hoover, referring to him as a "do nothing" president who should be held responsible for the deepening depression that was gripping the nation. Even as some states began to shut down their banking systems, Hoover refused to take any aggressive steps to slow the panic.

By the time Roosevelt took office, the country's banking system and economy nearly had ground to a halt. It would take a world war some seven years later to lift the country out of the economic quagmire it had gotten itself in.

An earlier presidential election that ended in a virtual tie ironically led to a serious and long setback for Blacks in the South. Presidential scholars long have regarded the 1876 election as perhaps the most controversial of all.

With a steady stream of Republican victories since the presidential election of 1860, Southern Democrats were anxious to attract someone who finally gave them a good chance of winning. Their candidate, Gov. Samuel Tilden of New York, fit the profile of an honest, solid and competent executive who could run effectively against a record of corruption and incompetence in sitting President Ulysses S. Grant's administration.

The Republicans nominated Civil War veteran Rutherford B. Hayes, three-time governor of Ohio, advocate of civil service reform and a man with a reputation for integrity.

In an extremely tight and fiercely fought race, both sides claimed victory with a virtual tie in electoral votes and a close popular vote. Thrown to Congress to break the deadlock, the dispute dragged on for weeks, with the distinct possibility that no one would be selected in time for the inauguration of the new president in March. Threats of violence swept the nation, to which Grant warned that he would declare martial law, if necessary, to quell the civil unrest.

With concern that the situation was worsening, leaders from both parties began complex and often heated negotiations. Finally, with only two days before the inauguration, Southern Democrats worked out a deal that solved the dilemma and actually worked to their advantage.

Knowing that Hayes was a moderate and no radical, they threw their votes to him. In return, they gained a number of concessions, including federal government subsidies for Southern railroads, federal assistance for internal improvements and, perhaps most important, the removal of all remaining federal troops from the South.

Since the end of the Civil War, Union soldiers had occupied the former Confederate states to, among other things, ensure that the recently emancipated slaves were not mistreated, and their civil rights were not violated. White Southerners had resented the presence of what they considered an occupying army and took whatever opportunity they could to intimidate African Americans. The presence of Union soldiers kept that threat at bay.

With the troop removals, however, Southern states began passing so-called Jim Crow legislation that restricted voting rights for Blacks, imposed rigid segregation of the races in public places and imposed a system that relegated them to second-class citizenship for nearly a century.

Historian Eric Foner described this set of events as "one of the most significant setbacks in American history." It relegated a large portion of the nation's population to decades of grinding poverty, severely limited educational opportunities, disfranchisement from the political process and a long legacy of inferior health care.

Trump still is proclaiming victory in the recent election, refusing to acknowledge a growing mountain of evidence revealing the opposite. Little by little, his supporters are beginning to face reality and are leaving the administration. The time has come for him to face reality and admit defeat. To do otherwise only makes his behavior seem more childish and could do serious harm to the nation.

Richmond *Times-Dispatch*, December 13, 2020

37

DEMAGOGUERY AND
THE GREAT INSURRECTION

Since the deadly assault on the U.S. Capitol by an angry mob, any number of people have asked me to put that unsettling event in historical perspective. I answer that frankly, I can cite nothing from our history that helps us understand the January 6th orgy of violence and destruction.

If anything, I keep thinking about Eric Larson's bestselling book, *In the Garden of Beasts*, an account of William E. Dodd's term as American ambassador to Germany in the 1930s.

Dodd, a one-time history professor at Randolph-Macon College, and his wife and two adult children arrived in Berlin in late 1932. His daughter, Martha, soon became enamored with the handsome young men who enthusiastically supported restoring Germany to world prominence as promised by Adolf Hitler and his Nazi followers.

On the other hand, Ambassador Dodd soon grew concerned over Hitler's rhetoric, and the actions he and his supporters took. He watched the persecution of Jews with mounting alarm. He witnessed the elimination of personal freedoms, including muzzling of news sources that dared question the actions of the Nazis.

Dodd reported his concerns to his superiors in the State Department and President Franklin D. Roosevelt to little avail. State Department officials doubted Dodd's claims, and argued that Hitler merely was a flash in the pan. The German people surely would come to their senses and reject him and his cronies, they argued.

Their prediction turned out to be horribly wrong. Hitler continued to strengthen his position and increase his power. By the time Dodd left his post in 1937, he was convinced that his voice was not being heard in Washington.

In the meantime, the dictator was poised to conquer much of western Europe and to begin the mass murder of millions of Jews and others deemed as "undesirables."

How does Dodd's story relate to this past week's attack on the U.S. Capitol? The common element that ties them together are the roles played by two demagogues - Adolf Hitler and Donald Trump - who attracted huge followings despite the unsavory characters of both men.

The word "demagogue" is Greek in its origin and has been applied to the likes of Caesar, Napoleon, Benito Mussolini, Josef Stalin and Venezuela's Hugo Chavez.

By spreading a message of fear and hate, demagogues have a genius for attracting large numbers of followers. They heavily rely on repeated lies to convince people to become their followers.

They persuade those followers to believe they are victims of any number of grievances caused by "enemies of the people," often in the form of a conspiracy. Hitler singled out Jews, while Trump has targeted, among others, immigrants.

They often reach out to other demagogues to strengthen their own positions, as Hitler did with Mussolini, Spain's Francisco Franco and, at one time, Stalin. Trump has shunned many of our traditional allies, while cozying up to the likes of Russian's Vladimir Putin and Kim Jong Un of North Korea.

The advent of modern communications such as radio became powerful tools for Hitler to get his message across, while Twitter and Facebook have allowed Trump to reach even larger audiences.

Whatever the January 6 event is labeled, it likely is to be considered a turning point in history. Pundits already have posited that it was "the worst day in American history" and "another date that will live in infamy."

The perspective of time should tell us just how serious it was. But as more information about the insurrection leaks out, the more we realize just how much worse it could have been.

Based on evidence found after the insurrection, we now have good reason to believe that some of the protesters (terrorists) apparently came prepared to commit mass murder and kidnapping.

God forbid that we have another such attack on a national treasure. Going forward, what we say to each other and how we say it can make a difference between civility and rudeness. The words we use can be hot buttons.

How, for example, does calling Republicans "fascists" or "Nazis" and Democrats "socialists" and "Communists" advance civil discourse? The words we use can result in insurrection and the trashing of a national icon, or in a Kristallnacht that singled out Jews to suffer beatings and mass destruction of property.

One of the first steps is for everyone, especially those in public office, to tone down the angry and insulting rhetoric.

Most of us are familiar with the response of the late U.S. Sen. John McCain, R-Ariz., to a woman who accused Democrat Barack Obama of being a Muslim and of not being a native-born American. McCain, who lost the 2008 presidential race to Obama, stopped her in her tracks saying that she was wrong, and that Obama was a good American and a decent man.

In today's charged political environment, we desperately need more elected officials and candidates for office who have the courage not to give in to insulting their political opposition, particularly with lies.

We as a people should not tolerate lying by our leaders. But lying has become so commonly used by those in positions of authority that we almost have become numb to it.

As we prepare to inaugurate a new president, let us hope that there is no more bickering over the number of votes cast in the last election or the size of the crowd that shows up for the inauguration or anything else that does not help the nation heal.

Words from President Abraham Lincoln's second inaugural address seem most appropriate now:

"With malice towards none, with charity for all, with firmness in the right as God gives us to see the right, let us strive on to finish the work we are in, to bind up the nation's wounds . . . and to do all which may achieve and cherish a just and lasting peace among ourselves and with all nations."

Richmond *Times-Dispatch*, January 17, 2021

PART VI

FALL IN: HOW THE MILITARY HAS SHAPED AMERICA AND AMERICANS

Most veterans cite their military service as a turning point in their lives. People who have served in uniform often recall the heavy responsibilities thrust upon them at a young age, the experience of working as a team to carry out difficult tasks, and for many, leaving home for the first time for places far away. For veterans of combat, the experience is indelibly part of their persona. As Chief Justice Oliver Windell Holmes, a Civil War veteran, recalled: "in our youth, our hearts were touched by fire." Without question, that observation applied to George Washington. His experience in the military served him and the infant American republic well as our first president.

38

THE WAGES OF WAR - NOW AND THEN

Later this year, the United States will mark the 75th anniversary of its entry into World War II. The way we waged that war and financed it stand in contrast to how we have conducted the war on terrorists for the past 14 years.

When war erupted in Europe in 1939, most Americans had no desire to join the conflict. Still suffering from a decade-long depression and questioning the nation's involvement in World War I, they endorsed President Franklin Roosevelt's call for American neutrality.

Of course, Roosevelt knew that it would be difficult to keep the United States out of the war. Adolph Hitler's powerful legions seemed unstoppable as they easily rolled over one European country after another - and appeared ready to invade Great Britain.

The rise of an increasingly militaristic Japan threatened to spread its imperial power throughout the Pacific Rim. In response to these growing threats as 1940 ended, Roosevelt proclaimed in a radio address that "we must become the arsenal of democracy."

Bucking public opinion and ignoring potential political damage when he successfully ran for an unprecedented third term, Roosevelt had already been preparing the United States to fight. The president secured a huge increase in spending from Congress to enlarge the armed services and better arm and equip them. He instituted the first peacetime draft. He allowed American factories to supply Great Britain and its allies with war-related materials.

***

Americans continued to hope that their nation would remain at peace. Yet within a year, the United States was thrust into the global conflict when the Japanese launched a devastating attack on Pearl Harbor on December 7, 1941. The next day, President Roosevelt delivered his famous "Day of Infamy" speech before Congress, and received a declaration of war as prescribed by Article 1 of the U.S. Constitution.

The Japanese attack and a subsequent declaration of war by Germany on the U.S. brought the American people together as no other event could have. They responded with anger and determination. Over the next four years, some 15 million men and women served in all branches of the armed forces. Most American families had someone in uniform, many in harm's way. More than 400,000 sons and daughters paid the ultimate sacrifice.

People adjusted to a wartime footing on the home front by learning to live with less. Rationing of food, gasoline, clothing, metal products, and a host of other items became a way of life. Citizens volunteered in a variety of ways, from helping with scrap metal drives to promoting war bond sales.

Throughout the nation, industry shifted into high gear to support the war effort. The output of American manufacturing astonished almost everyone, especially considering how quickly it was able to reach such high levels of production.

The German war machine had taken eight years to build before it launched its attacks to overrun Europe. In 1940, U.S. arms production was negligible. Yet within two years, American factories churned out as much war material as Germany, Italy, and Japan put together. By 1944, U.S. production levels were more than twice as great.

***

Many pundits did not believe that a democracy could successfully wage a major war, especially on a worldwide scale.

The utter defeat of Germany, Italy, and Japan, all ruled by strongly centralized governments led by dictators or a small coterie of strongmen, laid that doubt to rest.

How the U.S. financed this massive effort is instructive. To reach the same percentage of gross domestic product that they did in World War II, today's federal budget expenditures would have to almost double - to about $7.2 trillion.

The country financed the huge budget expansion in World War II by raising taxes and getting citizens to invest in the war. The so-called Victory Tax of 1942 sharply raised income tax rates; but the chief source of funding came through the issuance of war bonds. Americans purchased some $186 billion worth of the instruments that paid for nearly three-quarters of federal spending from 1941-45.

How does this compare to the current war on terrorism? Today it has come almost entirely through borrowing - about $4 trillion so far. As one pundit put it: "We're putting it on a credit card with no real plan or schedule to pay it off." The only other time the U.S. financed a war solely by borrowing was during the American Revolution when France bankrolled the infant nation. During the Civil War, both federal and Confederate governments raised taxes to finance the conflict.

***

The United States has not formally declared war since 1941. Our involvement in Korea, Vietnam, and the Middle East has been conducted by congressional authorizations to use force as prescribed by the president.

In a recent speech at a Virginia War Memorial Foundation event, Sen. Tim Kaine expressed grave concern about this practice of ignoring Article 1 of the Constitution. He blamed both the legislative and executive branches of government for their failure to follow this clearly mandated constitutional provision.

Kaine contends that by fighting a war circumventing Article 1, the president is allowed to conduct matters, for better or worse, with limited legislative oversight. At the same time, members of

Congress are absolved from having to make a vote that could come back to haunt them in their next re-election. Political expediency outweighs constitutional responsibility.

The public, not to mention their elected representatives, seem oblivious to both the legitimacy and the cost of a war that has been going on for fourteen years. An all-volunteer force that comes from a small minority of American families is fighting it. The proportion of veterans serving in Congress is now less than twenty percent, compared to almost 80 percent, for example, in the late 1970s. An even lower percentage has children or grandchildren in the military.

Taxes have not been raised to wage the current war, while many members of Congress advocate for even lower taxes. Ironically, not a single candidate in the current presidential election has addressed this problem. Oh, each says he or she knows how to win the war - from carpet-bombing to "putting more troops on the ground."

Without question, the likes of ISIS must be hunted down and destroyed with the U.S. in the lead. That said, let's do it the way the so-called Greatest Generation did, by adhering to Article 1 of the Constitution and by no longer charging it to the nation's credit card.

Richmond *Times-Dispatch*, January 17, 2016

39

VIRGINIA ON THE CUSP OF WAR

A hundred years ago, Virginians watched with growing concerns (and sometimes mixed sentiment) as World War I - the so-called Great War - resonated in ways similar to our own Civil War. And the state's economic and demographic patterns shifted as U.S. intervention neared.

A century ago, newspaper headlines from Europe reminded Virginians of their own costly war not long before.

During the hard winter of 1864-65, entrenched Confederate and Union forces confronted each other in a standoff from Petersburg to Richmond. A half-century later, World War I - the so-called Great War - had descended into a grim stalemate, with the Allies and the Central Powers mired along trenches that stretched from the North Sea to the mountains of Switzerland.

Not unlike the Civil War, millions of casualties on the Western Front in France and Belgium had created an appalling image - one that Virginians watched with growing concern, and sometimes mixed sentiment.

Most Virginians were sympathetic to Great Britain and its French and Russian allies. But many people of German descent, especially in the Shenandoah Valley, sided more with the German-Austrian coalition at first. Regardless of their leanings, few people wanted to become involved in the conflict. They applauded Virginia-born President Woodrow Wilson's declaration of American neutrality, hoping the war would be short.

But as the conflict dragged on, it became clear that neutrality would be difficult to maintain. Germany had unleashed hundreds of submarines to strike merchant and passenger ships without warning, touching a raw nerve among Americans. To them, this new form of warfare was appalling, in part because of its disruption of commerce. And Virginians had much to lose from this new weapon.

With proximity to Washington and the cluster of military and naval centers around Hampton Roads, the Old Dominion was soon drawn into the European conflict. The Allied Powers quickly became dependent on America's great industrial and natural resources, much to the benefit of Virginia's economy.

The demand for agricultural products boosted farm prices, and Virginia farmers responded by increasing crop levels almost twofold, especially tobacco and wheat. Manufacturing also expanded dramatically in response to wartime needs. The giant DuPont plant in Hopewell hired thousands of additional workers in 1915 to keep up with the Allies' insatiable requirement for gunpowder. Tobacco manufacturing plants in Richmond and Petersburg accelerated production to meet European demand, and textile plants in Southside added workers.

Overseas shipments from Norfolk, Portsmouth and Newport News reached unprecedented levels in 1916. Coal from Southwest Virginia was the chief export, with shipments to Europe and other American ports reaching nearly 10 million tons that year. Coal and freight trains rumbled along Virginia rails day and night to meet demand.

Mineral resources and manufactured goods were not the only Virginia export. In a movement that would become known as the Great Migration, black Virginians from rural areas began to leave the state in growing numbers. Fed up with limited economic opportunities, exclusion from the political system, a frightening increase in lynchings and more restrictive segregation laws, many African-Americans throughout the South headed north to take advantage of a need for industrial workers.

This phenomenon began earlier in the century, but its pace picked up in 1916 as more jobs became available above the Mason-Dixon line. Because of recent laws limiting the number of immigrants to the U.S. from eastern and southern Europe, cheap labor became harder to procure. As a result, industrial jobs in the North that had not been available to blacks now became more accessible.

The bustling factories in Virginia cities also began to draw people, black and white, from farms in the state and North Carolina. Seeking good-paying jobs, they were a key component of another great American migration - from country to city, from farm to factory. By 1916, fewer than 4 in 10 American workers made their livings on farms. (A century before, nearly all were involved in some form of agriculture.)

This rural-to-urban migration changed the nature of farming not only in Virginia but the nation as a whole. The exodus of farmhands and sharecroppers to the cities coincided with advances in the internal combustion engine. Although farmers saw their labor force shrink in the first quarter of the 20th century, the introduction of motorized tractors, mechanized reapers, combines and harvesters more than made up the difference. Farmers could produce more with fewer people, and with rising demand for agricultural products from a Europe at war, the process of making farms less labor-dependent accelerated dramatically.

While this profound social and economic transformation may not have been obvious to most people at the time, the war in Europe and a civil war in Mexico made them realize that American neutrality was becoming increasingly difficult to maintain. The Preparedness Movement sought to expand the military in preparation for war, and numerous cities held preparedness parades - in June 1916, a Norfolk event had roughly 11,000 marchers and tens of thousands of spectators, according to a Richmond *Times-Dispatch* account. Virginia Congressman James Hay helped push through the National Defense Act of 1916.

In his bid for re-election that year, Wilson ran under the slogan "He kept us out of war," to appeal to the sentiments of most voters. His Republican opponent, Charles Evans Hughes, advocated a more interventionist policy and accused Wilson of pandering to Germany. Wilson narrowly won and desperately tried to steer a neutral course. At the same time, he worked to broker a peace settlement between the warring nations, to little avail.

Only months after the election, Germany reintroduced unlimited submarine warfare. Now any and all shipping in the Atlantic, neutral vessels included, could be sunk without warning. Wilson immediately severed diplomatic ties with Germany in hopes that it would suspend its campaign. The sinkings continued, and in early April 1917, Wilson asked Congress for and received a declaration of war.

This conflict was far different from previous American campaigns. The five earlier major wars - Revolutionary, 1812, Mexican-American, Civil and Spanish-American - were fought on U.S. soil or nearby foreign soil. Now the country was engaged in fighting thousands of miles away. From then on, the U.S. "would be a force, or at least a presence, in the affairs of all nations everywhere," according to historian Ernest May.

In the coming years, Virginia would be a key component of the nation's emergence as a superpower. So while one war in the 1860s devastated the state, another war a half-century later - and a continent away - began to yield prosperity not seen before.

Richmond *Times-Dispatch*, April 18, 2016

40

"Hearts Touched by Fire:"
A Community of Warriors

I grew up among warriors, men who had experienced armed conflict on a scale that is hard for us to comprehend today. I did not realize this until I recently purchased a history of Warren County, Tennessee, where I was born and raised.

A section of the book on the county's military heritage was an eye-opener for me. Turning the pages, I saw photographs and biographical sketches of men I knew only as my teachers, coaches, deacons in my church, and as lawyers, merchants, farmers, and doctors.

Yet what I read about them revealed a whole other aspect of their lives to me. Borrowing from Oliver Wendell Holmes's comment about his Civil War experience, their "hearts were touched by fire" — in this case by World War II.

The book contains a profile of Jonah Fitch, who was the stern but respected principal of my high school. I often wondered why he limped slightly, only to find out later that he lost several toes to frostbite while serving as an infantry soldier during the Battle of the Bulge.

The entry on Carl Campbell, superintendent of city schools and father of one of my friends, revealed that he served as a squadron commander of B-17s in the 8th Air Force, and flew dozens of bombing raids over Germany. He was awarded the Distinguished Flying Cross for extraordinary heroism.

Howard Locke, the mild-mannered, soft-spoken owner of a five-and-dime store on Main Street and father of one of my classmates, also earned a DFC for dropping paratroopers behind German lines in Normandy, flying through heavy flak during the opening hours of D-Day.

Robert Boyd, one of Warren County's most prominent citizens and owner of its largest wholesale nursery, served in the Navy, and survived numerous kamikaze attacks on his ship.

Then there was my Uncle Tom Bryan, who became a highly respected physician in Nashville following the war. After receiving his medical degree and completing his residency, he joined the Army in 1943.

His son, John Bryan, former director of CultureWorks in Richmond, said my uncle rarely talked about his war experience. Yet he learned later in life that his father was awarded a Bronze Star for rescuing and treating wounded soldiers while under enemy fire during the bloody Okinawa campaign in 1945.

***

Since moving to Richmond nearly 30 years ago, I have met scores of men like Tom Bryan and Jonah Fitch. Bob Bluford, for example, is a retired Presbyterian minister who led bombing missions over Germany as a B-24 pilot.

The late Stuart G. "Punky" Christian, a retired tobacco executive, who carried pieces of shrapnel in his leg from a wound he received in Normandy, served as chairman of our board at the Virginia Historical Society.

Dr. Bruce Heilman, chancellor of the University of Richmond, joined the Marine Corps at age 16 and experienced combat at Okinawa.

Civil Rights attorney Oliver Hill once told me about the challenges he faced as a black officer in a segregated army that was fighting to preserve freedom — but denied many of its fundamental tenants to him and his fellow African-Americans.

One thing that all of these men had in common was that each returned to civilian life soon after the conflict ended. They were civilians before and after World War II, yet they performed their duty in uniform when called on to serve their country.

Although most were not professional soldiers, Americans in uniform were as courageous and effective as the soldiers of any nation. German prisoners testified "to the fear of these silent soldiers moving remorselessly forward that grew in the ranks of the German divisions."

Having grown up during the Great Depression, they rolled up their sleeves and went to work when they returned from war. As historian Stephen Ambrose argued, "they were the men who built modern America."

Most had learned to work together while in the military. They learned the advantages of teamwork and organization.

They understood the importance of taking responsibility for their actions. Most seemed reluctant to talk about their war experience.

***

I have never cared for the label "The Greatest Generation" that Tom Brokaw bestowed on them. I have no doubt about the World War II generation's greatness, but I question that it is the greatest generation.

To me, those who shed blood for American independence and those who fought and won the Civil War, preserving the republic, were no less great than the generation that fought and won in the 1940s, preserving the republic from a foreign threat.

Soon our nation will mark the anniversary of one of the most important events in American history — the Japanese attack on Pearl Harbor and the entry of the United States into World War II.

Virginia is the first state in the country to take steps to commemorate that significant anniversary. Last year, the General Assembly created a commission chaired by Del. Kirk Cox to mark the 100th anniversary of America's entrance into World War I and the 75th anniversary of World War II.

The commission has started a number of initiatives, including a ceremony to honor all living Virginia World War II veterans on December 8 at the University of Richmond. Dawn of

Infamy: America Goes to War will feature a parade of World War II veterans, remarks from dignitaries, and a keynote address by Pulitzer-Prize winning historian Rick Atkinson.

There is precedent to this event. Like the last major reunion — attended by a shrinking number of living Civil War veterans in 1938 at Gettysburg — this event will carry significant poignancy. At that time, Americans were aware that the last living links to a turning point in our history was slipping away.

The roll call of living World War II veterans has been winnowed from 16.1 million to about 500,000 today. And they are in the last years of their lives.

Nationally, we lose about 600 veterans every day. Fortunately, we have an opportunity to thank some of these special people on December 8 before taps blows for them.

In the words of historian Ambrose: "So they fought and won, and all of us, living and yet to be born, must be forever."

Richmond *Times-Dispatch*, November 20, 2016

41
HOW WORLD WAR I SET VIRGINIA
IN MOTION

When World War I began in Europe the summer of 1914, President Woodrow Wilson declared strict American neutrality. But within three years, German aggression - notably all-out submarine warfare that could target American shipping - left the Staunton native little choice but to side with Great Britain and France.

In April 1917 - 100 years ago this month - America declared war on Germany, but it found itself largely unprepared. Its armed services were small, poorly equipped and virtually untrained for modern warfare, let alone the notion that young American boys would be sent to fight 3,000 miles across the Atlantic. For the most part, the economy was still in peacetime mode.

Virginia, though, had a jump-start on war. At Hampton Roads, construction on one of the world's largest naval bases and a nearby Army supply depot had begun before America joined the conflict. Trains delivered huge shipments of coal from Southwest Virginia to the expanded ports of Newport News, Portsmouth and Norfolk. Other commodities - food, tobacco, cotton, iron and steel - and finished products were shipped from Virginia to satisfy ongoing demand from the Allied powers. After the U.S. declared war, activity and production accelerated dramatically.

Even though Virginia was becoming increasingly industrialized by 1917, it was still primarily a state where most people earned their living from the soil. Nearly two-thirds of its 2.3 million residents lived and worked in rural areas, and most black Virginians (a third of the state) were involved in farming.

Richmond's population of about 170,000 trailed the totals of other Southern cities, such as Atlanta; Nashville; Louisville; and Birmingham.

But the war would change Virginia and its people, as well as the nation as a whole.

The American homefront experienced a rapid and systematic mobilization of the entire population and economy. Federal and state governments set up dozens of temporary agencies and bureaus to direct the economy and society into the production of goods and services needed to mobilize the armed forces.

In Virginia, garden clubs - as part of the Woman's Land Army of America - provided support by shifting their emphasis from flowers to vegetables. Red Cross chapters sprang up in most counties and provided medical supplies - the Northampton chapter produced 20,000 surgical dressings, 2,000 hospital gowns and thousands of towels and handkerchiefs. In Richmond, churches prepared comfort packets of tobacco products, sweets, socks and Bibles to send to American soldiers in Europe. Even the Boy Scouts sold liberty bonds and collected food and clothes for European orphans.

In rural areas, farming began to take on 20th-century qualities. Some 50 Virginia Tech-trained county extension agents introduced farmers to scientific practices, including the use of fertilizers and the introduction of new types of seeds. Many farmers prospered as wartime demand for tobacco, wheat, fruit, livestock and poultry boosted prices. They in turn invested in tractors, trucks, mechanical reapers and other modern equipment, which soon reduced the need for farmworkers while helping greatly increase crop yields. By 1918, wheat and tobacco harvests nearly tripled their pre-war totals.

Yet as work for farmhands declined, new opportunities developed in Virginia's towns and cities, where manufacturing was rapidly transforming the economy. Textile mills in Southside, tobacco factories in Richmond and Petersburg, the DuPont plant in Hopewell, the large Roanoke Machine Works - all were part of growing job opportunities tied to wartime demand, and rural Virginians moved to manufacturing communities in large numbers.

And with many men going into military service, employment expanded for women. For example, women in Henrico County and Richmond were recruited for the Women's Munitions Reserve to work in a large gunpowder plant at Seven Pines. In all, some 2,000 women signed up to load bags of explosive material.

For African-Americans, Virginia was still a state of Jim Crow laws, segregated transportation and schools, and job discrimination. Opportunities, though, rose elsewhere.

The rise of manufacturing in the North had turned the United States into one of the world's industrial giants, thanks largely to low-paid European immigrants. World War I curtailed that labor supply, so Northern industry began to hire African-Americans in large numbers for factory jobs. Known as the Great Migration, this shift resulted in about 6 million African-Americans leaving the South between 1910 and 1970. While 90 percent of black Americans lived in the South in 1910, nearly 50 percent lived in Northern cities six decades later.

The war affected other elements of Virginia culture. The federal Committee on Public Information sought to influence American opinion, and the 1917 Espionage Act and 1918 Sedition Act criminalized negative expression about U.S. involvement in the war. Americans began to distrust other Americans, especially people with German connections.

Many Virginians were gripped by fear that enemies lurked within their midst - particularly in the Shenandoah Valley, where German ancestry was widespread. Near Winchester, a rumor ran rampant that an apple grower was operating a wireless radio that sent signals directly to Berlin. The rumors remained unfounded, but the man eventually left the community.

The mayor of Charlottesville outlined plans for guarding against sabotage by Germans in the area, warning that they could poison the city's reservoir, destroy bridges and derail trains.

In Richmond, a large second-generation German population felt the tension. The city's German Catholic and Lutheran churches reported an "unhappy period" for their parishioners, with declining enrollment in the parochial schools. Because of the German origin of his name, young Dewey Gottwald, a Richmond native who later led Ethyl Corp., was rejected when he tried to enlist in the Army.

Distrust of fellow citizens abated after a while when no incidents of sabotage or evidence of spying were uncovered. By the end of 1917, Virginians were largely mobilized toward the war effort - both at home and overseas.

Near Petersburg, the Army's Camp Lee was constructed in three months and trained 45,000 soldiers, including the 80th Division, which included large numbers of Virginians. The state supplied more than 20 units to the American Expeditionary Forces, who steamed out of Hampton Roads en route to the Western Front in France. By the time peace was proclaimed in November 1918, about 1,200 Virginians had died during the conflict, mostly in its final few months.

The formal Treaty of Versailles did not suspend the changes that were sweeping Virginia. Indeed, World War I proved to be a catalyst for more. Virginia grew and prospered on a scale not seen since pre-Civil War days, and the Old Dominion was well on its way to becoming a New Dominion.

Richmond *Times-Dispatch*, April 17, 2017

42

CARING FOR THOSE WHO HAVE BORNE THE BATTLE

VCU AND MCGUIRE VA HOSPITAL

In recent years, the Department of Veterans Affairs has come under intense scrutiny and heavy criticism for a variety of reasons. My experience with the VA, however, has been nothing but positive.

I was diagnosed with Parkinson's disease 13 years ago. My service in the Army during the Vietnam War qualified me for drug trials at the comprehensive Parkinson's disease center at the McGuire VA hospital in Richmond.

McGuire is one of seven of the 162 VA hospitals in the nation to have such a program. Specialists in movement disorder diseases who have treated me have helped slow the progression of my Parkinson's, which has allowed me to live a relatively normal life.

One factor that helps explain my good fortune is something I began to notice early in my visits to McGuire: the large number of medical personnel holding joint positions with McGuire and VCU.

I had assumed that all personnel at veterans hospitals practiced exclusively for the VA. I have subsequently learned that the presence of VCU clinicians represents one of the most comprehensive academic health partnerships in American history, a cooperative arrangement that began as a result of World War II.

***

Following the Allied victory in 1945, the then 26-year old VA system faced a crisis because of the overwhelming number of veterans requiring immediate medical attention from injuries suffered in the war.

With fewer than 100 hospitals nationwide, mostly in rural areas, and less than 1,000 physicians in the system, the VA found it nearly impossible to meet the demand.

To address this new challenge, President Harry Truman, himself a veteran of World War I, directed the VA to sign a revolutionary agreement with medical schools throughout the country. Under the new arrangement, the VA would work with nearby universities with medical schools to help train resident physicians and students. They in turn would provide high-quality health care for veterans.

For 70 years, the VA has worked hand-in-glove with medical schools across the country to care for veterans, while simultaneously training clinicians to treat the general public. Nearly 70 percent of physicians in the country have received at least some training through the VA.

For that matter, the VA conducts the largest education and training program for health professionals in the United States. Working in partnership, VA hospitals and their affiliate medical schools have been a driving force in health care and innovative education. While the VA's primary mission is to serve veterans, many of its developments have benefited non-veterans alike.

In the 1950s, for example, the VA and its partner universities led the way in the development and accreditation of clinical psychology, helping build greater awareness of it as a legitimate field of medicine and developing ways to treat mental illness as a disease.

In the 1960s, the VA helped promote physician assistants as professionals who could bring needed help to the practice of medicine. A decade later, it recognized the concerns unique to treating the elderly and developed the field of geriatric medicine as a specialty. It introduced hospice and palliative care to veteran patients several years ahead of the general patient population.

The VA was in the lead in the 1980s in developing the technology to create electronic health records and then link the whole VA system into a single database. This model became increasingly standard in non-VA hospitals, thereby transforming the nation's record-keeping system.

***

Over the past 16 years of the seemingly endless war on terrorism, the VA has seen a significant increase in new patients with a variety of injuries caused by insidious devices that kill and maim our men and women in uniform.

McGuire is well known throughout the VA system for its Polytrauma Center of Excellence and is regarded as a leader in the treatment of traumatic brain injury. In 2005, McGuire was designated as one of only four polytrauma centers in the entire VA system.

Again, the involvement of VCU medical personnel and other resources has played a crucial role in the development of this center. A recently announced $62 million Department of Defense grant to the VA for a study on rehabilitation for patients with brain injuries will again prove the value of the VA/VCU partnership.

The first heart transplant in the VA system was performed at McGuire in the mid-1990s by a surgeon working jointly for the VA and VCU. Since then, nearly 400 of these procedures have been performed.

And another example of how VA leadership in the field of medicine has helped non-veterans can be seen at the new VCU comprehensive movement disorder treatment complex located near Short Pump Town Center. Having opened last year, it is modeled after the one at McGuire, and is available to anyone, not just veterans, who need treatment for the disease.

***

The VA has been accused of wasting taxpayer dollars; of being incompetent; however, we are fortunate to have a hospital for our veterans working hand-in-hand with VCU to provide the care they deserve.

The partnership will become increasingly important going forward. Virginia has the fastest-growing veterans population in the nation and has the largest number of veterans under the age of 25.

Whenever I go to McGuire for my Parkinson's, I cannot help but be moved by the sight of the veteran patients I see there. Almost every one of them wears a ball cap with his military branch or the outfit he served with proudly displayed on the front crown.

People on staff, whether they are physicians, nurses, nurses' aids, or volunteers, will tell you what a privilege it is to help work with patients who served their country, many of whom bear the scars or have lost limbs from combat.

As far as I am concerned, they do a remarkable job of fulfilling President Abraham Lincoln's promise: "To care for him who shall have borne the battle."

Thanks to the partnership between the VA and VCU, our veterans receive the best health care possible. They deserve no less.

Richmond *Times-Dispatch*, July 9, 2017

43

Ten battles that changed American history

urning points are events that, had they gone another way, could have led to a significantly different future. For example, had Abraham Lincoln not been assassinated, the history of post-Civil War America probably would have turned out quite differently.

A surprisingly large number of military engagements qualify as turning-point moments in our history. Here are my candidates for turning point battles and campaigns, with an explanation of why they helped shape our nation's history:

The Battle of Saratoga (1777)

This American victory over a smaller British force is considered a turning point of the Revolutionary War. Actually two battles were fought over 17 days in upper New York state. American commander Horatio Gates defeated and captured a British army, including its commander, General John Burgoyne. The victory swayed France to officially recognize the Patriot cause and enter the war as a key ally, resulting in American independence.

The Yorktown Campaign (1781)

After weeks of intense campaigning in the South, British General Sir Charles Cornwallis marched his nearly exhausted army to Yorktown with plans to escape by sea to fight another day. French forces under the Marquis de Lafayette, however, pinned Cornwallis's army down.

The Continental Army under George Washington then joined Lafayette's forces and laid siege to Yorktown. When a large French fleet moved into the Chesapeake Bay to block the British from escaping, Cornwallis surrendered his army, thereby assuring American victory and independence.

Battle of New Orleans (1815)

Who would have thought that a ragtag American army composed of state militia, pirates, and regular troops could handily defeat a larger army of hardened British regulars? American commander Andrew Jackson posted his men and artillery behind strong earthworks and mowed down row after row of attacking redcoats under General Sir Edward Pakenham, who was mortally wounded.

This last battle of the War of 1812 was one of the most lopsided defeats in British military history, but it made Jackson an overnight American hero - and contributed greatly to his election as president in 1828.

Campaign to Mexico City (1848)

Gen. Winfield Scott boldly landed his army on the beaches near Vera Cruz, Mexico, in the first amphibious operation in American history. He then marched his troops westward some 250 miles, fighting six battles along the way, and eventually arrived at the gates of Mexico City, which surrendered a few days later.

Regarded as one of the most brilliantly conceived and executed campaigns in American military annals, it served as a model that inspired U.S. Grant during the Civil War. It also resulted in the U.S. acquiring a huge block of land in the American southwest that contributed to a growing debate over slavery's expansion into the territories.

Vicksburg Campaign (1863)

Taking a page from Winfield Scott's book, U.S. Grant crossed the Mississippi River and after a series of battles, brilliantly maneuvered his army to trap a Confederate army at Vicksburg. After a month-long siege, Grant forced the Rebel commander to surrender on July 4, thereby completely opening the Mississippi River to navigation for Federal forces.

The day before, Robert E. Lee had suffered a devastating loss at Gettysburg, Pennsylvania. The war continued for another year and a half, but the Confederacy never fully recovered from these twin blows.

The Meuse-Argonne Offensive (1918)

Although the U.S. did not enter World War I until April 1917, three years after the beginning of hostilities in Europe, it was unable to commit its troops to actual combat for more than a year.

In their first large-scale engagement, half a million Doughboys under Gen. John J. Pershing attacked a bulge in the German lines in September 2018. Within a day, the bulge was cut off and the Americans captured large numbers of Germans. Over the next two months, the German forces were gradually worn down until they finally gave up on November 11.

Once in battle, the American forces helped turn the tide of the war in favor of the Allies, but at a cost of nearly 120,000 casualties- in only a matter of months. Never before had so many Americans served and died so far from home, a trend that continues today.

The Battle of Midway (1942)

Arguably the most decisive naval battle of World War II began in June when the Japanese attempted to seize Midway Island to use as a base for attacking Hawaii and eventually the U.S. West Coast. Although outnumbered in ships and planes, the Americans delivered a stinging defeat to the Japanese navy, which lost four aircraft carriers and nearly 300 planes. Never again would the mighty Japanese navy hold sway over its American foe.

D-Day at Normandy (1944)

When weather conditions changed to their advantage on June 6, the Allies launched a massive invasion of Western Europe along 50 miles of the Normandy coastline, under the command of Gen. Dwight D. Eisenhower. Despite fierce enemy resistance at some of the beaches, the Allies eventually gained a firm foothold in France, and during the next 11 months steadily drove Nazi forces back to Germany - and to ultimate surrender that closed World War II's European Theater.

Okinawa (1945)

While the war wound down in Europe and Hitler's Nazi regime collapsed in May, the conflict was far from over in the Pacific. This large, island located within striking distance of Japan could have served as the jumping-off place for an allied invasion.

In the last major battle of World War II, and one of its bloodiest, American forces came ashore to meet only light resistance. Once inland, however, well-entrenched Japanese troops fought savagely to hold the island, with most fighting to the death. After more than two months of almost continuous combat, and some 45,000 American and nearly 120,000 Japanese casualties, Okinawa finally fell to the Americans.

Convinced that the next step - the invasion of mainland Japan - would be even more costly to American troops, President Harry Truman decided to drop two atomic bombs on Japan, which forced it to surrender and ushered in the age of atomic warfare.

The Tet Offensive (1968)

For nearly three years, American military commanders and President Lyndon Johnson's administration had convinced themselves and the public that the war in Southeast Asia was going well. But in a massive series of well-coordinated attacks by North Vietnamese and Viet Cong forces throughout South Vietnam, the Americans were at first caught by surprise.

After recovering from the initial shock, superior American forces eventually turned the tide of battle in their favor. Despite victory on the battlefield, American public opinion grew increasingly disillusioned with the war in Vietnam and over the next few years the peace movement in America grew to the point that the war effort could no longer be sustained.

***

Turning points in history often come at a cost - in terms of money, power, prestige, and, in some cases, lives. Let us not forget that the turning points fought on the fields of battle resulted in hundreds of thousands of deaths.

As Sir Arthur Wellesley, the Duke of Wellington, wrote many years after his signal victory at Waterloo: "Next to a battle lost, nothing is so sad as a battle that has been won."

Richmond *Times-Dispatch*, April 22, 2018

44

REFUSING THOSE WHO WANT TO SERVE
IMMIGRANTS IN THE MILITARY

Over the years, I have visited numerous World War I and II battlefields in Europe and their accompanying military cemeteries - American, British and German. The immaculately ordered American cemeteries stand out for their stark beauty and order, with graves laid out in strict military precision. British cemeteries have a certain poignancy about them with their individual flower plantings on most graves.

While the Allied burial grounds are in a way awe inspiring, German military cemeteries from World War II are dark, somber places, leaving no doubt as to which side lost the war. I learned that many World War II German grave plots have up to four or five sets of remains in them. As one cemetery caretaker told me, "A soldier should never be alone. He should be with his comrades, especially for eternity."

Going from grave to grave, you see the final resting places of young men and boys from all regions of Germany. Most were members of the German army, the Wehrmacht, but many had served in the dreaded SS, the elite, fanatical shock troops of Hitler's. All were buried under Christian crosses. Unlike American and British World War II cemeteries, not a single grave is marked with a Star of David.

Go to a German cemetery from World War I, however, and you will find Star of David headstones with Jewish names on them scattered throughout. These were the final resting places of German Jews who had fought and died for their country.

Some 100,000 Jews served in the German army during World War I, and more than 12,000 died in combat. More than 18,000 received the Iron Cross, of which about 1,000 received the Iron Cross First Class for exceptional gallantry in action. Most German Jews supported Kaiser Wilhelm and his decision to invade Belgium and France. Of course, none of them would have suspected that their country would begin one of the most despicable mass crimes in history by attempting to exterminate Europe's Jewish population.

In the post-World War I years, anti-Semitism, which had long simmered underneath the surface in Germany, became intensely virulent especially after Hitler rose to power. Jews became the target of blame for the country's post-war problems. They were accused of betraying Germany for self-gain. In 1935, the new Nazi regime under Adolph Hitler announced that henceforth, it was "forbidden to list the names of fallen Jews on Memorials of the World War." Jewish veterans were removed from civil service jobs, and Jews were no longer allowed to serve in the military. Nazi doctrine basically held that Jews were not real Germans.

Germany's treatment of Jewish veterans in denying their military service makes me think in some ways of the immigrants who want to serve our country in uniform. Today recent immigrants serve in the American armed forces in large numbers ' some 80,000 in all branches of the military, including the Coast Guard. The U.S. has had a long-standing tradition of allowing immigrants to serve in its military as a path to gaining citizenship. But immigrants serving in uniform are being denied citizenship at a much higher rate than in previous years, according to recent government sources. Stricter policies by the Trump administration explain most of this reversal. Major General Paul Eaton, U.S. Army retired, notes, "To have this [reversal], where they are actually taking a back seat to the civilian population, strikes me as a bizarre turn of events."

Eaton also questions why the Defense Department is willing to make it more difficult to recruit eligible immigrants, particularly with the challenges recruiters face today. The rush to the colors immediately following the 9/11 terrorist attacks has long lost its momentum as the subsequent conflict enters its 19th year. As reported last fall in the *Army Times*, the army missed its annual recruiting goal by more than 6,000, its worst record in years. The Coast Guard fell short on its recruiting goal as well. The remaining three service branches met their respective goals, although barely.

It is impossible to accept everyone wanting to serve in the military, but why deny immigrants who are willing and able to put their lives on the line for this country in exchange for citizenship? Such a policy is shortsighted because it denies a place for those who deserve it for the sacrifices they have made and will continue to make on our behalf. At least their plight is not as consequential as that of the German Jews who had fought bravely and sacrificed in great numbers during World War I, yet were persecuted and killed en masse simply because of their religion and ethnicity.

Richmond *Times-Dispatch*, July 14, 2019

45

HONOR TO THE SOLDIER AND SAILOR EVERYWHERE

A few years ago, I was flying back to Richmond from a business meeting. I had a tight connection in Atlanta. As often was the case in those pre-pandemic days, the terminal teemed with thousands of people dashing from one concourse to another, desperately trying to make their connections. I cannot remember the year of that trip, but I distinctly remember the date: November 11, Veterans Day.

Soon after I arrived at my gate before boarding began, the Delta agent announced: "Please raise your hand if you are a veteran of one of the U.S. armed forces."

Having served stateside in the Army during the Vietnam War, I slowly raised my hand, along with perhaps half a dozen other passengers, not quite knowing what to expect. The agent then asked all other passengers to give us veterans a round of applause in honor of Veterans Day.

Much to my surprise, my fellow passengers broke into a loud and sustained ovation. Then the agent invited all veterans to board first. I proceeded to my seat, and for the next 20 minutes, almost every passenger who walked past me thanked me for my service.

Suddenly tears welled up in my eyes. Never since being discharged from the Army had anyone offered me a gesture of appreciation for my military service, especially in the years immediately following my time in the Army.

Although I never experienced the open hostility and taunts of "baby killer" directed by some people at service members returning from Vietnam, the public for the most part ignored the former warriors. But it was unthinkable then that an airport gate agent would recognize veterans the way the woman in Atlanta did.

Veterans definitely are "in" now, which no doubt is related to the high regard the military enjoys. We are asked to stand and be applauded when our respective service songs are played at July 4 celebrations. It is not unusual for people to say, "Thank you for your service," when they discover that I am a veteran.

It has not always been that way. For that matter, the United States has a long and checkered history with its veterans. From the earliest days of the republic, elected officials have debated how to treat those who risked their lives for their country.

After the American Revolution, Congress awarded land grants in the western territories to those who had served. Pensions, bonuses, medical care and financial support for education have been granted by Congress to veterans of subsequent wars.

After the Revolution, veterans who had been guaranteed pensions and land grants saw their promised benefits reduced because Congress lacked the funding to pay for them. War of 1812 veterans received no support for more than 50 years.

After the Civil War, Union veterans received modest pensions, while former Confederates had to rely on the limited benefits made available to them by their cash-strapped states.

World War I veterans received minimal federal benefits immediately following the war. Unless the veteran had been wounded, benefits were limited to a $60 bonus and a ticket for a train ride home.

After considerable lobbying on their behalf, however, veterans were promised benefits that would be made available to them in 1945. Congress also created the Veterans Administration (VA) in 1930 that, among other things, administered retirement homes and small hospitals for needy veterans.

Then veterans saw promised benefits become victims of the Great Depression. In 1932 some 50,000 demonstrators, who called themselves the Bonus Army, marched on Washington demanding early distribution of the bonus promised to them in 1945. Arguing that they needed the money then, not later, the veterans set up an encampment at Anacostia Flats, pledging not to leave until their needs were met.

After being told that some of the protesters were communists and other left-wing radicals, President Herbert Hoover was convinced that the veterans posed a threat to the government. After negotiations broke down, Hoover sent federal troops in to disperse the Bonus Army encampment, resulting in the death of several veterans and the eventual failure of their cause.

The tragic irony of regular army soldiers firing on veterans who wanted financial relief helped lead to Hoover's crushing defeat to Franklin D. Roosevelt in the 1932 presidential election.

World War II, however, brought about the most significant developments for veterans. For one, the war led to the passage of arguably the most important piece of legislation of the 20th century - the GI Bill. Provisions of the bill included low-cost mortgages, low-interest loans to start a business or farm, unemployment insurance, tuition payments for attending college or a vocational school, and several other benefits.

The provisions of the original GI Bill expired in 1956, having served the nation well for more than a decade. In addition to helping GIs adjust to civilian status immediately following the war, it had other long-term benefits for the nation, particularly its economy, by providing the country with the most educated and skilled workforce in the world. That, in turn, led to an economic boom that lasted for more than two decades.

Even with the GI Bill's expiration, Congress continued to provide benefits to veterans, including a greatly expanded health care system.

At the end of World War II, the VA was overwhelmed by the huge number of veterans requiring treatment for wounds they had sustained. With fewer than 100 hospitals located mostly in rural areas and barely 1,000 doctors, the VA could not meet the demand.

To address this challenge, President Harry Truman signed a revolutionary arrangement with medical schools throughout the country. Under this agreement, new VA hospitals would partner with nearby medical schools, sharing physicians, interns and other health care professionals in treating veterans. It is an arrangement that for the most part has worked well.

As a result of this and several other factors, the U.S. has the most comprehensive system of services for its veterans in the world. However, the VA - now formally called the U.S. Department of Veterans Affairs - faces huge challenges with soaring demand coming from aging Vietnam-era veterans who require increased medical care. Additional claims created by the war on terrorism are placing even more stress on the system.

Given their age and general health, the current COVID-19 pandemic is hitting veterans to an unusually high degree. If that isn't enough, nearly 300,000 people who have served their country are living on the street. For that matter, the number of homeless Vietnam veterans is far greater than the number who died in that war.

Come Veterans Day this year, it is well worth remembering the words of Abraham Lincoln:

"Honor to the soldier and sailor everywhere who bravely bears his country's cause. Honor also to the citizen who cares for his brother in the field and serves as best he can, the same cause."

Richmond *Times-Dispatch*, November 11, 2020

46

OKINAWA: THE LAST GREAT BATTLE
OF WORLD WAR II

On Wednesday, April 1, many people will mark the day with practical jokes and pranks. But it is well to remember that April Fools' Day 75 years ago signaled the beginning of one of World War II's longest, bloodiest and most desperate battles. With the war in Europe winding down and the enemy armed forces disintegrating in the face of the Allied onslaught, Germany formally surrendered on May 7, 1945, thereby ending six years of combat operations. Soon after millions of people throughout Europe and the U.S. celebrated the return of peace on VE (Victory in Europe) Day.

For many Americans, however, it was premature to celebrate. The war seemed far from over to those who had loved ones serving in the Pacific. Indeed, the U.S. and its allies faced the possibility of the most costly campaign of the entire war - the invasion of Japan.

Nevertheless, there was one more obstacle in the way before an attack on the mainland could begin. The capture of the nearly 460-square-mile island of Okinawa, located 325 miles south of the mainland, was essential to the success of the invasion. The island would serve as a jumping-off place for more than a million troops who would be engaged, as well as the site of numerous air bases needed to continue a devastating bombing campaign against Japanese cities.

Based on the experience from earlier island campaigns - Tarawa, Saipan, Iwo Jima and others - planners for the invasion of Okinawa expected even heavier losses. The Pentagon ordered a million Purple Hearts in anticipation of a long and bloody struggle. Many of those medals awarded today are from that surplus stock.

Army Lt. Gen. Simon B. Buckner, son of a Confederate general, served as commander of this combined U.S. Army-Navy-Marine Corps operation. Early in the morning of April 1, the American Fifth Fleet opened up on Japanese positions with the war's heaviest bombardment, hoping to prevent the casualties experienced at Normandy's Omaha Beach the previous year.

When the first wave of Americans waded ashore, they were stunned that Japanese defenders put up little resistance. They immediately pushed inland, many reaching their objectives within two hours. Soon wave after wave of reinforcements, ammunition, supplies and equipment came ashore effortlessly. As one Marine officer observed, the landing looked "more like a pastoral scene than a battle. We were all incredulous, as if we had stepped into a fairy tale."

It did not take long for this fairy tale to turn into a living nightmare. The tableau being rolled out had been carefully planned by Japanese Gen. Mitsuru Ushijima. He allowed the Americans to come ashore virtually unopposed after pulling most of his force back to the hilly southern part of the island. After reducing the lightly held northern defenses, U.S. troops began to concentrate their efforts on the southern sector. There they ran into formidable defenses that stopped them in their tracks.

Then the Japanese struck. On April 6 and 7, nearly 700 enemy aircraft, including 350 kamikaze suicide planes, pounded the American-controlled beaches and the naval task force offshore. They unleashed the huge battleship Yamato and several other ships to attack the American fleet and troops ashore, only to see the entire Japanese flotilla sent to the bottom. In the meantime, the suicide attacks on the American fleet continued unabated for weeks, eventually sinking 34 ships and inflicting 9,700 casualties, the most the Navy suffered during the war in one battle.

Back on land, as the days passed into weeks, U.S. forces became locked in a relentlessly brutal fight as they challenged deeply entrenched Japanese troops backed by heavy artillery. This made for a slow, grueling bloodletting that some compared to the battles of World War I. Progress was measured in feet amid drenching rain and deep mud. As the Americans became bogged down, Ushijima launched a desperate counterattack in early May that resulted in nothing but 6,000 more Japanese deaths.

By late May, Ushijima, having lost more than half of his troops, backed up to a shorter defensive line near the southern tip of Okinawa where they continued the fight for several more weeks. Realizing the futility of continued resistance he, along with most of his remaining troops, committed hara-kiri in late June. Control of Okinawa now belonged to American forces.

More than 170,000 Japanese and native Okinawans died during this brutal campaign. Some 12,000 American service members were killed, including Buckner, who was felled by a sniper. He was one of two of the highest ranking Americans killed during the war.

Planners for the invasion and eventual defeat of Japan estimated that it would cost a million American lives. "Victory was never in doubt," observed Marine Maj. Gen. Graves Erskine. "What was in doubt in all our minds," he continued, "was whether there would be any of us left to dedicate our cemetery at the end."

The feared bloodbath that Erskine and others predicted never occurred. With the dropping of atomic bombs on Hiroshima and Nagasaki, the Japanese surrendered within days.

Those who survived Okinawa carried awful memories of that experience with them for the rest of their lives. I sometimes wonder if that was true of my Uncle Tom Bryan, who became a prominent physician in Nashville after the war. I knew that he had served as an Army doctor in the Pacific, but it wasn't until after his death that I learned that he had been awarded a Bronze Star for valor for an incident on Okinawa when he risked his own life to drive a jeep that came under enemy fire to treat three badly wounded soldiers.

His son said he rarely talked about the war. When asked about the medal, he would say that it was only for performing his duty. Duty, indeed. As historian Stephen Ambrose wrote about men like my uncle: "So they fought, and won, and all of us living and yet to be born, must be forever profoundly grateful." Amen!

Richmond *Times-Dispatch*, March 29, 2020

PART VII

LIVING AND DYING

The average life expectancy of human beings changed little from the time of the birth of Christ until about two centuries ago. Skewed to some extent by horrifically high infant mortality rates, the average life expectancy of our species hovered in the mid-twenties. Now that number is well into seventy years, although it has receded slightly since the recent coved pandemic. What has caused such a dramatic drop in deaths in only two centuries? The following essays should provide most of the answers to that question. After reading them, I wonder how many people would want to return to a past that was far from perfect when it comes to the practice of medicine?

Pedro Ramirez, M.D.

47

HIGH HOPES FOR THE FUTURE

We are bombarded with news on immigration. Prior to the launching of the Republican primary campaign this year, immigration was low on the list of issues concerning voters. But candidate Donald Trump has made it central to his campaign and forced his opponents to defend their positions on this divisive issue. Several European countries are caught in an immigration dilemma of their own as refugees pour across their borders to escape the violence in the Middle East.

The subject is nothing new in America. Over the centuries immigrants have come here in waves from around the world, giving credence to the oft-quoted statement: "We are a nation of immigrants."

Controversy surrounding immigration is also long-standing. Americans have rarely greeted immigrants with open arms. The current presidential campaign is by no means the first to have immigration play such a key role.

The Know-Nothing Party, which was formed mainly in opposition to Irish Catholics immigrants, was strong enough in the 1840s and '50s to influence state and national elections. The re-emergence of the Ku Klux Klan in the 1920s not only targeted African-Americans, but also the large number of Catholic and Jewish immigrants who had come in large waves from Southern and Eastern Europe.

Americans may disagree over the subject of immigration, but there is little question that the contributions of many of those who have moved here - from Alexander Hamilton to Albert

Einstein to architect I.M. Pei - have helped make the United States a great nation.

***

I met someone recently who immigrated to the United States nearly 40 years ago and now is making important advances in the fight against cancer. The circumstances of our meeting came in a way that I would not have preferred.

In May, my wife was diagnosed with stage four ovarian cancer. We were devastated by the news, but we were determined to fight it any way we could. We started with the excellent healthcare facilities and capable cancer specialists in Richmond. A friend, however, urged us to seek treatment at the University of Texas's M.D. Anderson Cancer Center in Houston, regarded by many experts as one of the foremost medical institutions in the world in fighting this insidious disease.

Through our Richmond connection, we were able to secure an appointment at M.D. Anderson, where my wife became a patient of Dr. Pedro Ramirez.

An internationally renowned physician in gynecologic oncology, he has pioneered numerous advances in cancer surgery and post-operative treatment.

Thanks to the work of Dr. Ramirez, in coordination with our family physician and our oncologist in Richmond, a once desperate situation for my wife now has been replaced by one of hope for the future.

***

It was shortly after Dr. Ramirez performed surgery on my wife that I learned his remarkable life story. Born in Cuba in 1968, Ramirez spent his first 11 years in a country controlled by the iron fist of Fidel Castro's regime. His memories of Cuba are one of a police state where distrust reigned and everyone seemed to live on the edge of poverty. People spied on their neighbors and would turn them in to the authorities if they spoke against the Castro government. Even though it was an island nation well suited for agriculture, food shortages were common.

In 1969, Pedro's parents, an accountant and a teacher, tried to leave the country with their two children - only to be turned back at the last minute, thereby marking them as potential enemies of the state. His father was imprisoned for four years.

Ten years later, the family was able to leave Cuba under a new mandate from Castro allowing some political prisoners to seek asylum in another country with a pledge to never return to the island nation. The Ramirez family moved to Spain, their family's ancestral homeland, hoping to eventually enter the United States.

For young Pedro, Spain was a breath of fresh air compared to the oppressive environment he had grown up with in Cuba. Even though the family was forced to live in a shelter at first, he later said "we were extremely happy because we felt as if we had reached heaven. We were free!"

The move to the United States two years later, however, proved more difficult. Arriving with little money, the family moved to a poor area near Newark, N. J., where the parents took any job available just to keep the family fed and clothed.

Pedro and his sister attended schools that drew students from impoverished neighborhoods. Student dropout rates were high, and hopes for a bright future were limited. By the time Pedro was a high school senior, despite his good grades and obvious potential, he seriously considered going to work for UPS at $8 an hour, which seemed like a princely sum to him.

His older sister, who at the time was earning a degree in industrial engineering and went on to become an executive with IBM, forcefully told her brother that his parents had sacrificed too much for him not to set his sights higher.

Eventually giving in to the not so gentle prodding of his sister, the young immigrant went on to earn his college degree from Rutgers, a M.D. from Albert Einstein Medical School, and he did his residency at Columbia University. He then received a fellowship from M.D. Anderson in Houston, where he now serves on the faculty of the University of Texas Medical School and is one of its star professors, both as a practicing physician and a medical scientist.

***

Numerous studies have demonstrated that in most advanced countries immigrants actually bolster economic growth by increasing the labor force and consumer demand. Immigrants tend to pay more taxes than they claim in government benefits. They often come with skills and expertise that are not readily found in their new home country.

It was a lucky day for the United States and for my wife and countless other cancer patients when Pedro Ramirez immigrated to this country nearly 40 years ago.

Richmond *Times-Dispatch*, November 15, 2015

Pedro Ramirez, M.D.

48

BANDING TOGETHER TO CONQUER POLIO

A sk almost anyone 60 years and older about polio, and inevitably you will stir up memories of seeing its victims lying encased in iron lungs that emitted deep, rhythmic, mechanical breaths every few seconds. Two of my high school teachers were confined to wheelchairs, victims of polio when they were young. One summer, public health officials closed the municipal swimming pool in my hometown, deeming it too risky for spreading the disease.

Many of us remember how the American public rallied and came together to fight polio: How school children contributed millions of dollars in dimes in what would be the first truly national fundraising campaign. How Hollywood celebrities such as Eddy Cantor, Bing Crosby, and Jack Benny took on the disease as their cause célèbre.

Poliomyelitis has been around for thousands of years, but it was not recognized as a distinct disease until the late 18th century. A virus that spreads among people by fecal matter or saliva found in food or water, it leaves its victims fully or partially paralyzed - and sometimes dead. Severe breathing problems often accompany polio.

Medical scientists finally isolated and identified the virus in 1908, a time when doctors became increasingly concerned about major outbreaks in Europe and the U.S. The number of polio cases rose dramatically in the 20th century, reaching a peak in the years following World War II.

***

President Franklin Roosevelt, who was stricken with polio as an adult, became its most visible symbol, although he tried to hide its consequences from the public. On the other hand, because most of its victims were young, especially the very young, and the publicity polio generated, it became the most visible childhood disease of the century.

Polio reached epidemic levels in the early 1950s. In 1950 alone, more than 33,000 Americans, half of whom were age 10 or younger, contracted the disease. Wytheville in southwest Virginia gained national attention when polio struck it with a vengeance, resulting in nearly 200 cases.

The following year, the number of cases nationwide continued to rise, as did the public clamor for a solution. Americans then began to band together, much as they had during World War II. Government agencies on all levels joined forces with non-government organizations to combat the disease.

Volunteers by the millions offered their assistance. Medical scientists sprang into action when federal funding, along with corporate and private philanthropy, began to flow into research institutes, led by the March of Dimes.

Soon an intense rivalry developed between the two leading polio scientists - Jonas Salk and Albert Sabin. Both men were raised in Jewish immigrant neighborhoods in New York and New Jersey respectively. Both finished medical school preferring the challenges of medical research rather than the practice of medicine.

During World War II, Salk started work in virology, and in 1947 began studying polio at the University of Pittsburgh, where he concentrated on developing a vaccine against the disease. Because of the risks surrounding the use of live virus, "killed virus" vaccines delivered by injections would be safer and more effective.

Established researchers, however, rejected Salk's idea and his methods. Leading the opposition was Sabin, who believed that an oral vaccine would destroy the virus in the intestines and prevent it from entering the blood stream.

The two rivals were unrelenting in their search for a "magic bullet," but Salk introduced his vaccine first when he began field trials at an elementary school in McLean, Virginia, in April 1954. With these early experiments deemed a success, more than two million children received Salk vaccines by the end of the year. Within the next few years, millions more young people in the U.S. lined up for the vaccine, and the number of polio diagnoses plummeted.

In the meantime, Sabin first tested his oral vaccine in Europe in 1957. Delivered in sugar cubes, easily administered, and inexpensive, it became the standard vaccine around the world. Its use, however, was severely limited in the U.S. for several years after a federal advisory panel determined that it was still too risky.

Although Jonas Salk is credited with ending polio because his inoculation was the first to be administered to the public, Sabin's vaccine actually was used on a greater worldwide scale and is the preferred preventative treatment for polio today.

***

Thanks to both vaccines, the U.S. was declared polio-free in 1979. Through the efforts of Rotary International, the World Health Organization, UNICEF, and the U.S. Centers for Disease Control and Prevention, polio was reduced 99 percent globally by 1988.

The international effort to rid the world of polio was set back in 2011 when the CIA orchestrated a fake polio clinic in Pakistan in an effort to capture Osama bin Laden. Since then, polio workers in Pakistan and Afghanistan have been distrusted, and suicide bombers have murdered more than a dozen. Sadly, they are the only two countries on Earth where the disease continues to claim victims.

In the U.S., reminders of polio can be observed almost anywhere. John Hager, former lieutenant governor of Virginia, has been confined to a wheelchair since contracting the disease when he was in his early 30s. Like Franklin Roosevelt, he has refused to let polio prevent him from continuing an active and productive life.

Gordon Kerby of Richmond, who grew up in Waynesboro, has no memory of life without polio. He was only 2 and a half years old when he and his seven-month old brother were diagnosed. Kerby was confined to an iron lung for five years, but thanks to physicians and physical therapists at the Medical College of Virginia, he learned how to breathe on his own, to walk with braces on his legs, and eventually ride a bicycle.

Kerby went on to become a respected environmental engineer, get married, and become a competitive bicycle rider. In recent years, however, he has suffered from post-polio syndrome, a condition that brings back many of the disease's manifestations 30 and 40 years later. Unable to walk very far, he relies on a motorized scooter to get around.

The story of the fight against polio reveals a time in our history when Americans came together to conquer a terrible disease. The combination of millions of people giving their dimes, volunteering, and working in private-public partnerships to fight a common enemy led to a medical breakthrough that saved countless people from a crippling disease and possible death.

Unfortunately, national unity, even facing a dangerous common enemy, has been difficult to achieve and nearly impossible to sustain in today's fractious political and social environment. If the current concerns over the zika virus were to reach the same level as they did for polio, would we as a nation respond as rapidly and effectively as we did in the 1950s? I wonder.

Richmond *Times-Dispatch*, February 21, 2016

Loosening a demon's grip

49

Loosening a demon's grip
Parkinson's

By my count, this column marks my 100th for the Richmond *Times-Dispatch*. I have published only one essay on Parkinson's disease, a chronic, degenerative neurological illness that has governed my life for more than 12 years. Why have I devoted so little attention to the disease in my pieces?

In all honesty, I welcome any escape from the grip of Demon Parkinson's, and I find that writing is one of the best ways for me to do that. Unfortunately, its grip is growing tighter on me with each passing year. Despite my best efforts and those of a first-rate medical team, the disease is gradually robbing me of a once-vibrant and fulfilling life.

I was diagnosed with PD in 2004 at age 58, which put me in the unenviable category of "early onset." After the initial shock of my diagnosis, I learned that my service in the Army during the Vietnam War qualified me to be treated at the Parkinson's disease center at McGuire VA Medical Center in Richmond, one of only seven such centers in the entire veterans hospital system nation-wide.

The results of the care I began to receive were almost immediate and dramatic. Thanks to the expertise of a superb medical team at McGuire, I was prescribed the medications and given the expert counseling I needed to help slow the disease's progression.

For nearly 10 years, I kept the disease at bay. Friends seemed amazed at how many of the manifestations of Parkinson's were reduced by the care I was receiving. And most people I met for the first time never guessed that I had the disease.

Gone was the blank facial expression of most Parkinson's sufferers. I started swinging my arms again and taking full strides when I walked, rather than the stutter steps so common with PD patients.

My handwriting improved from a scrawl to a reasonably legible script. I felt fully confident around people, and was completely comfortable in my public speaking. My wife and I traveled extensively overseas, realizing that we needed to take advantage of my relatively good health while we could.

With my friends David Reynolds and Kit Lephart, who have PD, we formed a support group that we named the Movers and Shakers. Together we became active in helping raise $5 million to establish a comprehensive Parkinson's disease center at Virginia Commonwealth University, one that has begun treating patients with movement disorders throughout central Virginia and beyond.

I have spoken at many Parkinson's disease seminars and participated in a number of related fundraising events. People began to refer to me as the "Parkinson's Poster Boy of Richmond."

***

It was a honeymoon of relatively normal living that lasted about 10 years, longer than it does for most Parkinson's patients. I knew, however, that the honeymoon had a time limit on it. Parkinson's is a cruel disease, patiently taking its time to shut its victims down, playing with them like a cat slowly but deliberately torturing a young rabbit it has caught.

Little by little, it began to age me and sap me of my ability to do things that once came naturally. I began to occasionally freeze and felt unable to walk through doorways, terrified that I would fall.

I would go into the grocery store at a full normal stride, yet halfway through shopping, Parkinson's would suddenly take control of me. I would begin shuffling my feet, gripping the cart in fear that I would fall. When I got to check out, I struggled to retrieve my wallet to pay for my purchases. I couldn't help but notice people staring at me, making me want to flee the store in embarrassment.

I am still able to drive a car without difficulty, but recently my children won't let me drive my grandchildren to McDonald's or the movies, fearful that they are at risk with me behind the wheel. It makes me sad, but I can't blame them.

While most people think of Parkinson's as an illness that affects people physically, it can have profound mental and psychological consequences. Depression is one weapon in its arsenal. Fortunately that weapon has failed with me. But another one bothers me no end - the loss of executive function.

Executive function is a skill that most of us have that allows us to get things done such as arrange your schedule for the day, organize your personal finances, remember where things are, multi-task, or analyze a complex problem and find a solution. At times, it drives my wife to her wit's end.

I know that part of it is the aging process, but hardly a day goes by that I can't find my keys or a bill I had intended to pay. I get frustrated trying to find a memo I had received from someone, only to realize that I had stuck it in the wrong file. I find myself putting off decisions until the last moment, something I never used to do.

***

People ask me what it feels like to have Parkinson's. Is there pain and discomfort? Not really, but it is more of the latter. The best description I have heard is that it's like driving with your parking brake on. Every motion seems to slow to half speed, whether it's buttoning a shirt, tying your shoes, getting in and out of a car, or typing.

It is the last that has really bothered me. I get great joy out of writing, which I have done initially on typewriters and then on computer keyboards. Although I have never been a speedster with my typing, up until a few years ago I could pound out words at a fairly fast clip. Although I have no problem finding the words, committing them to my computer screen comes more slowly now.

What can I do? I am getting ready to take a big step to try to loosen the grip of Demon Parkinson's. Until a year or so ago, I was able to control the disease by taking increasing amounts of the wonder drugs that curtail the disease's symptoms and actually slow its progression.

Unfortunately I have reached the point of maxing out on these drugs. I am a veritable walking medicine cabinet, taking near 20 pills a day. Their effectiveness and duration little by little is lessening.

As a result, I will soon take another step in this journey - deep brain stimulation surgery (DBS). In an operation that could take up to six hours, the surgeon will insert two thin, insulated wires through small openings in my skull and implant them in a targeted part of my brain.

These wires will be passed under the skin on my head, neck, and shoulder, connecting to a neurostimulator that will be implanted under the skin near my collarbone. Once turned on, the device will send out regular electrical impulses that will block the electrical signals that cause my PD symptoms.

Assuming it works, I can reduce the amount of my medications, and I will experience a reduction of my PD symptoms. Are their risks? Yes, anytime one undergoes brain surgery, there is the risk of infection, stroke, excessive bleeding in the skull, or complications associated with anesthesia.

But I am willing to assume those risks. If this procedure works, I can anticipate a better life for years to come. Frankly I am tired of being tossed around and tortured like a young rabbit.

I look forward to giving you a post-surgery report - a good one I hope.

Richmond *Times-Dispatch*, July 17, 2016

50

TAMING THE DEMON PARKINSON'S

The human brain is an amazing organ. It accounts for only 2 percent of the body's weight, but it consumes 20 percent of the body's energy. Every physical move we make, every word we utter, every problem we solve originates in the brain.

When the brain comes under attack, those functions can be affected seriously. More than a decade ago, I began to suspect there was an assault on my brain when I started to show signs of Parkinson's disease. My wife and I were devastated when our family doctor confirmed that our fears were justified.

Parkinson's is an incurable neuromuscular illness that strikes the substantia nigra section of the brain, ruthlessly mounting a slow and deliberate siege on the mind and body. Little by little, it ages and slows you down. It makes you feel awkward in public. It makes you chronically tired. Simple actions such as buttoning a shirt, keyboarding, tying shoes, rolling over in bed, or getting in and out of a car turn into major, time-consuming chores.

Balance becomes a cause for concern, with many Parkinson's patients experiencing serious falls and resulting injuries. Although people do not die of the disease, they often succumb to other causes that it has exacerbated.

***

This catastrophic illness was named for English surgeon and apothecary James Parkinson, who officially identified the ailment when he published "An Essay on the Shaking Palsy" in 1817. Parkinson classified the disease, and for the next century and a half, doctors and scientists looked for a cure and ways to treat it.

Finally in the 1960s, with the introduction of the drug Levodopa, doctors had the first weapon available to them that actually worked in fighting Parkinson's. Most patients receiving Levodopa experienced significant improvement in their condition.

Over the years other drugs were introduced to slow the progress of the disease and to further minimize symptoms. These medications brought about a revolution in the management of the disease.

But diagnosing and treating Parkinson's is a tricky business, usually requiring the skills of well-trained and experienced specialists. As an Army veteran, I was fortunate to qualify for comprehensive treatment at the Parkinson's Disease Center at McGuire VA Medical Center. McGuire is one of seven VA hospitals nationwide to have such programs.

The team of specialists there was able to prescribe just the right combination of drugs to treat me. Almost as soon as my neurologist put me on them, I felt better and my Parkinson's symptoms were reduced significantly for more than a decade.

People often expressed surprise when I told them that I had Parkinson's. Having a positive attitude and adhering to a rigorous exercise schedule contributed to my overall well-being.

***

Nevertheless, Parkinson's proved to be a relentless demon that can be slowed but not stopped.

Gradually, the symptoms I had experienced when I was first diagnosed began to subtly reappear - a slight tremor in my right hand, an unsteadiness while on my feet, occasional falls, and increasing difficulty in performing simple tasks that require some degree of manual dexterity.

Realizing that more drugs would no longer provide the help I needed, early this spring my neurologist and I began to discuss the next option - Deep Brain Stimulation surgery (DBS). DBS is a major surgery that if successful could diminish my Parkinson's symptoms.

I am fortunate that one of the country's most experienced and accomplished neurosurgeons specializing in DBS is located in Richmond. Dr. Kathryn Holloway, director of the DBS program at VCU Medical Center, has performed more than 500 (I was number 510) of these complex surgeries.

My wife and I met with her in early April, and Dr. Holloway explained that during the six-hour surgery she and her team would insert two thin, insulated wires through two openings in my skull and implant them in a pre-determined portion of my brain.

The wires would then be slipped under the skin on my head, neck, and shoulder and be connected to a neurostimulator they would implant under my skin near my collarbone. When they turned it on, she explained, this device would send out a steady stream of electrical impulses that would block the electrical signals that caused my Parkinson's symptoms.

If the surgery was successful, I could limit the amount of drugs I was taking, while enjoying a reduction in my symptoms. Dr. Holloway warned, however, that the operation was not risk-free.

Anytime brain surgery is performed, the patient runs the risk of a stroke, infection, and excess bleeding in the skull, or having a bad reaction to anesthesia. Given the alternative, I decided to take those risks.

***

To qualify for the surgery, I had to pass a series of tests to determine that I responded well to my medications, that I did not have other ailments not related to Parkinson's, and that I was not suffering from depression. I passed easily, and was given a date for my surgery - July 26 - more than three months in the future.

I had to wait in line for my turn for the DBS, and the next three months seemed excruciatingly long. The closer it got, time seemed to slow to a crawl. It reminded me of those few days before Christmas when I was a child and the hands on the clock never seemed to move.

Finally the big day came. A small contingent of family and friends took me to McGuire Hospital for my 6 a.m. surgery appointment.

In many ways the rest of the day is a blur, but here are some impressions: an exceptionally friendly and welcoming medical staff who helped ease any worries I had; endlessly repeating my full name and social security number; being told to count backwards from ten and not quite reaching five before the anesthesia kicked in; waking up to the voice of Dr. Holloway and some of her team members and realizing that they were in the middle of my surgery; hearing a strange, fluctuating noise in the background that I was told - after asking - was the sound of my brain as Dr. Holloway guided a probe to find a "sweet spot" to place my implants.

I remember my neurologist commanding me to move my arms and legs at intervals to ensure that the implants had been properly placed - and waking up in the recovery room, my head still foggy from the surgery and the affects of the anesthesia.

The total time for the surgery was a little more than six hours. I was then kept in the hospital for five days, including one for Dr. Holloway to place the stimulator device in my chest. Once she did, to ensure there was no infection or other complications, I had to wait two weeks for the stimulator to be activated.

***

My wife and I went back for my appointment on August 12 to have me "turned on." As we made the 21-mile drive to McGuire, I thought again of Christmas during my childhood. What would be under the tree? A bright, new, shiny toy, or a pair of pajamas and some socks?

Fortunately my device was the new toy. After they turned it on, I soon felt like a new person. No more shaky hands. No more freezing when I came to a doorway. No more falls. No longer having people stare at me as I stutter-stepped my way through the grocery store.

I know that the DBS has its limitations and that a time will come when it, too, will no longer be as effective as it is now. But if

I can have another 10 years, even five years, of the way I feel now, it was well worth the effort, despite the risks involved. Thanks to a gifted surgeon and her team, I have been given back a way of life I thought I had lost forever. They have truly turned me on.

Richmond *Times-Dispatch*, August 21, 2016

51

THE HIGH COST OF LIVING THE GOOD LIFE

Increasing mechanization of agriculture made it possible for millions of people to leave their farms and move to a more reliable source of income in factories in those cities.

The images coming out of Houston and Florida of the devastation caused by the spate of recent hurricanes have seemed almost unbelievable. Although the death toll was higher from Hurricane Katrina 12 years ago, the destruction of property and disruption of business and commerce are proving much greater than the earlier storm.

Scientists have been telling us to expect more of these incredibly destructive events as the globe's oceans warm.

One factor that's often overlooked: The extent of destruction is caused by where most people live today. Some 81 percent of Americans now reside in urban areas. The more population is concentrated, the greater the risk of loss of lives and property by weather, earthquakes, volcanoes, and nuclear warfare.

Urban historians point out that cities were relatively few until the 19th-century. Only two cities in the ancient world (Rome and Alexandria) had populations of around half a million people. Archaeologists estimate that the Inca city of Cuzco had nearly 500,000 residents in the 13th century.

By 1800, Rome and Alexandria had declined and were succeeded by Paris and London, with a million people each. Only one century later, however, the United States alone had six cities with more than half a million inhabitants.

This congregating of people can be traced to the Industrial Revolution and advances in technology beginning in the late 18th century in Western Europe.

The growth of the factory system led to the concentration of work forces in burgeoning cities. Increasing mechanization of agriculture made it possible for millions of people to leave their farms and move to a more reliable source of income in factories in those cities.

***

Technology also played a crucial role in urbanization. In the centuries before the Industrial Revolution, the size of cities was determined by the transportation available. The footprint of cities could only be as large as a person could walk, ride on horseback, and travel by wagon to a job or marketplace and then back home again.

By the 1880s, however, cities began to experience a transportation revolution, changing from "walking cities" to "streetcar cities." The introduction of electricity made it possible to replace slow horse-drawn trolleys with fast streetcars, trains, and subways, allowing people to live many miles from their place of work and still be able to return home to suburbs in the evening. The growing dependence on the automobile in the 20th century accelerated the process.

As cities began to expand horizontally they also began to rise vertically. In the 1880s, buildings began to incorporate steel girders in a skeleton-like frames, resulting in skyscrapers 20 stories or higher. Inventions like the elevator, flush toilet, telephone, and air-conditioning contributed to urbanization as well as suburbanization. The advent of artificially cooled air had perhaps the most profound consequence of all.

By mid-20th century, an ever-increasing dependence on air-conditioning made working and living bearable even during the hot days of summer. Mechanically cooled air began to reshape the nation's economy and demographics. The great migrations, industrial development, and urbanization in the Sun Belt would not have been possible without it.

It is no coincidence that since 1940, the South has urbanized more than any other section of the country, from 36 percent urban to more than 75 percent in 2010.

The exploding population of Florida is tied closely to the spread of air-conditioning. In 1920, the Sunshine State was home to barely a million people. By 1960, it had jumped to some 5 million. With artificially cooled air becoming standard throughout Florida, the state has become the country's third largest, with 20.6 million people, many of whom are retirees. The majority of Floridians live within 25 miles of the coast.

Houston experienced similar growth. A century ago, it had only 138,000 residents, but today Houston's metropolitan area's population approaches 6.9 million, making it the nation's fourth largest.

***

Technological advances turned cities into points at which power, wealth, and influence came together. A relative recent development - the ability to retire and move to milder winter climates - has also led to the concentration of people in the South. It has made them extremely vulnerable to natural disasters as well.

Ironically, the things that contributed to the growth of cities - electricity, indoor-plumbing, elevators, air conditioning and refrigeration, modern transportation systems - when lost, can virtually paralyze millions of people. The unchecked growth and expansion of cities have caused their own set of problems.

Houston, for example, has had a laissez-faire attitude toward growth, refusing to impose zoning codes on its people. As a result, more and more of the city's once-green surfaces are covered either in asphalt or concrete for parking lots, highways, and buildings.

As woods and fields are cleared for suburban expansion, rainwater is less effectively absorbed by groundwater aquifers. Runoff from rain showers and storms also becomes polluted as gasoline, motor oil, and heavy metals are washed away. Hurricanes like Harvey demonstrate that such growth comes at an extremely high price.

What is the answer? The term "smart growth" has been used for nearly 50 years to slow the pace of urban and suburban sprawl. Some cities like Portland, Oregon, have adopted slow-growth policies that have sought to make the city more compact.

Smart growth, however, can run counter to the American ideal of property rights and real estate development. The industry contributed $1.2 trillion to the nation's economic output, representing 6 percent of the U.S. gross domestic product. The combined costs of recent hurricanes, however, will run in the tens of billions.

There is no easy answer to the complex dilemma in which we find ourselves. One thing is certain, however. We can anticipate that massive storms will continue, yet people will keep developing property in the path of these meteorological monsters. Let's not forget that we have more than a month to go before the end of this hurricane season.

Richmond *Times-Dispatch*, October 15, 2017

52

THE EXQUISITE TRAUMA
OF DOWNSIZING

I was looking for my hammer the other day, and couldn't find it anywhere. I know where I kept it for some 30 years, but now it's nowhere to be found. Why? It's because my wife and I have recently moved for the first time in three decades.

Surveys reveal that moving is one of life's most traumatic experiences, ranking only behind the death of a loved one and divorce. By my count, I have now moved 13 times, my wife a dozen, which is just about the average number of moves that most Americans make before going to their just reward.

Some Americans, particularly those who are career military or who have corporate jobs that require frequent relocations, move 20 or more times.

Why do people move? It boils down to two or three basic factors. They are either pushed or pulled to do it; or it can be a combination of the two.

People are often pulled to move when presented with an opportunity, as I was 29 years ago when I moved to Richmond to take a job as head of the Virginia Historical Society.

On the other hand, some people are pushed or forced to move because of economic circumstances or because their jobs require them to relocate.

The move that we just made, however, entailed both push and pull factors, and was heavily influenced by issues of age and health.

We became septuagenarians last year. And I was diagnosed with Parkinson's disease 14 years ago. As of yet incurable, Parkinson's probably will eventually render me an invalid and would make living in our two-story home difficult for both of us.

My wife developed ovarian cancer two years ago, and then suffered a recurrence earlier last year. Fortunately, thanks to aggressive treatments, her latest checkup determined that she is NED (no evidence of disease), but we are fully aware that ovarian cancer has a risk of returning.

With those two traumatic life events in mind, we decided that it was time to begin thinking about moving to a continuing care retirement community.

We considered going to my wife's hometown of Lexington, Virginia, or to Chapel Hill, North Carolina, where our daughter and her family live, but we decided to stay in Richmond.

We both had lived in our Richmond home longer than any other place in our lives.

Richmond offers a rich cultural and arts community, relatively low cost of living, a pleasant climate (except for July and August!), and, most important to us, first-class medical care. Also, over the years, we have built many strong friendships that we were reluctant to give up.

After visiting several retirement communities, we chose Cedarfield in western Henrico, which was only two miles from our current home and near all of the shops, stores, and restaurants we have patronized for years.

Knowing that we would be moving eventually, we began the unpleasant process of downsizing from a 2,300-square-foot house to a 1,200-square-foot apartment last summer.

Our adult children had little interest in our collection of so-called "brown furniture," nor did the china and silver collections we had inherited from two sets of grandparents appeal to them. Young adults today are more informal in the way they live and entertain.

During my career as a professional historian, I had accumulated an extensive book collection that filled the shelves of my study and had long since spilled over onto the floor and to other rooms.

Years ago, my wife unsuccessfully tried to rein in my book purchases saying, "No more books! Just download them on your I-Pad." Indeed, I cut back on buying real books, but there were certain ones that I just had to have.

But the closer we came to moving, the more I realized that we simply didn't have the space to take my full library. I ended up donating a large number to the Virginia Historical Society (now known as the Virginia Museum of History & Culture), which in turn put them up for sale at its annual fall used-book sale, the proceeds of which go to a collections fund.

Our biggest downsizing challenge, however, was our attic, which has accumulated three decades' worth of stuff, including more brown furniture, clothing that we haven't worn in years, — my VMI uniforms, for example — and dozens of boxes containing who knows what.

Some of that stuff came from the homes of our parents after they died. These included my Lionel electric train set, my wife's dolls, my class notes from VMI and graduate school, my childhood drawings that my mother had saved, and many things we had said we would decide what to do with later.

Suddenly we were discovering that later is now. Thanks to Goodwill Industries, Sisters of the Poor, the Historical Society, and Hope Church, which collects used furniture, we were able to rid ourselves of a good bit of material.

Then came the time for us to get ready to move. We had not sold a home in 30 years, and we soon discovered that the rules of the real estate game have changed. Fortunately, we chose experienced and engaged agents, a couple who live in our neighborhood. From beginning to end, they worked closely with us to get our home sold.

First, they told us that we would have to "stage" the house to make it more marketable. Rather than calling it "staging," I would describe it as "sterilizing" the house.

We had to remove almost anything left that was of a personal nature. So down came all of our family pictures; into boxes went my wife's shelf of collectable trinkets that she had accumulated from our travels abroad, along with the majority of my history books.

Our interior began to look more like a nondescript furniture storeroom display than a real home.

Staging must have worked because our house sold just 16 days after going on the market — and attracted dozens of prospective buyers. The young couple that bought the house wanted to move into our neighborhood and liked the idea of raising a family in our home.

The physical move to Cedarfield proved to be much more difficult than we ever imagined. Although our home is nearby, it may as well have been 2,000 miles away. Thank goodness for the help of neighbors, friends, our daughter, and a good moving company — we transported stuff from one place to another over a two-week period. Yet the real burden fell on us, which made us realize that moving is not for people our age.

Despite having downsized what seemed like tons of stuff, we discovered that it was by no means enough. As I write this column, I see boxes yet to be emptied everywhere I look. My wife says anyone walking in to our apartment now would think we are hoarders.

We have been reassured by our new neighbors that this is not unusual and to take our time. Those are words of wisdom, but I still wish I could find my hammer!

Richmond *Times-Dispatch*, March 4, 2018

53

WHY MODERN AMERICANS LIVE LONG AND PROSPER

I n recent years I have reflected on my father's death soon after he turned 43. I was only 8. We were returning from family vacation by car. My mother was driving, while my father was resting in the passenger seat with his eyes closed. My sister and I were in the back seat.

Suddenly my father sat up, reached for my mother, and then collapsed. She slammed on the brakes and turned the car off the road. Other cars stopped to help, but it was too late. My father had died of a massive heart attack.

In retrospect, his death should have come as no surprise. He had been afflicted with rheumatic fever as a child. And when he tried to join the Army during World War II, he was declared 4-F because of a heart murmur.

He had a series of heart-related episodes prior to his death. But cardiology in 1955 was primitive compared to now, which leads to the conclusion that if those episodes had occurred today, he could have lived many more years.

His premature death bucked a trend that had been going on for more than a century - the lengthening life expectancy of the human being. Statistics tell the story.

***

According to several studies, the average human life expectancy of an American in 1800 was only about 30 years. That figure includes all births and deaths in a given year and is skewed somewhat by a high infant mortality rate. For each 1,000 babies born, 400 did not reach adulthood.

Go another hundred years to 1900, however, and the average American life expectancy had leaped ahead to 47 years. And by 2000, it had soared to an astonishing 76 years. This was no accident. Three major factors contributed to the phenomenon.

First was the development of the practice of medicine as a legitimate profession. For most of recorded history, self-proclaimed healers treated the injured and ill. Their knowledge of the nature of illnesses and how to treat patients was primitive at best.

But beginning in the 19th century, physicians started a concerted effort in Western Europe and the United States to set certain standards for practicing medicine.

The establishment of the American Medical Association in 1847 led to stronger educational requirements and the improved practice of medicine. Schools like the Medical College of Virginia sprang up throughout the country. For their time, they provided decent training with a greater emphasis in science than ever before.

By the end of the 19th century, a degree and professional licensing became required to practice medicine. No longer could a self-taught person hang a shingle out and declare himself a doctor.

By the early 20th century, the profession developed an increasing number of specialists who limited their practice to specific ailments. Also, by the early 1900s, physicians began to receive higher pay for their work. Practicing medicine would be regarded as a true profession rather than a trade.

***

The second factor that contributed to humans living longer was the development of a strong public health system nationwide. Modern, well-equipped hospitals and clinics staffed by trained doctors and nurses sprang up around the country in the first half of the 20th century.

Fewer babies were born at home, resulting in a significant drop in infant mortality. Major funding from government and private sources led to increases in research and effective treatment of numerous diseases.

Mass inoculations for polio, smallpox, measles, mumps, and influenza became standard procedures for most American citizens.

The production, manufacturing, and distribution of pharmaceuticals became strictly regulated by governmental and professional authorities to ensure that patients were being properly medicated.

Preventative medicine came into its own by the mid-20th century. Exercise and diet became a mantra for doctors and their patients, with most having adopted sedentary lifestyles associated with a non-agrarian society.

A large and concerted anti-smoking campaign was launched as a result of the U.S. surgeon general's report in 1964. That eventually led to a significant reduction in tobacco use, along with serious ailments associated with smoking, including lung cancer and heart disease.

***

The third development contributing to longer living was the application of research science to the everyday treatment of patients, also known as translational research.

Well into the 19th century, some doctors resorted to bleeding their sick patients, under the belief that it would rid the body of its bad elements. And it was nearly the end of the 19th century before doctors accepted the germ theory, which in turn led to basic sanitation by physicians in treating ill and injured patients.

By the mid-20th century, medicine began to be practiced in ways that would have seemed like science fiction only a few decades earlier. Organ transplants, valve replacement surgery, joint replacements, and deep brain stimulation surgery to treat Parkinson's disease have become almost routine procedures and have extended the lives of countless numbers of people.

MCV was one of the leading medical centers in the country to launch an organ transplant program. Dr. Christiaan Barnard of South Africa is credited with having performed the first human heart transplant 50 years ago.

A little-known fact is that prior to performing this path-breaking surgery, Barnard spent three months in Richmond studying the organ transplant program under the direction of MCV surgeon Richard Lower. Since then, more than 6,000 heart transplants have been performed between VCU and Richmond's McGuire Veterans Hospital.

***

Will humans continue the trend of living longer? Actually, over the past few years, the opioid epidemic that is afflicting the country is slightly reversing the longevity trend. But I sense that is a temporary development. A recent report by the U.S. Census Bureau noted that by the year 2035 "senior citizens will outnumber children for the first time in American history."

With Americans having fewer babies and seniors living longer than ever, the consequences are profound. Will strains on the Social Security system increase a rapidly growing trend of people delaying retirement for many years? Will the need for assisted living facilities begin to outnumber those for elementary schools and playgrounds?

Perhaps the late journalist Andy Rooney said it best: "It's paradoxical that the idea of living longer appeals to everyone, but the idea of getting old appeals to no one."

Richmond *Times-Dispatch*, April 1, 2018

54

LESSONS LEARNED FROM EARLIER PANDEMICS

As the coronavirus continues its seemingly relentless march around the globe, I have been thinking of historical comparisons to make sense out of the unfolding drama. Pundits are equating it to the 1918 flu pandemic that killed tens of millions of people over a relatively short period of time.

In some ways, the coronavirus pandemic seems almost the stuff of science fiction. It's odd, but a few months ago, my wife and I watched the 1971 movie "The Andromeda Strain," based on a bestselling novel by Michael Crichton.

The plot revolves around a team of scientists investigating the outbreak of a deadly, invisible microorganism in Arizona. The team determines that the lethal microbes, which they name Andromeda, kill their victims by rapidly clotting their blood. Furthermore, the deadly agents came from outer space, having been attached to a man-made satellite that had recently crashed in the Arizona desert.

Soon, this invisible enemy begins to mutate by transforming itself into an unstoppable force. The scientists isolate themselves in a sealed chamber, but a mutated form of the microbe attacks its synthetic rubber door and hatch seals, and rapidly migrates toward the chamber containing the scientists.

In case you haven't read the book or seen the movie, I won't spoil the ending for you. But more than once over the past couple of weeks, I have thought about "The Andromeda Strain." History, however, tells us that there have been real Andromeda-like pandemics that killed countless numbers of people.

Recorded accounts of mass deaths by disease go back nearly 2,500 years, when smallpox swept through ancient Greece in 430 B.C., killing an estimated 30,000 people or about 20% of Athens' population.

Next came the Plague of Justinian that appeared and reappeared periodically for nearly 200 years in the Middle East, parts of Asia and then the Mediterranean Basin. First reported in 541 A.D., it was transmitted by rats that had been bitten by fleas carrying the deadly bacteria. Scholars contend that at least 50 million people died as a result, making this the first real pandemic the world experienced.

Probably the most infamous of all plagues was the Black Death or bubonic plague. Thought to be one of the deadliest of all pandemics, it led to the deaths of an estimated 200 million people in Eurasia. Apparently starting in China in 1334, it spread gradually along trade routes to Europe, wiping out villages and towns along the way.

Like the Justinian Plague, its root cause came from rats that had been bitten by plague-infected fleas. It struck crowded Paris, London and Rome, and modern scholars estimate that it killed up to 60% of Europe's population.

The long-term consequences were profound. It took another two centuries for the European population to recover to its previous level. It also resulted in major social, religious and economic upheavals that shaped the course of world history for centuries to come.

A pandemic that struck the Western Hemisphere in the 16th century often is overlooked because of little written evidence. When Christopher Columbus arrived in the New World in 1492, archaeologists now estimate that the native population numbered nearly 100 million. Yet a century later, it had declined some 90%. The cause?

For one, the American natives had been isolated from the rest of the world's population, and had never been exposed to the diseases that Europeans had experienced and to which they had developed immunities. When the latter arrived in America, they were virtual germ and virus machines, unknowingly spreading disease everywhere they went. Smallpox, measles, pneumonia and influenza wiped out huge portions of the population, making the conquest of today's South and Central America a relatively easy undertaking.

Numerous epidemics have occurred since then, many in the United States, such as smallpox in New England in the 1640s; yellow fever in Philadelphia and the surrounding countryside in 1793; cholera in the American Midwest in 1832 and again in 1848; and polio in the 1940s and 1950s.

Breaking out during World War I, the great influenza pandemic of 1918-19 presented the world with the most widespread and deadliest of all modern-day mass killing diseases. Debate still surrounds the location of the microbe's origins, but whether it was in Kansas, New England or Europe, it struck rich and poor, urban and rural, old and young alike.

This particular virus could attack a perfectly healthy person one day, and by the next day, that person was dead. Soldiers being transported to the war in Europe by train and ship spread the virus everywhere they went.

It came in two waves, and by the time the disease had run its course, an estimated 675,000 Americans died as a result, along with nearly 100 million people worldwide.

What can we learn from these periodic visits from the angel of death? First, in each instance, the outbreak of a deadly disease caught everyone unprepared. Modern pandemics have occurred despite warnings from scientists. As a result, the response from those in authority was too slow to prevent its rapid spread, in turn resulting in a huge loss of lives.

Next, as trade routes developed and modes of transportation improved over the centuries, epidemics turned into pandemics. By the 20th century, they spread throughout the planet rapidly, greatly disrupting world markets.

Then there were the economic consequences caused by pandemics. After the 1918-19 influenza pandemic, for example, life insurance claims soared, driving many companies out of business. Small businesses that had been forced to shut down during the pandemic or lost workers to death often went bankrupt. This, combined with the disruptions caused by the transition to a peacetime economy, led to a major post-war recession.

Pandemics vary from one to another, but there are enough similarities to give us pause. The truism "It ain't over 'til it's over" should serve as a warning to us all.

Predictions and promises as to when we can start celebrating victory over the coronavirus are premature and irresponsible. Scientists tell us that the end is no more predictable than the beginning. Let us hope that our political leaders will heed the warnings being issued by members of the scientific community. To not do so is tempting fate.

Richmond *Times-Dispatch*, April 12, 2020

55

ALL IN THE FAMILY:
WHAT TO DO WITH THE OLD FOLKS?

As I approach my mid-70s, I'm finding life to be a greater challenge with each passing year. For one, more and more of my relatives and friends who have been an important part of my life are dying.

Pain is an almost constant companion now as arthritis has settled in for a long siege of my lower back. Since being diagnosed with Parkinson's disease 17 years ago, I am finding it increasingly difficult to do routine things that I once took for granted.

I had to give up driving this past year. Dressing myself is becoming a chore. And my voice is beginning to soften, prompting people to frequently ask, "What did you say?"

On the other hand, I have much to be thankful for.

In the decade leading up to my retirement, I socked away every dollar I could from my paycheck into a 401(k) account. As a result, my wife and I have a modest nest egg. That, plus monthly social security checks, ensures a fairly comfortable but not extravagant lifestyle for us.

Three years ago, we moved into Cedarfield, a continuing care retirement community in western Henrico County that satisfies most of our basic needs, while relieving us of many of the hassles that go with home ownership. We have been well looked after during the COVID-19 pandemic.

Our situation makes me realize just how fortunate we are when compared to previous generations of senior Americans and many elderly people living today. Until the 1920s, most Americans lived in rural areas and made their livelihood on farms, when there was no real retirement as we know it today. People simply worked until they physically were unable to or they died.

Taking care of the elderly mostly fell on family members, especially for the very old, infirmed and poor. Genealogists researching census records long have discovered that it was not unusual to find three or four generations of a family living under one roof.

But in many instances, it was not feasible for families to care for their elderly parents and grandparents. Throughout the country in the 19th century, town and county governments began to build "poor houses" that took in seniors who had no family or other means to support themselves.

At the same time, reform-minded advocates led a movement to establish asylums for the mentally ill and orphanages for parentless children. Built with charitable intentions, many of these places were underfunded and had barely tolerable living conditions. They were regarded by most people as the last stop in the game of life.

By the late 19th century, the first elements of a modern care system for the elderly began to take shape. Religious, fraternal and veterans groups started opening living facilities for seniors. These "retirement homes" were a welcome alternative to most state and local government-run institutions.

Often referred to as almshouses, a term that was borrowed from the English model, they provided shelter and regular meals for the elderly in need of support. Almshouses continued well into the 20th century but became overwhelmed during the Great Depression when the poor and indigent population virtually exploded.

Little by little, interest increased in how society treats its senior population as people began to live longer with healthier lifestyles and the advent of modern medicine. The average life expectancy of an American nearly doubled in the 19th century from age 28 to age 47. It nearly doubled again during the 20th century.

In addition, unheard of wealth was created, as various national economies shifted from agricultural to industrial. Governments throughout the western world instituted social welfare programs that provided an income to seniors who no longer could work.

Led by the German government in the late 19th century, the U.S. eventually created an old age pension plan that led to passage of the Social Security Act of 1935 under the leadership of President Franklin D. Roosevelt. In 1965, President Lyndon B. Johnson led the effort to create Medicare and Medicaid to ensure that all seniors would have access to medical care regardless of their financial situations.

At the same time, our elderly population continues to steadily grow. The percentage of Americans age 65 and older nearly has quadrupled from 4.1% in 1900 to 15.2% in 2016 with no evidence that it is slowing. By 2030, seniors are expected to make up more than 20% of the population.

Despite this growth in the elderly population, according to the Social Security Administration, the poverty rate for people 65 and older has declined almost 70% in the past five decades. That trend does not appear across the board as the population of elderly Latinos and African Americans living in poverty actually has grown by as much as 8.6% during that same period.

This will require the government to spend almost double what it does today on programs like Medicare. As a result, senior care will have to develop quickly to meet this growing demand.

In response, an increasing number of residential living facilities for the elderly have emerged since the 1970s, from elegant facilities to those that offer the barest of amenities. For those who do not require a nursing home environment, assisted living communities providing intermediate care have proliferated as well.

The competition to attract residents is keen. Many offer excellent dining services, a full range of exercise equipment, regular entertainment and a variety of other amenities.

Seniors living in those centers sometimes don't realize how fortunate they are to spend their last years in relative comfort and security. People increasingly are not viewing senior living as a final stop, but rather someplace to age with dignity and to be cared for when needed.

Unfortunately, there still are far too many people out there who still aren't able to take advantage of a comfortable retirement, and who might have to rely on the support of family members simply to stay afloat.

Richmond *Times-Dispatch*, March 21, 2021

56

WHY DO WE LIVE SO LONG?

The COVID-19 pandemic has made us painfully aware of the fragility of life. More than a half-million Americans have died of the virus, and deaths worldwide now number more than 3 million. It again is raging in India.

Despite this catastrophic health crisis, scientists predict that human life expectancy will continue to increase, as will world population. Indeed, the average life expectancy of the human has jumped from about 28 years to 77 since 1800, and it keeps rising.

What caused this phenomenon? To answer that question, I interviewed some two dozen people in the health care profession. Dr. Peter Buckley, dean of Virginia Commonwealth University's School of Medicine, helped in my project by posing my question to many of his department heads.

My survey should not be considered comprehensive nor as a rigorous scientific exercise. Nevertheless, I was impressed with the thought the respondents gave to my question.

Many of the suggestions I received overlapped enough for me to determine five fundamental developments that led to a longer life expectancy and quality of life for humans. Some of these advances originated outside of the United States, but they eventually profoundly affected Americans.

The answers to my question are as follows (arranged chronologically):

1) Acceptance of the germ theory (1860s)

Until the mid-19th-century, numerous reasons were given for the causes of illness and death. The most common was the miasma theory that held that infectious diseases such as cholera, malaria, typhoid fever and the Black Death were attributed to "bad air," composed of decomposed matter carried by mists.

Even when surgery initially was deemed successful, patients frequently died from postsurgical infections such as gangrene and sepsis. No one understood the causes of these infections or their complications, and how they spread.

French scientist Louis Pasteur proved infectious diseases were a result of an invasion of microscopic organisms (germs) into living hosts. Furthermore, the spread of germs in the body could explain infectious diseases.

Known as the germ theory, Pasteur never tested the concept. Instead, Glasgow University Professor Joseph Lister studied Pasteur's theory and tried it in surgery. In the 1880s, he applied a "chemical barrier" (that he called antiseptic) using germ-killing carbolic acid. His techniques seemed to work, despite initial mixed reaction within the medical profession.

Despite initial reluctance by many doctors to endorse his methods, by the turn of the 20th century the number of surgery-related deaths significantly fell, providing solid evidence that his antiseptic worked.

Also, sterilizing surgical instruments, wearing gloves during surgery and dressing wounds with antiseptic solutions became standard procedure for doctors, resulting in the saving of untold numbers of lives ever since.

2) Internal imaging (1895)

This development changed the practice of medicine almost overnight. German physicist Wilhelm Rontgen was experimenting with electrical currents through glass cathode-ray tubes and discovered that X-rays could provide images inside the body. X-ray machines allowed doctors to examine broken bones, tumors, internal injuries and other irregularities that are not visible to the eye alone.

Later medical imaging such as computerized tomography (CT) scanners and magnetic resonance imaging (MRI) created even sharper images within the body and have become fundamental diagnostic tools in modern medicine. Rontgen's early work using electrical currents eventually opened a whole new therapeutic element.

3) Penicillin, the world's first antibiotic (1928)

Scottish biologist Alexander Fleming accidentally discovered mold in a petri dish that killed deadly bacteria on contact. Most doctors were slow to recognize penicillin's significance until World War II, when it went into mass production. This crucial development has saved tens of millions of lives but over the years, certain bacteria have become increasingly resistant to antibiotics and raise the fears of some scientists about the ability to stop their spread.

4) Antiviral drugs (1960s)

We only have to look at the past year to comprehend the devastation that viruses can cause. From smallpox, to influenza, to hepatitis, to polio, to the coronavirus, these microorganisms at times nearly have destroyed whole populations.

Scientific journalist Charles Mann notes that on the eve of Christopher Columbus' first visit to the New World in 1492, the total native population in the Western Hemisphere is estimated to have numbered some 100 million.

Yet within a century, that figure had plummeted to only about 10 million. The native population had been isolated from the rest of the world's population and had not developed immunities like the invading Europeans who practically were germ- and virus-spreading machines.

The development of antivirals did not take off until the 1960s. Medical scientists found it difficult to conquer viruses because of their complex structure and their ability to mutate to other forms. The development of several different types of antiviral drugs that stimulate the body's immune system to attack the coronavirus has been a game saver during the past year. Medical scientists, however, constantly are watching for any new virus strains that could prove more devastating than any seen before.

5) Stem cell therapy (1970s)

When stem cells were discovered inside the cord blood of infants, therapy under certain circumstances could be used to make any type of human cell, giving it huge potential to treat various blood cancers, as well as bone marrow transplantation.

Two things make stem cells unique: They can renew themselves through cell division and they can be used to make any kind of human cell. This discovery has great potential for the future of medicine and already is being used to treat leukemia and other blood disorders. Research is underway to use stem cells to treat spinal cord injuries, Alzheimer's disease, Parkinson's disease, strokes and other afflictions.

Other significant developments

Respondents to my question suggested a number of other factors that easily could be listed in the five mentioned above. They include:

The public health movement calling for, among other things, clean drinking water, proper sewage disposal, food inspections, regulation of drugs, personal sanitation and hygiene, particularly in urban environments (mid-to-late 19th century), and the building of hospitals and clinics throughout the country.

The professionalization of the practice of medicine, requiring educated, licensed medical personnel and the elimination of quackery.

Organ transplants. First tried in the 1840s, anesthesia enabled doctors to perform both minor and major surgery on patients without pain.

Acceptance of mental health as a legitimate medical concern deserving treatment.

Immunotherapy, especially in the treatment of cancer.

It would be interesting to see the list of developments 50 years from now, such as the application of focused ultrasound in a variety of ways. As VCU's' Buckley observes: "Thanks to the tireless work of today's medical scientists who stand on the shoulders of others before them, we can anticipate the eventual end of , Parkinson's, Alzheimer's and various cancers, among other debilitating scourges."

For some of us, those developments cannot come soon enough.

Richmond *Times-Dispatch*, May 2, 2021

PART VIII

THIS AND THAT

None of the following essays fits neatly into the previous seven categories, so I have consigned them to this catch-all section.

57

VIRGINIA, THE UNSETTLED STATE IN THE EARLY 19TH CENTURY

Virginia was a central point in America in Revolution and Civil War eras. But in between, even as Virginia's population grew, other states surged ahead in growth and power. Indeed, more than a million people moved out of Virginia during that span.

The journey west always began with a decision, one that hundreds of thousands of Virginians made in the first half of the 19th century. Their decisions were an integral part of a huge population movement never seen before or since in the Old Dominion.

From the end of the American Revolution until the Civil War, even as Virginia's population grew, other states surged ahead in growth and power. Indeed, more than a million people moved out of Virginia during that span.

Most of them had come to the conclusion that lands to the west offered opportunities that could not be realized in their native state. As one emigrant later noted: "They agreed on the one general object - that of bettering their condition."

Tobacco, the crop that underpinned Virginia's agriculture-based economy for nearly three centuries, seemed to have run its course by the early 19th century. To meet a soaring demand for tobacco products worldwide, farmers in Tidewater and Piedmont Virginia overplanted the crop, unaware of its leeching effects on the soil.

Crop rotation and the use of fertilizer were well into the future, and as a result, soil exhaustion became widespread. One observer noted that the land was so washed out and gullied that after a heavy rainfall, rivers and creeks "appeared like a torrent of blood."

Meantime, even as wheat production held steady in the Shenandoah Valley, statewide land values plummeted from $207 million to less than $100 million in the first quarter of the 19th century.

"The times are dreadful," Elizabeth Trist proclaimed in 1823, "if we may judge from the numbers that are migrating to different parts of the continent. Scarce a day passes that families are not going to Alabama, Missoura [sic] or some other places."

Reports of a happier and more prosperous life in the states and territories farther west convinced many farmers that remaining in Virginia presented a grim future. Virginians who had gone ahead of them were only too glad to point this out. Writing to his sisters from Texas in 1848, Branch Archer warned: "Virginia is waning fast. ... Quit her as rats quit sinking vessels, and take a home in this land of promise."

A once-mighty Virginia - the most populous, wealthiest and politically influential of the original 13 states - had slipped on the national scene by the 1830s. Its presence in Congress dropped sharply in the first half of the century. While four of the first five presidents were lifelong Virginians, three of the four remaining presidents who were born in the Old Dominion had long left their native state and were elected from elsewhere.

But Virginia's loss did result in the westward spread of its culture, political ideas, laws, surveying practices, labor systems, concepts of honor, architectural styles - and a number of its talented natives, some who would play key roles in the history of the westward movement. Among them were John Sevier (first governor of Tennessee); Sam Houston and Stephen F. Austin in Texas; James Denver (a Kansas Territory leader and namesake of the Colorado city); politician Henry Clay in Kentucky; mountain man Jim Bridger; artist George Caleb Bingham; and inventor and philanthropist Cyrus McCormick.

Virginia's agricultural depression also resulted in the involuntary exodus of another significant component of its population: enslaved Africans.

Despite the hard times in Virginia, agriculture was thriving in the developing Deep South and the trans-Mississippi West. With the rapid rise of clothing made from cotton rather than from wool, demand for the new fabric soared. The shift resulted in increased use of slave labor in cotton-growing states.

With Virginia's land and crop values declining, maintaining slaves became more costly, and their monetary value declined as well. A slave appraised at $1,000 in Richmond could be sold in the New Orleans market for three or four times that amount. As a result, hundreds of thousands of slaves were sent involuntarily from Virginia, only to be sold at high prices in markets farther west. Virginia became a leader in this business, and nearly 30 auction houses in Richmond sold thousands of slaves every year. By 1850, the city was second only to New Orleans as the nation's slave-trading center.

Virginians reacted in different ways to the state's decline: One group of concerned men convened in 1831 to form the Virginia Historical Society to ensure that its glorious past would not be forgotten.

Others attempted to transform Virginia into a more industrialized state that would be less dependent on the vagaries of agriculture. As a result, the General Assembly authorized a spate of canal building that by the 1850s gave way to the construction of railway lines. At the same time, manufacturing became an increasingly important component of the Virginia economy, with large factories springing up, especially in Richmond. Even agriculture changed as men including Edmund Ruffin and Peter Minor introduced scientific farming methods such as crop rotation and the use of fertilizer.

After Virginia seceded and joined the Confederacy in 1861, pro-Union counties in the western part of the state broke away and formed what became West Virginia in 1863. Virginia became the great battleground of the Civil War, the bloodiest stretch of real estate in the Western Hemisphere. By 1865, thousands of graves, burned-out homes, denuded forests, destroyed bridges, bankrupt railroads and untilled farmland littered Virginia's landscape.

It would take another war nearly 80 years later for Virginia to fully recover from the setbacks of the 19th century. When World War II broke out, the U.S. economy shifted to wartime footing, much to the benefit of Virginia. The state was transformed as the defense buildup raised Virginia to unprecedented levels of employment and prosperity.

Virginia became a more urban and cosmopolitan state. Mechanization of agriculture spurred by a wartime labor shortage freed vast numbers of workers for a postwar boom in retail and other sectors of the economy. The federal government became Virginia's largest employer. And the commonwealth experienced steady population growth a century later.

One constant in U.S. history is that Americans are movers: If you have studied your family history, you probably have found that once your forebears arrived here, they and their offspring moved to other places. History tells us that this centuries-old phenomenon will continue.

Richmond *Times-Dispatch*, February 22, 2016

58

A Year With No Summer

Almost anyone living on earth two centuries ago never forgot the year 1816. Crop failures, disease, widespread hunger, financial ruin, civil unrest, and abnormally low temperatures throughout the year convinced many people that the world was doomed. Known as the "Year Without a Summer," this natural catastrophe had its origins in the massive volcanic eruption of Mount Tambora in Indonesia in 1815.

The largest volcanic explosion in some 1,300 years, Tambora followed a centuries-long period of global cooling and four other significant volcanic events since 1812. Tambora's eruption thrust an immense plume of gas and ash into the stratosphere, creating a great sun-obscuring dust cloud that circled the globe in a matter of weeks, and played havoc with weather systems for another three years. Worldwide temperatures plunged between 3 and 6 degrees Fahrenheit. Rainfall patterns were seriously disrupted.

Accounts in North America in the spring and summer of 1816 tell of a persistent "dry fog" that dimmed the sky during the day and turned a reddish hue at twilight. Even rain and wind could not disperse this "fog," which scientists now say was caused by ash from Tambora creating a "stratospheric sulfate aerosol veil."

The New England and Mid-Atlantic states experienced abnormally cool temperatures, frost, and snow all spring and well into the summer. Snow was reported in Maine, Massachusetts, and parts of New York state as late as the first week of June.

Killing frosts were even more widespread, especially at higher elevations. For a people accustomed to living through harsh winters, lower temperatures were not the real problem. Most of the world's population depended on subsistence farming to provide their daily sustenance, thus the year-round cool temperatures were a disaster.

In upstate New York, temperatures dropped below freezing every day in May, destroying an entire range of budding crops. One farmer recounted that fields normally green with tender new shoots "were barren like winter." Damage was extensive in Cape May, New Jersey, after five nights in a row of heavy frost in June. Thin layers of ice formed on some rivers and lakes in northwestern Pennsylvania in July.

***

Virginia could not escape the abnormal weather, experiencing wide swings in temperatures and lower than average precipitation. Reports of frost followed soon by daytime highs in the 80s came in from numerous locations in August.

In July, a Norfolk newspaper opined that "we have not had what could properly be called summer. Easterly winds have prevailed for nearly three months past. The sun during that time has been generally obscured and the sky overcast with clouds; the air has been damp and uncomfortable, and frequently so chilling as to render the fireside a desirable treat."

Thomas Jefferson, who had retired to Monticello after serving two terms as president, suffered from sustained crop failures that year, which in turn helped plunge him deeper into debt.

The corn crop in the Old Dominion ended up only a third the size of the previous year's harvest. As one account lamented, "the cold as well as the drought has nipt (sic) the buds of hope."

If anything, the people of Europe suffered more. Great Britain and Ireland experienced bitterly cold temperatures and heavy rains throughout the year that led to widespread harvest failures and resulting famine.

The crisis was even worse in Germany, where food prices skyrocketed, causing great civil unrest. Riots, arson, and looting were reported in cities throughout the country. Some experts describe the 1816 famine as Europe's most severe and widespread in the 19th century.

***

In the months following 1816, the veil of Tambora ash began to dissipate, and weather patterns gradually returned to normal.

Scores of scientists and historians have long studied how the Tambora eruption and subsequent "Year Without a Summer" shaped the course of history. Some scholars, for example, argue that the widespread crop failures may have helped persuade farm families in huge numbers to leave the eastern United States in search of more hospitable weather and better growing conditions farther west.

One result of this climatic phenomenon was creation of a literary classic that has terrified readers - and future moviegoers - for two centuries.

In June of 1816, writer Mary Shelley and a group of her literary friends were forced to spend most of their holiday inside their villa overlooking Lake Geneva because of the incessant rain and cold "that wet, uncongenial summer." Someone in the group suggested they hold a contest to determine who could write the most frightening story. Two classics came out of that contest - Shelley's *Frankenstein* and John W. Polidori's *The Vampyre*, the precursor to Bram Stoker's *Dracula*.

Could we experience another year without a summer? Historian Will Durant observed that, "civilization exists by geological consent, subject to change without notice." Most scientists agree that another massive volcanic eruption like Tombora is within the realm of possibility. The consequences are almost too frightening to contemplate given today's world population as compared to 1816 - 950 million then, 6.2 billion now.

It can also be argued that the human race may be acting as a Mount Tambora in slow motion. Since 1816, human activities have contributed to an estimated 40 percent increase in atmospheric carbon dioxide. Over time it has created its own toxic veil that is heating rather than cooling the earth.

There is little we can do to mitigate another Tambora, but we should do everything we can to stop our own self-destruction.

Richmond *Times-Dispatch*, April 3, 2016

59

FROM FIELD TO FACTORY:
THE GREAT MIGRATION

Several years ago, I had the pleasure of sitting next to legendary basketball player Bill Russell at a dinner. You would think our conversation revolved around sports, but Russell wanted to talk about history and genealogy.

He was born in 1934 in Monroe, Louisiana. His earliest memories were of living in a strictly segregated society. He told me about the time his father was refused service at a gas station until later-arriving white customers were tended to first. When his father tried to leave and go to another station, the white attendant pulled a gun on him and told him to wait his turn or suffer the consequences.

After years of accumulated insults like this, Russell's father moved his family to Oakland, California, at the beginning of World War II. Although the Russells struggled financially for years, their new environment allowed young Bill to go on to become one of the greatest NBA players ever, something that would have been nearly impossible had he stayed in Louisiana in the 1940s and '50s.

Stories like Russell's were not unusual in the mid-20th century, and they were symbolic of one of the great social movements in our history. Called the Great Migration by historians, it was a phenomenon that resulted in a transformational redistribution of the country's black population in the first half of the 20th century - from the South to the North and the West, from country to city, from farm to factory. In all, some 6 million African-Americans moved out of the rural South between 1910 and 1970.

***

In 1910, nearly 90 percent of America's black population lived south of the Mason-Dixon Line, mostly in rural areas, where they often toiled as farmers for their livelihood, many as share-croppers who could barely make ends meet. By 1970, however, the numbers had shifted dramatically. By then nearly 50 percent of blacks lived in the North or West, mostly in cities.

Why such a significant change? As is often the case when people leave their homes and old lives behind, there were push-pull factors involved. Pushing them were a number of things that made life in the South unbearable for many blacks.

Although African-Americans had been granted freedom from slavery during the Civil War, the rights and privileges they obtained immediately after the conflict were taken from them when Southern state legislatures passed a series of so-called Jim Crow laws beginning in the 1890s.

These severely limited blacks from participating in the political process. Segregation of public places and transportation was imposed. African-American children received less-than-adequate educations in shabby school buildings and with hand-me-down books from white students. Wages paid to blacks were much less than their white counterparts'.

African-Americans received far from equal treatment under the law, and they often were victims when whites took the law into their own hands and meted out justice on their own terms. Black males were particularly susceptible to having vigilante justice handed down to them in the form of lynching. Although the total number of lynchings dropped from a peak of 211 in 1886 to 67 in 1910, black males still lived in fear that one misstep or ill-timed word uttered to a white woman could lead to a brutal death at the end of a rope.

***

While many factors pushed African-Americans out of the South, a number of incentives pulled them northward and to the West. At the turn of the 20th century, the United States had developed into one of the world's industrial giants. Although factories began springing up all over the country, most were concentrated in an area stretching from New England across the Great Lakes states and on past Chicago.

Initially, low-paid European immigrants made up a large percentage of the industrial labor force until the outbreak of World War I in 1914, when they were not allowed to leave their native countries. Post-war congressional legislation setting immigration quotas also made it more difficult for them to settle in the U.S. Still needing an inexpensive labor force, for the first time Northern factories began to hire African-Americans.

Given the choice of doing backbreaking work in tobacco or cotton fields with little to show for it financially, it is little wonder that so many African-Americans headed north and west in hopes of finding much better lives for themselves and their families.

The Chicago Defender, and other influential black-owned newspapers in the North, encouraged African-Americans to leave the South. They portrayed the North as "the promised land."

Richard Wright, who became an internationally acclaimed writer, recalled how the North beckoned him as he grew up in the Deep South. "The North symbolized to me all that I had not felt or seen," he wrote; "it had no relation to what actually existed. Yet by imagining a place where everything is possible, it kept hope alive inside of me."

Black Southerners moved as individuals or in small family groups. Government assistance was unheard of, but some Northern industries and railroads recruited black workers and paid for transportation and relocation.

The migratory patterns were closely tied to the regional railroad lines of the time running north and south. Blacks from Virginia, North and South Carolina, Georgia, and Florida tended to ride the rails paralleling the East Coast and settling in Washington, Baltimore, Philadelphia, New York, and other smaller cities. Migrants from Tennessee, Alabama, Mississippi, and Arkansas took the trains to Cleveland, Chicago, and Milwaukee, while blacks from Louisiana and Texas, like Bill Russell's family, headed west.

**

How did this great movement of people change America? In her Pulitzer Prize-winning book, *The Warmth of Other Suns* (2010), author Isabelle Wilkerson identifies some of the transforming effects. Because black immigrants settled in cities in the North and West, their influence was profound. Cities that had been virtually all-white in the early 20th century became centers of black politics and culture.

Did the North and West turn out to be "the promised land?" Yes and no. Because large numbers of blacks moved into cities so rapidly, European-American immigrants resented these newcomers from the South, and many felt threatened by the influx of new work competition.

Also, European ethnic groups created neighborhood boundaries that precluded blacks from moving in - leaving them only the crowded, run-down sections in which to live. In recent years, many of these black neighborhoods have boiled over as local police and residents have clashed violently.

Despite these obstacles, most blacks who left the South had no desire to return until the end of the 20th century, when the region underwent significant changes.

By then Jim Crow was for all intents and purposes dead. Job opportunities opened up thanks to air-conditioning, interstate highways, and federal civil rights legislation, which helped the South become the nation's fastest growing region. Despite subtle efforts to curtail black voting rights now, African-Americans can be found in public offices throughout the South. And the South's more laid-back pace beckoned many to return.

Charlie Cox and his wife Darlene, who spent 35 years in Detroit, have come back to their native Mississippi. For years they had been eager to trade the cold, the crime, and the frenetic pace of life for the relative peace and quiet of the South. Now, Mrs. Cox says, "You couldn't get me to leave here for anything" - a sentiment that would have seemed fantastical only a few decades ago.

Richmond *Times-Dispatch*, May 1, 2016

60

WE'VE ALWAYS BEEN PEOPLE ON THE MOVE

Immigration has been a hot-button issue during the current presidential campaign, but the subject is nothing new under the sun. People have been moving from one corner of the globe to another since before recorded history.

Humans have migrated for a number of reasons - to escape tyranny and oppression, to seek new opportunities, because of environmental disasters, and numerous other reasons. No matter where they moved, if their numbers were large enough, immigrants often have changed their new homelands for better or worse.

The subject of human immigration has become a major field of scientific and scholarly study involving the fields of archaeology, anthropology, genetics, geography, historians, and several other disciplines. What is being discovered is changing our perceptions of our species and the past. It reveals more than anything that we are a restless lot, and probably will always be.

***

The latest research on the subject reveals that our prehistoric ancestors evolved into hominids about 200,000 years ago in present-day Ethiopia.

Several key factors gave Homo sapiens key advantages over other species. By learning to stand erect, for example, humans for the first time had two limbs that could be used to make tools and weapons. These, along with an ability to analyze situations and communicate, separated humans from other similar species.

Our human ancestors tended to be taller and slimmer than other hominids, like the heavy-set, big boned Neanderthals.

Humans and Neanderthals had similar brain sizes, but their skulls were shaped differently, with the latter having prominent jaws and straight foreheads without heavy brow ridges.

Humans and Neanderthals interbred, but the latter became extinct for reasons that are not certain. Was it disease? Did their human rivals wipe them out?

Some experts argue that early humans required less food, which gave them a competitive advantage during hard times. Regardless, geneticists have determined that up to 3 percent of the DNA of a person of western European ancestry is Neanderthal.

More than 60,000 years ago, humans triggered perhaps the most important event in prehistory, when they began to leave Africa to eventually occupy every corner of the earth. We are not certain what set this event in motion, but most experts argue that it was related to major climatic shifts.

A sudden cooling of the Earth around 70,000 years ago made life difficult for those early Africans, and archaeological evidence indicates a dramatic reduction in population, almost to the point of extinction.

When the climate began to improve some 10,000 years later, however, the population recovered rapidly and expanded its footprint well beyond Africa. These ancient immigrants dominated their competitors everywhere they moved, particularly in Asia and Europe, including scattered groups in the Far East.

***

Archaeological evidence reveals that soon after 50,000 years ago, humans had reached large parts of the Middle East, south central Asia, and Australia, which was at that time connected by land to Asia. They subsequently moved to the northern latitudes of Asia and Europe.

About 20,000 years ago, during the last Ice Age, successive waves of Asian hunters began to cross a large land bridge made of ice and snow connecting Asia to the Americas. Within another 5,000 years, people had penetrated all the way to the tip of present day South America.

By 3,000 years ago, humans had discovered and occupied the remote and isolated islands of the South Pacific, an incredible feat of discovery that baffles scholars even today, given the great distances between these far-flung dots of land in a vast ocean.

Perhaps more than anything, the rise of agriculture about 10,000 years ago led to human dominance of the globe. Thought to have begun in the Fertile Crescent of the Middle East, the systematic cultivation of crops soon followed in Asia, Africa, New Guinea, and several regions of America.

With the advent of agriculture and the development of domesticated animals, humans evolved from hunter-gatherers dependent on the uncertain availability of wild prey into farmers with a steady food source available to them.

The spread of humans throughout the world has had profound consequences for our planet, both good and bad. On the one hand, no other species has been able to control the destiny of the Earth like ours.

We have used the bounty of natural resources available to us to our advantage. Humans have evolved into the rulers of the globe. But are we ruling wisely?

***

As the human population has grown, the demands it makes to sustain itself have grown as well. It is little wonder that our species has begun exploring worlds beyond. Only recently, astronomers identified a planet similar to Earth circling a nearby star, an exciting development that is part of a concerted scientific effort to discover as many human-friendly planets as can be found. Scientists estimate that there are trillions of planets in the universe, billions of which have environments capable of sustaining life.

Mars is the focus of scientific study about possible human colonization. Its surface conditions and the possible presence of water make it arguably the most hospitable place in our solar system, other than Earth.

Human survival would require complex life-support measures, including the creation of a sophisticated artificial environment. Preparations are underway to train a team of astronauts with various scientific backgrounds to establish a colony on the red planet.

If the past serves as an indicator of the future, our species will continue to seek new opportunities and escape adversity, like those first immigrants. It is a phenomenon set in motion 60,000 years ago, and it will continue for ages to come.

Richmond *Times-Dispatch*, October 30, 2016

61

AMERICA'S RISE TO PROSPERITY

A century ago, the United States was in the midst of a significant transformation. The country was rapidly changing from a nation of farmers to one of blue-collar factory workers and white-collar professionals; from a nation where most people lived in the country to one primarily of city and town dwellers; and from a people mostly of Anglo ancestry and Protestant faith to one that included more eastern and southern Europeans who were mostly Catholic and Jewish.

A great revolution in the way things were produced caused this significant shift.

Industry is as old as human society. Archaeological evidence reveals that even pre-historic humans and Neanderthals made crude tools, weapons, clothing, and jewelry. But beginning in the second half of the 18th-century, the ability to manufacture goods increased dramatically as machines began to replace humans in the production of goods.

The so-called Industrial Revolution originated in England and spread rapidly to the rest of western Europe and the United States.

By the time of the Civil War, this revolution was well underway in the U.S. For that matter, the internecine conflict actually accelerated the process, in which inventions such as the cotton gin, steam engine, and agricultural machinery served as catalysts.

After the war, industrialization drastically altered the basic patterns of life in the country. By the turn of the 20th century, America had emerged as an industrial giant and was well on its way to becoming a superpower.

***

Like a complex watch, a new system called the industrial order emerged. It involved a large number of parts that had to fit together if the system was to work.

An abundance of natural resources, a habitable climate, and a terrain that was relatively easy to develop were essential for its emergence. It also entailed concentrating large numbers of workers in relatively small places, thus leading to a dramatic increase in the number of large American cities.

Huge deposits of raw materials such as coal and iron ore for making steel existed in the U.S. During this period vast quantities of coal were discovered and mined in southwest Virginia, West Virginia, Michigan, and Minnesota.

Cost-effective transportation like railroads had to be built to bring raw materials to factories and then take finished products from them. Just like farming, railroads benefitted from technological developments such as steel rails that could bear the weight of heavier locomotives pulling much larger loads. This led to an explosion of railroad construction, including transcontinental lines in the postwar years. Rail mileage increased from 60,000 in 1870 to 250,000 in 1900.

A spate of late 19th-century inventions and related products duplicated what happened to the steel industry and had a huge ripple effect. Manufacturing increasingly relied on electric power. Sewing machines, telephones, batteries, dynamos, lubricants, gasoline, batteries, light bulbs, and lumber could be produced much more rapidly and in larger volume.

Factories required workers to operate them at the same time that agriculture became more mechanized, requiring fewer farmers to grow crops. More and more farm workers left rural America for good-paying factory jobs in towns and cities. As farms lost their labor force and began to rely more on machinery, ironically crop production increased.

Despite this move of Americans from farm to factory, it wasn't enough to supply the voracious labor demands of industry.

Industrial growth also drew women and children into the labor force. Between 1870 and 1900, the number women working in factories increased from 1.9 million to 5.3 million. During the same period, children under the age of 15 entering the labor force rose from 750,000 to 1.75 million. Many worked in dangerous jobs in coal mines and factories where permanent injuries and death were common.

Immigrant labor, however, supplied most of the workforce. In all, more than 14 million immigrants mostly from eastern and southern Europe came to America between 1860 and 1900. Some 16 million more followed between 1900 and 1920.

***

The way labor was employed underwent a revolution of its own. Until the Civil War, most people worked in small traditional shops where work centered on the individual, who was usually skilled in a particular craft. But under the new system, low-skilled workers using machinery could significantly increase the volume of their work.

Richmond's Lewis Ginter provides a perfect example of this transition. Entering the tobacco manufacturing business in 1873, the Allen & Ginter Company initially employed 20 women who hand-rolled up to 5,000 cigarettes a day. In the 1880s, however, Ginter replaced his workers with newly invented cigarette-making machines that could turn out the popular product at a much higher rate.

By the late 1880's, Ginter's factory employed a thousand workers, who produced more than a million cigarettes daily. Cigarette prices plummeted, and worldwide demand increased at a phenomenal rate. As a result, Ginter became an extraordinarily wealthy man.

His story could be repeated thousands of times over in a variety of industries. By 1900, the U.S. had more rails, steel, electric trolleys, telephones, and electric lights, not to mention more millionaires, than any other nation on Earth.

American industrial and economic might, however, came at a price. By the turn of the 20th-century, American cities had grown so rapidly that housing, city services, traffic flow patterns, and law enforcement proved inadequate to the demands placed on them.

Cities might tower with tall buildings and glisten with electric lights, but they began to fill up with poverty-stricken immigrants. The term "on the other side of the tracks" entered the American vocabulary, and referred to the poor neighborhoods on the downwind side of the railroad lines and factory smokestacks.

Indeed, the new industrial order meant more than growth and wealth. It created new problems that Americans were slow to recognize and even slower to solve. Division along class lines disrupted the old social order. The growing immigrant population lived in deplorable conditions. Factory workers began to resent poor living conditions and low wages, and they developed a deep dislike of eastern industrialists and financiers who seemed to grow wealthier with each passing year.

Farmers expressed mounting discontent as crop and livestock prices plummeted and remained low for years. Many were angry that the world around them was changing faster than they could adapt. If these problems could not be soon addressed, some observers warned that the great American experiment in self-government would collapse.

Richmond *Times-Dispatch*, April 9, 2017

62

In Praise of a Vast Wasteland

I don't quite know what to say when some people tell me with an air of superiority that they never watch television. I must confess that I have watched a lot of TV in my lifetime, going back to 1956 when my family purchased a large, boxy Zenith tabletop model that sat in our living room.

We could tune to only three stations that were beamed to us from Nashville, Tennessee, some 75 miles away. I was nine years old when television entered my life.

Has TV warped me as a person? Did it dumb me down? I'll let others determine that, but I am reminded of the famous speech given in 1961 by Newton Minnow, chairman of the Federal Communications Commission. In it, he declared that, "When television is good, nothing ... is better. But when television is bad, nothing is worse." He then urged his audience to sit in front of a TV and glue their eyes to the small screen for a day. "I can assure you that what you will observe is a vast wasteland," he declared.

Wasteland or not, I am convinced that TV was a factor in my lifelong love of history. In addition to reading lots of books and listening to my grandfather's stories of the past, you could often find me in front of the TV watching shows such as The Gray Ghost, You Are There, and Walt Disney's Davy Crockett and Swamp Fox. None of those programs can be considered good historical narrative, but they reinforced my fascination with the past.

Thanks to YouTube, I can watch many of those old shows. Recently I started thinking about which were my favorite programs over the years. Note that I said "favorite" programs, not necessarily the most influential in shaping my life, nor most notable for their artistic significance. Here are some of my choices from the past 60 years.

***

(1) "Victory at Sea" was a 26-segment documentary about the U.S. Navy in World War II. First broadcast in 1952, relying solely on wartime moving picture film and accompanied by a dramatic musical score by Richard Rogers and Robert Russell Bennett, "Victory at Sea" set the example for future television documentaries for years to come. Episode No. 25, "Suicide for Glory," the account of the Japanese Kamikaze attacks on the American fleet, is some of the most gripping viewing in 70 years of television broadcasting.

(2) "Have Gun Will Travel" (1957-63) was originally conceived as an episodic story of a modern day bounty hunter set in New York City. But with cowboy-themed shows dominating the airwaves then, the producers gave it a western setting. The enigmatic Paladin, portrayed by actor Richard Boone, was a refined gentleman living in a posh San Francisco hotel, who also happened to be a gun for hire. He used his keen mind, strong sense of fairness, and cunning to settle disputes in the American West.

(3) "Leave it to Beaver" (1957-63) has been condemned by some social critics for being an overly simplistic portrayal of an idealized white family that never existed, but this program, nonetheless, has attained iconic status. Each episode revolved around the adventures and misadventures of Theodore ("the Beaver") Cleaver.

Parents, Ward and June, and brother Wally, helped get him out of youthful scrapes that were often created by their scheming neighbor, Eddie Haskell. Unlike other domestic comedies of the time, Leave it to Beaver focused on the children, not the adults. Its writers found inspiration for the characters and story lines from their own children. I enjoyed the show when it was first broadcast, and then watched it with my daughter and son, gaining a far different perspective, learning that patience and tolerance are keys to raising children.

(4) "What's My Line?" (1950-67) was a popular game show in which four panelists questioned contestants to determine their occupations. The panelists were blindfolded for the last contestants, who were well-known celebrities speaking in disguised voices. Journalist John Daly served as the show's moderator. Although dozens of people sat as panelists over the years, regulars Bennett Cerf, Arlene Francis, and Dorothy Kilgallen, decked out in formal attire, and conversing in light repartee, provided viewers a window into high society in New York in the mid-20th century.

(5) "The Carol Burnett Show" (1967-78) was one of the most popular comedy shows of all time, having garnered 25 Emmy awards. A few years ago, it was voted 16th out of television's 50 greatest shows. As the show's centerpiece, Burnett demonstrated a variety of talents, including comedy, choreography, and singing. Supported by a splendid cast of actors, including Tim Conway, Harvey Korman, and Vicky Lawrence, Burnett produced sketches, such as "Went With the Wind" and "The Family," that have become classics.

***

(6) "Cosmos: A Personal Voyage" (1980) was a 13-part series about a wide range of scientific subjects, including the origin of life, space, and time written primarily by the program's host and narrator, astronomer Carl Sagan. The great value of Cosmos was Sagan's ability to make complex subjects like quantum physics, Einstein's theory of relativity, pulsars, and black holes understandable to a large lay audience. When first broadcast, it attracted the largest audience ever on PBS, a record that lasted until 1990.

(7) "The Civil War" (1990) is one of the most successful documentary films ever. Produced by Ken Burns, the five-part series attracted an audience of some 40 million viewers, the most watched program in PBS history.

Narrated by David McCullough and accompanied by a haunting musical score, the film explored the military, political, and social aspects of the war using thousands of photographs, paintings, and comments from letters and diaries. TIME magazine described it as the "film that forever changed the documentary form and ... explained an incalculably important chapter in American history to a generation that needed the tutorial."

(8) "Rome" (2005-07) is the gripping HBO series about two Roman soldiers, Lucius Vorenus and Titus Pullo, who lived during the death of the Roman republic and its transformation to an empire. Both characters are caught up in the middle of political machinations, family feuds, betrayals, murders, wars, assassinations, and blood-curdling intrigue. The series features a variety of historical characters including Julius Caesar, Mark Antony, Cleopatra, Augustus, Marcus Brutus, and Cicero, among others. Noted for its attention to detail and historical accuracy, Rome is an example of how television can do an excellent job of portraying the past.

(9) "Masterpiece Theater" (1971-present) on PBS has consistently presented first-class television viewing for nearly half a century. Many of its programs are television renditions of classic British novels and biographies of famous and infamous historical figures. TV doesn't get much better than programs such as "The First Churchills," "The Jewel in the Crown," "Upstairs Downstairs," "Poldark," "Prime Suspect," "Sherlock," and "Downton Abbey."

(10) "Saturday Night Live" (1975-present) is the longest running comedy show in television history. Its creator, Lorne Michaels, has a genius for finding new talent that goes on to greater fame and fortune, including Dan Akroyd, Billy Chrystal, Tina Fey, and Bill Murray. The Donald Trump administration has proven to be rich fodder for SNL's political satire, resulting in the highest ratings the show has enjoyed in many years.

***

Some other shows I almost chose:

"Perry Mason" - a gripping courtroom drama that made me think about becoming a lawyer.

"Band of Brothers" - HBO's screen adaptation of Stephen Ambrose's account of a company of paratroopers serving in Europe in World War II.

"Twilight Zone" (1959-65) - Rod Serling created this wildly successful program that was an odd mix of science fiction, horror, mystery, and superstition.

For those of you who never watch television, I at least hope you have enjoyed reading this column. The cast of "Leave It to Beaver:" Tony Dow as Wally, Barbara Billingsley as June, Hugh Beaumont as Ward, and Jerry Mathers as the Beaver.

Richmond *Times-Dispatch*, November 12, 2017

63

WERE WE GREAT BRITAIN'S VIETNAM?

The PBS broadcast of the Ken Burns/Lynn Novick documentary on the Vietnam War was both compelling and disturbing. Most disturbing to me was listening to White House audiotapes of Presidents Kennedy, Johnson, Nixon and their advisors make decisions that in retrospect were horrendous mistakes resulting in death and destruction on a large scale.

Equally troubling was the dubious information military leaders and civilian officials fed the public that painted a more optimistic picture of the real situation.

The series reminded me of an insightful article by military historian Richard Ketchum published nearly 50 years ago in *American Heritage* magazine. Titled "England's Vietnam: The American Revolution," Ketchum pointed out just how much those three presidents could have benefited from examining "the ghostly footsteps of America's last king before pursuing their adventure in Vietnam."

***

King George III grew increasingly concerned with the growing discontent of American colonists and their calls for self-government. He was determined to preserve the British Empire, fearing that if the American colonies were lost, it would have a domino effect.

In the beginning, he noted that the rebellion was "the most serious in which any country was ever engaged. ... Should (it) succeed ... the West Indies must follow, not in independence, but for their own interest they must become dependent on America. Ireland would soon follow."

Like the U.S. in the mid-20th-century, Great Britain in the 18th-century was the mightiest nation on Earth. Its powerful navy and army were unequaled in strength and experience.

At the beginning of the conflict with the American colonies, King George and his advisers were convinced the war would be won quickly.

One British officer wrote that "I am satisfied that one active campaign, a smart action, and the burning of two or three of their towns, will set everything right."

As Ketchum notes, however, British hubris blinded them to what they would confront. Great Britain faced a set of complex problems in America, similar to the ones the U.S. would face in Southeast Asia.

For one, geography did not favor the British. Three thousand miles of ocean separated the mother country from its colonies. Providing supplies and fresh troops proved to be incredibly expensive, time-consuming, and wasteful.

Like the American experience in Vietnam, the war in the colonies was fought over a vast, rugged country that was heavily wooded. The British also found it nearly impossible to prevent arms, ammunition, and equipment from their archenemies, France and Spain, to be smuggled into the hands of the colonials.

King George and his advisers placed high hopes on the support of those Americans who remained loyal to the crown and joined forces with their British cousins to suppress the rebellion.

While the number of loyalists was impressive at the beginning of the war, particularly in the southern colonies, their numbers began to dwindle as the war ground on.

At the same time, army recruiting in England and Ireland began to lag badly. As a result, British commanders in America found it increasingly difficult to acquire replacement troops for their losses.

To make up the difference, King George turned to the Duke of Brunswick in Germany to supply well-equipped and veteran soldiers to fight in America.

Most Americans resented - with a passion - the use of these battle-seasoned mercenary troops, known collectively as Hessians. Their use hardened American attitudes toward the English. As a result, supporters of the patriot cause grew. Also, the longer British forces remained in America, the more their cause suffered.

***

Similar to the war in Vietnam, determining friend from foe during the Revolutionary War proved challenging. From the beginning of the war until its end, some Americans who proclaimed loyalty to the crown were in reality spies for the patriot cause.

Karl von Clausewitz, the 19th-century Prussian military theorist, declared that when war is mainly fought by an armed citizenry rather than by professionals, it "introduces a means of defense peculiar to itself."

At times, Americans resorted to a form of guerrilla warfare when the British left the coastal plain and advanced into the interior, a region unsuited to European combat and inhabited by people who fought according to their own rules.

When circumstances dictated and the odds favored them, Generals George Washington and Nathanael Greene played a brilliant game of hit and run. This strategy would later be labeled the "offensive defensive," and was a form of irregular warfare comparable to that used by Gen. Vo Nguyan Giap, commander of North Vietnamese forces.

***

With the war in America dragging on for more than eight years, and with British losses mounting, public support, which had been strong at first, began to melt away. The voices of a small, but increasingly influential, group of members of Parliament opposed to the war started picking up support.

Lord Effingham and William Pitt argued forcefully that bearing arms against their fellow citizens in America was wrong. Pitt exclaimed that if he were an American, "I never would lay down my arms - never - never - never. You cannot conquer America."

Pitt's prediction was eventually confirmed when Lord Cornwallis surrendered his army to George Washington at Yorktown in 1781. The signing of a formal peace treaty two years later guaranteed American independence.

The British Empire was not dealt a fatal blow by the loss of its American colonies. Indeed, Great Britain would be a world power for another century and a half. But the Revolutionary War demonstrated that the old saying "might makes right" is at times a fallacy.

American patriots had everything to gain from victory and everything to lose by defeat.

"Beaten frequently on the battlefield, inadequately trained, fed, and clothed, they fought against unreasonably long odds because of that slim hope of attaining a distant goal of gaining independence," observed Ketchum.

But with each passing year, more and more of the British people lost the will to keep fighting. For them, the end result was not worth the high cost the war extracted.

As Ketchum noted, there were enough parallels between the 18th and 20th centuries' conflicts "to make you wonder if Presidents Kennedy, Johnson, and Nixon had their ears closed while the class was studying the American Revolution."

Sadly, the failure of our leaders to heed the lessons of the past cost the lives of nearly 60,000 Americans and some 1.5 million Vietnamese.

Richmond *Times-Dispatch,* February 4, 2018

64

THE LONG CLIMB FOR
VIRGINIA'S VINEYARDS

When I was growing up in the 1950s and '60s, the eating and drinking habits of most Americans were very different from those of today. For one, it was the norm to have most meals at home. Eating out at a restaurant was a rare treat. Now, Americans dine out on average four to five times a week.

What we eat and drink has changed considerably as well. Pizza, tacos, orzo, couscous, and arugula were yet to appear on the plates of most of us. With rare exception, Americans drank little wine, despite its existence for several millennia.

Indeed, the making of wine is one of the oldest of human endeavors. Archaeologists have found evidence of grape fermentation in Armenia, which then spread to the Fertile Crescent and ancient Egypt. During the next several thousands of years, the fruit of the vine expanded to other parts of the world, including the Western Hemisphere.

Grapevine cuttings made up part of Christopher Columbus's cargo on his second voyage to the New World. Catholic priests introduced small quantities of grapes to California to produce ceremonial wine.

***

Virginia provides a microcosm of the American experience in winemaking. English settlers produced wine made from wild grapes in Jamestown. During the next two centuries, however, attempts to introduce grapes for winemaking in Virginia failed.

Thomas Jefferson spent considerable resources developing vineyards at Monticello, convinced that the surrounding region was well-suited for the growth of wine-producing grapes from Europe.

"We could in the United States make as great a variety of wines as are made in Europe, not exactly the same kind, but doubtless as good," he declared. Despite his best efforts, Jefferson was no more successful than others who tried it before him.

And after more than a decade of attempting to grow grapes for wine at Mount Vernon, George Washington abandoned the endeavor.

Hot, humid summers and frigid winters, not to mention a wide variety of plant diseases and insect enemies, conspired to prevent European grape varieties from flourishing in Virginia.

By the mid-19th century, growers began to develop hardy fusions between European and American grapes. As a result, grapes took root in the Virginia Piedmont. But just as the wine industry seemed to be gaining a foothold, the Old Dominion was plunged into destruction on a vast scale. The Civil War swept across Virginia, destroying almost everything in its path, including the infant wine industry.

It would take another century for wine production to return successfully to the commonwealth. Several factors contributed to this. For one, competition from the American West Coast proved intense.

After the Civil War, the new state of California, blessed with a near perfect grape-growing climate and immune from wartime destruction, began to dominate the small American market.

American drinking habits also limited the consumption of wine, as most citizens sated their thirst for alcohol with long-established beverages that were relatively easy and cheap to produce - such as whiskey, brandy, hard cider, ale, and beer.

Attempts to expand the wine market the first half of the 20th century suffered major blows with the imposition of national prohibition, followed by the Great Depression, and the disruptions caused by World War II.

***

Wine was an important cultural component for immigrants from eastern and southern Europe living in northern urban centers at the turn of the 20th century. But for other Americans, it played little role in our eating and drinking habits.

Little by little, though, wines (mostly European) were introduced to the American palate. Two brands from Portugal, Mateus and Lancers, became best-sellers. Presented in uniquely shaped bottles that seemed to be designed for one purpose only - to hold candles for romantic occasions - both offered a slightly sweet rosc wine.

Many American teenagers received their introduction to wine (and alcohol) from cheap wines and coolers that were once described as "bottom-shelf grape concoctions." Coming in various fruit flavors, they appealed to young adults with unsophisticated tastes. Other high-octane, ultra-sweet wines were known as "brown bag vino" because of their low price and the drinking habits of the customers who often bought them.

Eventually, however, like most Americans, Virginians became more refined in their taste for wine, graduating from rose to full-bodied cabernets and delicate chardonnays.

A television program in the 1970s profoundly influenced attitudes toward wine and helped make it an important component of the dining experience.

Julia Child's PBS program "The French Chef" ran for more than a decade and reached millions of households. Ms. Child's quirky way of preparing standard French cuisine, and her pronouncements on the perfect wine to accompany each dish, helped lead to its increased consumption by Americans.

Virginia has benefitted greatly from this trend when six vineyards were established in the 1970s. By 1995, the Old Dominion was home to 46 wineries. Ten years later, the number more than doubled to 105; and by 2015, it had reached more than 250. Only California, Oregon, and Washington have more wineries.

Today, Virginia wine contributes nearly $1.4 billion to the commonwealth's economy. The growth in the wine industry has greatly enhanced another important driver of the Virginia economy - tourism.

A recent survey of the Virginia economy reported an increase in visitors to wineries, from 1.6 million in 2010 to 2.25 million in 2015. The study further reveals that most of this growth comes from small vineyards in rural areas from the Eastern Shore to the far southwest corner of Virginia.

How competitive are Virginia wines? They have fared well in international competitions, garnering numerous awards. That said, inconsistency of product has been a problem, and helps explain why Virginia wines do well in competitions one year, then poorly the next.

Unlike the major wine-producing areas of California and Europe, where the weather varies little from year to year, Virginia's climate is more unpredictable. The extremely wet spring and roller coaster-like temperatures we have experienced this year can result in wines that have less body and flavor than those produced in years that are dryer and warmer.

Although Thomas Jefferson's dream of producing Virginia wines as good as those in Europe may not have turned into reality, wine growers in the Old Dominion can take pride in coming close almost every year now.

Richmond *Times-Dispatch*, June 10, 2018

65

FROM OBSCURE TO FAMOUS PLACES ON EARTH

Recently I spent a week at the Outer Banks of North Carolina with my family. In addition to enjoying the beach, we visited some of the area's historic sites. One of those was Kill Devil Hills, where because of the right conditions of wind and elevation Orville and Wilbur Wright launched the world's first mechanically powered flight in 1903. Although their first flight lasted only twelve seconds, subsequent developments in aviation transformed the world. As *National Geographic* writer Willie Drye concluded, this was the place where "the past and the future separated, and the world started shrinking."

As we walked along the actual flight path of the Wright brothers' prototype airplane, I started thinking about places that once were obscure dots on a map, yet they became famous or infamous because of significant events that occurred there. In 1903, hardly anyone in the world had heard of Kitty Hawk, yet only 66 years later, men left footsteps on the moon because of what the Wright brothers did there.

Or take Andersonville, Georgia, for example. Until the mid-1850s, Anderson Station was a small, obscure agricultural hamlet that got its name from a director of the railroad that ran through it. The U.S. post office name designation was changed to Andersonville to avoid confusion with the post office in Anderson, South Carolina. During the Civil War, the Confederate army established a prison there to house captured Union soldiers. Located in southern Georgia, the camp was chosen in part because of its remoteness from invading Union armies.

Designed to hold no more than 10,000 inmates at one time, by the summer of 1864, it contained more than 30,000 who existed in almost unimaginable squalor. Men died by the thousands. Andersonville was finally shut down when Union troops liberated it in the fall of 1864. Although there were other prison camps on both sides that were as reprehensible as Andersonville, the name would be forever the one most associated with perhaps the Civil War's darkest chapter. Still a small town, Andersonville is home of the National Prisoner of War Museum administered by the National Park Service.

Another example of the shift from relative obscurity to notoriety is a town in southern Poland. It became an important center of commerce in the late Middle Ages and changed hands among various contending factions numerous times. By the late 19th century, it had turned into an important rail junction, which would lead to its name becoming infamous - Auschwitz.

When Adolf Hitler's Nazi regime came to power Germany in the 1930s and adopted a strategy of destroying Europe's Jewish population, more than a dozen camps were initially set up to remove Jews from the mainstream German population. In 1940, the Nazis established several concentration and labor camps, some of which, including Auschwitz, were designated as extermination camps. All German concentration camps were evil places, but Auschwitz - with its estimated 1.1. million people killed, 90% of whom were Jews - was the nadir of human depravity. It is little wonder that Steven Spielberg's powerful movie "Schindler's List" was set in this small Polish town that most people had never heard of until it was turned into a charnel house.

Memphis, Tennessee, was long known for its barbecue, Beale Street blues and Graceland, the home of Elvis Presley. But the city had another site that was little known until an assassin's bullet ended the life of the leader of the civil rights movement ' the Rev. Martin Luther King Jr. An upscale overnight lodging that served an African American clientele, the Lorraine Motel traced its origins to 1925. Later named for its owner's wife, the Lorraine attracted such musical artists as Otis Redding, Aretha Franklin, Ray Charles and Lionel Hampton, who came to Memphis to perform concerts or make recordings at Stax Records. The Lorraine garnered international notoriety, however, when King was shot while standing on the balcony near his room.

The Lorraine never fully recovered from this tragic event. At one stage, it served as a home for low-income workers; but it was eventually purchased by a foundation that converted it into the National Civil Rights Museum, which opened in 1991. With more than 50,000 motels in the U.S. in 1968, the Lorraine became one with the most melancholy history.

These are only four examples of obscure places that suddenly became well known far beyond their immediate confines. Can you think of others that suddenly were recognized worldwide for better or worse? A number come to my mind.

Waterloo, Belgium, a quiet, rural village that would be forever associated with one of the great battles of all time when French forces under Napoleon Bonaparte were defeated by a British-led coalition army under the Duke of Wellington in 1815. It is hard for me to comprehend that many people at the time did not know where Pearl Harbor was before it was attacked by Japanese carrier launched planes, thereby resulting in America's entry into World War II. In fact, a significant percentage of Americans in the 1940s did not know that it was on American soil. Hiroshima, a relatively small Japanese industrial city that few people had heard of until it became the target of the first atomic bomb on August 6, 1945, thus hastening the end of World War II and ushering in the atomic age. Gettysburg, Pennsylvania, was a small farming community that had existed peacefully since its founding in the 1780s, but during the Civil War, it became the site of the largest battle fought on American soil. Its name also became attached to one of the greatest speeches of all time - Abraham Lincoln's Gettysburg Address.

I wonder about those obscure places on earth today that will suddenly gain notoriety for events that will make them household words.

Richmond *Times-Dispatch*, September 8, 2019

66

GLOBAL EXPANSION AND THE COLUMBIAN EXCHANGE

My wife and I love farmer's markets. This summer we visited one on the corner of Ridgefield Parkway and Gayton Road in western Henrico County nearly every weekend. We can buy most of the products at lower prices from area grocery stores, but there's something special about getting various fruits, vegetables, cakes, bread and pies from local farms.

Come July, I especially like buying sweet corn and tomatoes. There's nothing better than sinking your teeth into a bacon, lettuce and tomato sandwich dripping with mayonnaise or chomping on an ear of corn that had been ripening on the stalk earlier that morning.

Speaking of corn, my most recent purchase of it went into making a dish that brings back memories of meals at my grandmother's house in rural Tennessee. Throughout high school, I worked at my uncle's hardware store. Like most teenage boys, I had a ravenous appetite that went along with a high metabolism.

So with only a half-hour lunch break, I would rush to my grandmother's house, where she had prepared a veritable feast of fried chicken, green beans simmered all morning in a pot with salt pork, mashed potatoes, sliced tomatoes and my favorite, fried corn, all served with hot biscuits or cornbread.

Dessert quite often was fresh blackberry cobbler or apple pie topped with vanilla ice cream. None of those items are on any heart-healthy diet today and should be indulged rarely. Nevertheless at least once a summer I remember my grandmother by making a batch of fried corn.*

I never thought about it at the time, but eating corn, and the other items that were the staples of southern cuisine, represented a phenomenon identified in 1972 by University of Texas geographer Alfred Crosby as the "Columbian Exchange." Named for Christopher Columbus, it involved the widespread transfer of plants, animals, culture, human populations, technology and diseases among the Americas, West Africa and Europe in the 15th and 16th centuries.

When Columbus came to America in 1492, for example, there were no oranges in Florida or California, no pasta in Italy, no tomatoes in Italy, no chocolate in Belgium and no potatoes in Ireland.

Some scholars argue that this exchange might be the most important event in modern history. Crosby, for example, raised an interesting question: Why is it that most Africans live in Africa, most Asians in Asia and most Native Americans in the Americas? Yet people of European descent, by contrast, "are thick on the ground in Australia, southern Africa and the Americas."

Crosby went on to explain why Indian nations collapsed and European colonies thrived after the arrival of Columbus and the introduction of deadly diseases to the native population. In return, Europeans began to benefit from a cornucopia of fruits and vegetables coming from the New World. Before, their fundamental diet had consisted primarily of meat and a variety of grains such as barley, rye and wheat that were the chief ingredients in porridge and gruel.

On the other hand, for centuries natives of the Western Hemisphere consumed a more diverse diet. Maize or "Indian corn," for example, was first domesticated in southern Mexico some 9,000 years ago, and over the next several millennia spread throughout most of pre-Columbian America. It was eventually introduced throughout Iberia, North Africa, Italy and southern France. Likewise tomatoes, green beans, squash and potatoes originated in various regions of South and Central America at around the same time.

Simultaneously earthworms, mosquitoes and cockroaches, honeybees, dandelions, African grasses, bacteria, fungi, viruses and several species of rats came ashore, changing lives and landscapes in America forever. According to Crosby, the Columbian Exchange was neither controlled nor understood by its participants, but "it allowed Europeans to transform much of the Americas and Asia into ecological versions of Europe."

Prior to Crosby's thesis, historians tended to think that Europe's worldwide expansion was related mostly to superior armed forces and modern weaponry. Crosby argued, however, that Europe's crucial advantage was more biological than technological.

His pioneering work and that of subsequent scholars opened a whole new field of inquiry. Named environmental history, it is the study of human interaction with the natural world over time, with an emphasis on the role of nature in influencing human affairs and vice versa. One can only speculate on what future environmental historians will write about our generation's role in shaping the globe for better or worse. I wish I could say that I'm optimistic, but I'm afraid forces greater than any of us are at work to prevent that from happening.

*Here is my grandmother's recipe: *In a large cast iron skillet, fry five or six strips of bacon until crisp. In the meantime, shuck a dozen or so ears of fresh sweet corn and scrape the kernels into a medium size bowl. Remove bacon from the skillet, leaving enough sizzling drippings to cover its bottom. Pour the kernels into the skillet, and immediately stir in two-thirds a cup each of milk and water. Allow the mixture to simmer and cook down on medium to low for about half an hour, adding more milk and water if needed. Salt and pepper to taste. About five minutes before serving, crumble the set-aside bacon and add it to the simmering mixture.*

Richmond *Times-Dispatch*, October 13, 2019

67

BOOKS THAT CHANGED HISTORY

I have had a longtime fascination with turning points, those events that changed the course of history. They can be sudden, such as the assassination of Abraham Lincoln or the bombing of Pearl Harbor. But they can be subtle and evolve slowly, such as the advent of air conditioning or the spread of deadly diseases through the indigenous people of the New World.

From my study of history the past 50 years, I now realize that certain books can shape the course of history. A few years ago, I wrote a column in this newspaper that related the books that arguably changed America. Today's column expands its focus to books that helped shape world history.

They are based on at least one of the following criteria: They can be either fiction or nonfiction; they are not necessarily great literature or bestsellers; they shaped public attitudes and/or policy; they helped form people's beliefs and actions; and most importantly, there is no right or wrong candidate. These are my subjective opinions. I intentionally left the *Bible* and the *Quran* off my list, not because they do not deserve inclusion, but rather their choice is so obvious.

Here are my selections:

(1) ***The Travels of Marco Polo*** (c. 1300) When he was 17 years old, this son of a wealthy Venice merchant accompanied his father and uncle on what became a 24-year odyssey to the Near and Middle East, eventually traveling as far as China. Upon his return from the Far East, Polo fought and was captured in a war between Venice and Genoa. While imprisoned, he dictated an

account of his travels to his cellmate. When released from prison, he had his narrative published, thus giving its European readers their first comprehensive look into the exotic world of the Far East. Polo's words inspired European adventurers to begin looking for shorter routes to the Far East, and led to the Age of Exploration, including Christopher Columbus's voyages to the "New World."

(2) John Locke, ***Two Treatises on Government*** (1689) A physician by profession, Locke dabbled frequently in political issues and philosophy. He was an outspoken advocate of religious tolerance, and he argued that there is no "true religion." He further contended that trying to enforce religious uniformity by government led to civil unrest. To him, the primary purpose of government was to protect the rights of individuals, and that its powers should be limited. His words profoundly influenced intellectual thinking in Western Europe and America. Thomas Jefferson relied heavily on Locke in drafting the Declaration of Independence.

(3) Adam Smith, ***Wealth of Nations*** (1776) Born in Scotland and educated at Oxford, he joined the faculty of the University of Glasgow in 1751. There he developed the discipline of economics and coined the word "capitalism." His ***Wealth of Nations*** argued that industrial production and labor were more important than precious metals or land in creating wealth. He described the law of supply and demand, which leads to competition, and in turn leads to prosperity. Smith believed in "free markets" that operated without government interference and were guided by an "invisible hand." His book sold well, and eventually led to his being regarded as the father of free enterprise or modern capitalism. Many scholars regard him as one of the 10 most influential philosophers of all time.

(4) and (5) Karl Marx, ***The Communist Manifesto*** and ***Das Kapital*** (1848) An economist, historian and philosopher, among other things, Marx is considered one of the most influential persons in history. His ***Manifesto*** and ***Das Kapital*** asserted that the past is based on a struggle among the classes that would eventually end with the victory of the proletariat and the end of the class system. He frequently is referred to as the father of communism.

(6) Harriet Beecher Stowe, **Uncle Tom's Cabin** (1852) Described by many scholars as the most influential book published in America, this novel vividly described the ordeal of a Kentucky slave family and immediately became a sensation. Eventually published in multiple languages, the book influenced public attitudes as few others had, helping solidify both pro- and antislavery sentiment and fanned the flames that led to the Civil War.

(7) Charles Darwin, **On the Origins of Species** (1859) Born and raised in a wealthy English family, Darwin developed a keen interest in the natural world. Forgoing a medical career, he became a professional naturalist, biologist and geologist who argued that all forms of life have descended over time with common ancestors. His theory of evolution became one of the fundamental principles of science today.

(8) Alfred Thayer Mahan, **The Influence of Sea Power Upon History** (1890) Virtually unknown today, Mahan's book argued that throughout history powerful nations possessed strong navies and far-flung strategic outposts. Written by the president of the U.S. Naval War College and read by strategic thinkers beyond the United States, this book arguably led to the first worldwide arms race and contributed to the buildup of seagoing forces prior to World War I.

(9) Adolph Hitler, **Mein Kampf** (1925) In this autobiography, Hitler presented his radical political philosophy advocating transforming German society into one based on race. Written while he was jailed for treason, he singled out Jews as a threat to a stable society and advocated their removal from Germany and eventual extermination. Hitler's turgid prose did not deter more than a million readers from purchasing the book, and helped him rise to power and eventually became Germany's head of government.

(10) Your Choice - Now it's your turn to suggest one more book to add to the list. Here are a few possibilities: George Orwell, **1984** (1949); Rachel Carson's **Silent Spring** (1962); Betty Friedan, **The Feminine Mystique** (1963); and Mao Tse-tung, **The Little Red Book** (1964).

Modern readers might regard some books on my list as deadly dull. Nevertheless, each contains a message that changed or molded opinions that in turn led to new ways of thinking or acting.

Richmond *Times-Dispatch*, November 10, 2019

68

The Giant of the Sky
747 and the impact of air travel

The summer before my senior year in high school, I traveled to Europe for the first time. It was 1964, when few Americans had ventured outside the United States, other than millions of veterans of the world wars. I flew from Nashville to New York, where I joined a group tour organized by my uncle and aunt's newly founded travel firm.

Taking off from newly christened John F. Kennedy Airport the next evening, we flew overnight for seven hours to London Heathrow Airport via a TWA Boeing 707. Regular jet service was still relatively new then, having only been introduced in 1958. None of us on that trip realized that we were participating in the early stages of a revolution in aviation.

Recently I visited the Museum of Flight in Seattle that claims to be "the largest independent, nonprofit air and space museum in the world." It is, indeed, an impressive collection of planes that helped shape the course of aviation history.

Going through the museum, I thought about how much aviation has shaped the world we live in today in just a little more than a century. Air travel has evolved at a breathtaking pace since the first manned flight of the Wright brothers. From their flimsy biplane that barely traveled the length of a football field to spacecraft that have taken men to the moon and back, one cannot help but marvel at how quickly humans learned to defy gravity.

On display at the museum are a variety of planes that played key roles in shaping the future ' flimsy Word War I biplanes, World War II bombers and, of course, a B-29, the plane that ushered in the Cold War.

Not all planes in the museum, however, are military. For that matter, the majority had purposes other than waging war. Almost every kind of airliner caught my attention, starting with the DC-3, which went into production in 1936, yet is still being flown in some places throughout the world today.

Toward the end of the tour we came upon a gigantic Boeing 747, one of the largest and most influential planes ever developed. Of all the aircraft we saw, it arguably contributed more to shrinking the size of the globe and making it accessible to more people than anyone could have imagined.

Prior to the introduction of the 747, the largest airliners each carried only about 100 passengers, resulting in ticket prices that were affordable only for business travelers and the wealthy. In the early 1960s, a domestic ticket from Chicago to Phoenix went for nearly $1,200 adjusted to today's inflation. A flight from New York to Rome could set you back $3,000 today.

Look at any old film of commercial air travel then, and you will see most men wearing business suits and Stetson hats, with women sporting stylish dresses and suits with accompanying white gloves. Stewardesses, as flight attendants were called then, had been chosen for their personal appearance and had come through a rigorous regimen of training.

Nevertheless, with a growing public demand for long distance jet service in the 1960s, airlines began to think of ways to meet that need. Originally designed by the Boeing Airplane Company as a military transport, the huge plane caught the attention of senior executive Juan Trippe of Pan American Airlines.

He argued that converting the 747 from military to civilian use would help solve growing congestion at airports caused by planes with lower passenger loads. Bigger jets would allow airlines to take twice as many passengers than the largest airliners in use then. Bigger jets could also result in bigger profits.

In response to Trippe, Boeing assembled a design team to work on a larger airliner. Pan Am became the first to order the plane (25 initially), and as a result played a significant role in the final design and production of the 747. Initially, designers thought of having two decks of seating, giving the plane a capacity of more than 800. The ability to evacuate two decks of passengers in an emergency, however, forced them to nix that idea.

Nevertheless, from its earliest flights, skeptics wondered how the public would react to crashes that resulted in hundreds of deaths involving only one plane. After 50 years in service, however, 747s have had a solid safety record. It ranks third among the 19 jet models used in commercial travel today, having fewer crashes per miles flown.

After mounting a massive publicity campaign, the 747 made its inaugural flight from New York to London in January 1970.

Although Pan Am was the first airline to add 747s to its fleet, others major carriers followed suit. With their introduction, airlines could now sell low fare economy seats. Combined with airline deregulation in the late 1970s, travel by plane was now made affordable to a much broader public.

Are we better off with airplanes like the 747? On the one hand, they have allowed millions of people to see the rest of the world and to learn about different cultures. They have helped facilitate important business deals. They have reunited old friends and relatives. It has helped in the expansion of a hugely lucrative industry - tourism. Recreational travel has become one of the world's largest and fastest growing industries, accounting for about $7.6 trillion in receipts last year.

Many critics, however, point out the negative affect 747s and other jets have had on the environment. The rapid growth of air travel has led to a dramatic build up of greenhouse emissions in the upper atmosphere. While automobiles have greatly improved their emission standards, unfortunately the continuous increase in air travel has resulted in no reduction in pollution caused by these magnificent flying machines.

It makes one wonder if the damage being inflicted on our planet is worth it? Unfortunately, I don't see viable solutions to this problem anytime soon.

Richmond *Times-Dispatch*, January 26, 2020

69

SILENCE ON THE WESTERN FRONT: THE CHRISTMAS TRUCE OF 1914

Although World War I was only in its fourth month, the casualties were appalling in their scale. Since the opening of hostilities in early August 1914, nearly 1 million combatants had been killed, wounded, captured or declared missing in action.

These horrendous casualty numbers sent shock waves to people throughout the world, most of whom had predicted a relatively short war.

In its first three months, the conflict carried many vestiges of 19th-century warfare, with both sides relying on the offensive and large mass attack formations to punch through enemy lines. But two relatively new innovations immediately made offensive warfare unlike previous conflicts.

The machine gun, which was perfected in the late 19th century, could spew out 600 rounds a minute and was devastating when fired at massed troops.

And although artillery has been used to wage war for centuries, it mainly had been employed for close-up, direct fire. By World War I, however, direct fire gave way to indirect artillery barrages relying on deadly accurate howitzers and mortars. It now was possible to kill enemy soldiers in large numbers miles away and out of sight.

In response to these lethal weapons, a new form of warfare quickly evolved. By the end of 1914, the Allies and Germans had laid out a series of trenches stretching from the Swiss/French border some 475 miles west to the English Channel in Holland.

Periodic offensive operations mostly consisted of short, but costly, rushes against enemy trenches that seldom gained much more than a few acres of ground. The prevailing theory of trench warfare was that the other side eventually would exhaust its resources and have to sue for peace terms.

Between the respective trench lines, a no man's land evolved, monitored by snipers and warily ventured into by regular patrols. Behind rows of trenches and barbed wire, soldiers had constructed permanent defensive works, which provided the bulk of the respective armies with some shelter from deadly bombardments.

As Christmas and the new year approached in 1914, millions of men shivered in cold muddy trenches, suffering from ever-present rats and lice, and putting up with the constant acrid smells from exploded artillery shells and nearby latrines. Men occasionally lost their minds amid this hellish environment and the almost endless boom of cannon fire.

From these dismal circumstances came one of the most remarkable of Christmas stories. On Christmas Eve 1914, an officer in the Royal Irish Rifle Guard peered through his binoculars at the German trenches 100 yards away and saw something that astonished him.

He immediately reported to headquarters: "Germans have illuminated their trenches [with Christmas trees], are singing songs and wishing us a Happy Xmas." Concerned that what he was seeing was a ruse, he told his superior that he was "taking all military precautions."

He need not have been concerned as up and down the line, German and British or French soldiers began to serenade their enemies with carols and shouts of "Merry Christmas." Rival patrols stumbled into each other in no man's land with surprising results.

A British soldier later reported that, in the predawn light, members of the Scots Guards saw a German patrol headed their way. The Scotsmen halted and then sent a message forward saying that if they didn't fire at them, they would do likewise. The Germans agreed, and the two opposing patrols warmly greeted each other and exchanged whiskey and cigars.

As the sun began to rise in the east, soldiers gradually emerged from the opposing trenches and ventured into no man's land. At first cautiously, then enthusiastically, soldiers began shaking hands and greeting each other with wide grins and boisterous laughter. Even though few Allied soldiers spoke German, and most Germans spoke no English, the soldiers were able to communicate with gestures as if they were playing a game of charades.

As best as possible given the language barrier, they exchanged the latest professional soccer news, and according to some accounts, soldiers on both sides produced soccer balls and began kicking them back and forth.

Soldiers exchanged gifts up and down the long line of trenches, with schnaps going for whiskey from the Brits and wine from the French soldiers. Good tobacco was a prized gift from one enemy to another.

As the sun began to sink in the west, however, the day's revery began to fade with it. Up and down the line, soldiers - who seemed to understand that the truce would end soon - reluctantly headed back to their respective trenches, in some instances summoned by flares. For the most part, both sides refused to resume fighting until midnight, with some units wrapping up the remarkable day with singing a final round of carols.

The so-called Christmas Truce was one of the few and last examples of instances of chivalry between enemies at war. The following year, there was talk of another ceasefire, but generals on both sides refused to sanction one arguing that fraternization with the enemy lessened the ability of soldiers to fight effectively and ultimately kill the enemy. Such a truce never was repeated.

By the next day, December 26, the war again erupted. Soldiers who had cheerfully exchanged gifts with new friends the day before now were mortal enemies. There would be no real truce until the general armistice of November 11, 1918. Many, if not most, of those who participated in the unique Christmas celebration of 1914 did not live to see peace return.

With its mass slaughter, reliance on trenches, and use of new and insidious ways of killing the enemy, World War I has been described as the worst of wars for the soldiers who served their respective nations. But for those who were there and then survived the war, memories of the Christmas of 1914 would remain with them for the rest of their lives.

Sadly, the prospects of a Christmas truce virtually are unthinkable today. Although we have labeled the current conflict the "war on terrorism," in reality it is as much a religious war pitting Muslims against nations with Judeo-Christian religious traditions. Germany, France, Great Britain and eventually the United States all worshipped the same God and celebrated the birth of Christ despite being mortal enemies.

Unfortunately, religious conflict today makes it virtually impossible for the warring sides to cease the killing even for one day as was done during one of the worst of all wars.

Richmond *Times-Dispatch*, December 25, 2020

PART IX

FROM CONFEDERATE CAPITAL TO KING TOBACCO

In 2015, Lewis Brissman at the Richmond Times-Dispatch *approached me about writing a history of Richmond from 1850 to 1965 in five segments to mark 165 years since the paper published its first issue. The only rule he imposed on me was to break my narrative into segments of twenty-five years with the exception of the first essay that spanned only 15 years. In others words, I had to produce a snapshot of the city at twenty-five intervals—1850, 1865, 1890, 1915, 1940, and 1965. It was not an easy task, nevertheless I was able to fulfil my assignment as you will read.*

1850

THE COMING STORM: A CITY OF INDUSTRY AND INFLUENCE WAS GROWING, AS WAS ONE OF ITS DEFINING CHARACTERISTICS: SLAVERY

Visitors to Richmond in the mid-19th century were impressed with what they saw, especially its physical setting. It was a small but thriving city set on the churning falls of the James River, yet it was also a bustling industrial center.

A visiting Englishman was thoroughly charmed by the "friendly, cheery, little town [that is] the most picturesque I have seen in America."

It was also a community on the move after hard times. Like the rest of Virginia, Richmond had struggled in the first half of the 19th century.

Seeking opportunities elsewhere, nearly a million Virginians moved south and west, fleeing a seemingly endless agricultural depression and widespread soil exhaustion that plagued the commonwealth.

"The times are dreadful if we may judge from the numbers that are migrating to different parts of the country," lamented a woman from Tidewater in the 1830s.

By 1850, however, while rural areas of the commonwealth still struggled, conditions were improving in its capital city. Manufacturing had gained a strong foothold. Canals, railroads and the river linked Richmond to the rest of the state and beyond. As the center of state government, it was the nexus of power and influence in Virginia, creating both envy and resentment in rural areas, particularly west of the Blue Ridge.

At mid-century, Richmond had grown into the industrial center of the South and one of the most prosperous cities below the Mason-Dixon Line.

It led the country in manufacturing tobacco products. It was America's second-largest center for the milling of flour – the Gallego flour mill was said to occupy the world's largest physical plant. The city was the national leader in coffee imports. The Tredegar Iron Works, under the exceptional leadership of Joseph Reid Anderson, was the South's leading iron producer, forging track for the rapidly growing American railway network. Richmond's riverfront, with its humming factories, clanging iron works and teeming waterfront, resembled a frenetic beehive.

Ironically, in some ways Richmond seemed more Northern than Southern in 1850, and in the next decade, it would follow a national trend of growth and prosperity. The population of the United States would increase 35 percent in the 1850s, with most growth in Northern cities, but Richmond grew as well by 28 percent. The nation's manufacturing production rose dramatically, and rail transportation expanded with it, again mainly in the North but also in Virginia's city on the James.

Richmond also resembled its Northern counterparts in its ethnically diverse labor force who performed a variety of jobs. Many were whites who had moved from farms to the city under the promise of better jobs. Immigrants from Europe, especially from Germany and Ireland who had escaped civil war and famine in their native lands, could be found performing any number of jobs in Richmond.

One huge factor, however, made Richmond's labor force different from those in the North: A large percentage of its workers were not free. Nearly 11,000 slaves and some 2,000 free blacks made up more than a third of Richmond's population. Black Richmonders, both slave and free, were a crucial element of the workforce, especially in the ironworks and tobacco factories. They were also cooks, barbers, teamsters, dockworkers, street cleaners, railroad laborers and domestic servants.

Enslaved African-Americans were vital to Richmond's emergence as a flourishing city in another way: commerce and trade. The most lucrative export products were not tobacco, iron or flour but rather human beings.

Virginia's agricultural crisis coincided with the growth of cotton planting in the Deep South, so even as the value of slaves declined in Virginia, it increased elsewhere. A slave appraised at $1,000 in Richmond could fetch three or four times that amount in New Orleans. As a result, slaves by the hundreds of thousands left Virginia as "products" who were sold.

Although federal law had terminated the importation of slaves internationally to the United States in 1808, a booming interstate domestic slave trade took its place. The Old Dominion led the nation in this lucrative business, and in Richmond, thousands of slaves were sold every year from its nearly 30 auction houses. By 1850, only New Orleans surpassed Virginia's capital city as a slave-trading center. Shockoe Bottom at the corner of East Franklin and 15th streets became the center of the slave business and regularly drew gawkers and out-of-town visitors, many of whom chronicled this grim business of broken families and people auctioned off as if they were cattle.

The issue of race could not be avoided in Richmond because of the city's large African-American presence. Everyday life for blacks in the city was better than for those on farms and plantations, where freedom of movement was severely limited and the treatment of slaves harsher. Nevertheless, there was an almost constant underlying fear within Richmond's white population of a slave insurrection. The failed revolt in 1800 of Richmond slaves led by Gabriel Prosser and the bloody 1831 Nat Turner rebellion in Southampton County were fresh in the memories of whites. As a result, the city imposed restrictions on the movement, gathering and education of African-Americans. Despite imposing these measures, fears of insurrection would mount among whites in the coming decade.

By 1850, as political tensions between the North and South intensified because of a variety of complex issues, the people of Richmond began to worry that the nation could be torn asunder. But they had no idea of what lay ahead of them - a long and bloody civil war.

None of them would have guessed that their city would be the epicenter of that conflict, or that its population would explode to more than 100,000 almost overnight. They would have been astounded to learn that the land around the city would become the most heavily fought over and bloodiest in the Western Hemisphere, or that it would turn into a vast hospital for sick and wounded soldiers.

As people of any age do, the citizens of Richmond in 1850 muddled through life one day at a time, unaware that in a few years, their "friendly, cheery, little town" would be swept away by a terrible war in which the cost in human suffering was beyond their comprehension.

1865

The Fallen City:
In the heart of the Confederacy,
defiance gives way to defeat –
and uncertainty – amid the flames

As 1865 began, Richmond remained a defiant symbol of the Confederate States of America. Since being designated the capital of the infant nation in 1861, the city had frustrated one Union general after another who tried to take it.

But after four years of costly war, the people of Richmond knew that their city and the entire Confederacy were in dire straits. The South had managed to keep the war going by improvisation, determination and sheer stubbornness, but exhaustion was finally setting in.

White Richmonders had suffered through martial law, the draft, impressment of their slaves and the commandeering of homes and public buildings for the Confederacy's huge civilian and military bureaucracy.

The insatiable demand for space by government authorities was not the only reason for overcrowding on an unprecedented scale. Since 1861, the people of Richmond had seen their numbers explode from 35,000 to more than 100,000 at one point as tens of thousands of refugees sought safety from chaotic, war-torn rural Virginia. Like a medieval castle opening its gates to peasants in time of war, Richmond offered these desperate people the relative safety of a fortified city.

As the South's leading industrial center, Richmond's factories had been converted and expanded to full-time war production. The Tredegar Iron Works, the South's largest manufacturing establishment, turned out artillery pieces, projectiles, gun carriages, plates for ironclad ships, wheels, axles for railroad rolling stock, and furnaces for a chain of smaller factories throughout the South. Other plants produced small arms, percussion caps, cartridges, foodstuffs and tobacco products. To keep Richmond's factories humming around the clock, industry recruited workers, men and women alike, in numbers that were unimaginable before the war.

War profiteers, smugglers, con men, soldiers on furlough and women of the night, whose brothels always had a steady clientele, added to the throng of newcomers.

Richmonders saw their churches and school buildings turned into hospitals to handle the overwhelming number of casualties that poured into the city after each of the many battles fought nearby.

Tobacco warehouses and even Belle Island in the James River were converted into prisons for thousands of Union prisoners of war. At the beginning of the war, the belligerents exchanged prisoners, but when the Union ended that practice in 1864, the numbers swelled far beyond capacity to house them. As was true of all POW camps during the Civil War, conditions at Richmond's overcrowded prisons were miserable. Too hot in the summer. Too cold in the winter. Never enough food. Poor sanitary conditions.

By early 1865, many of Richmond's citizens felt little better off than those Union prisoners. Food was scarce. A clerk in the Confederate War Department confided in his diary that he had just enough to feed his large family for only a few more days. Firewood was scarce as well, making cooking and keeping warm a great challenge. "This is famine!" he exclaimed. With Confederate currency all but worthless, barter had become standard practice.

Many of these hardships were shared with the city's enslaved and free black population. From the earliest days of the war, however, slaves began to escape to freedom behind Union lines – first as a trickle, then as a regular stream with each passing year. By 1865, the institution of slavery in Richmond and the South was all but dead as more and more Confederate territory fell to the conquering federal armies.

Those armies would also seal the fate of Richmond. Since June 1864, Ulysses S. Grant and the mighty Union Army of the Potomac had been locked in an ever-tightening siege with Robert E. Lee's dwindling Confederate army at Petersburg, 20 miles south of the Confederate capital. Grant would soon be reinforced when another powerful Union force under William Tecumseh Sherman worked its way up through the Carolinas to Virginia. Once Sherman united with Grant, Lee's army would be forced to evacuate Petersburg or be crushed. Either way, Confederate Richmond would be doomed.

For three weary, cold months, Lee's men shivered in their trenches waiting for Grant's next move. Then suddenly, in the first week of April 1865, Grant unleashed his army. He moved a large force around Lee's right flank and slammed into it at Five Forks. Soon the entire Confederate line collapsed. Lee fell back, and triumphant federal troops marched into Petersburg on April 3. Richmond was next.

Word of the collapse quickly reached the capital city. Confederate President Jefferson Davis ordered the evacuation of his government and the army garrison. Fleeing Confederate troops torched factories, arsenals and mills. "The old war-scarred city seemed to prefer annihilation to conquest," one Confederate soldier mused.

Fires soon roared out of control. Fueled by liquor and pent-up deprivation, mobs of civilians and deserters roamed through the stricken city, burning and looting warehouses filled with rations and whiskey. According to one observer, "an ocean of flame is dashing as a tidal wave of destruction from street to street. … Miles on miles of fire; mountain pile on mountain pile of black smoke … one ceaseless babel of human voices, crying, shouting, cursing; one mighty pandemonium of woe."

While much of Richmond suffered widespread destruction at the hands of the Confederates, ironically, it was troops clad in blue uniforms who restored order and saved the city from further damage. Union troops marched into town and sprang into action dousing fires, stopping looters and restoring some sense of order to the city. Nevertheless, for many Richmonders it was a terrible day. A young woman remembered that she gazed upon "the horrible stars and stripes" floating from the Capitol building and compared them to "so many bloody gashes."

Once a semblance of order was established, Richmond received a distinguished visitor on April 4. With the city still smoldering, President Abraham Lincoln and his son Tad stepped from a Navy rowboat onto the north shore of the James River at Rocketts Landing. The president then set out on a tour of the devastated city, first on foot and then by carriage.

Everywhere he went, crowds of former slaves greeted the tall, bearded gentleman with loud cheering and ecstatic laughter. Some of them fell to their knees and tried to kiss his feet. He stopped at the Confederate executive mansion, where his counterpart and his family had lived. He visited Libby Prison and the state Capitol, where he met with officials to discuss what would happen to postwar Virginia. When asked that question, Lincoln pledged to "let 'em up easy." As the sun began to set, the president and his entourage slipped out of the city deeply moved by what they had seen.

Within a matter of days, Lincoln was dead at the hands of John Wilkes Booth. Five days earlier, on April 9, Robert E. Lee had surrendered his army at Appomattox. Except for a few minor actions in the Deep South and West, the war was over.

For the majority of white people in Richmond, the future was fraught with uncertainty. Many had lost almost everything – their homes, their bank accounts, their businesses, their slaves, their sons, their fathers, their husbands. Another fear emerged: What would life be like with Richmond's newly liberated black population? Some expected the worst.

For African-Americans, however, the future looked promising. Large numbers of them – of all ages – flocked to newly founded schools. Denied education before the war, they realized that learning to read and write was not only a symbolic step away from slavery but a way to enhance their ability to find good jobs. It would enable them to become active participants in the democratic experience – to vote and hold office, to make informed decisions, to be real American citizens.

Little did they know that within a matter of years, their postwar optimism would be undermined. Full citizenship would be denied them for a century. To borrow from a 20th-century observation of Winston Churchill, 1865 was not "the beginning of the end, but the end of the beginning" on the road to equality for Richmond's black community.

1890

THE GREAT TURN AROUND: TOBACCO AND TRANSPORTATION PUSHED THE CITY FORWARD EVEN AS CONFEDERATE NOSTALGIA HAD IT LOOKING BACK

In describing the late 19th-century rise of the United States as an industrial giant and increasingly urbanized nation, historian Bernard Weisberger observed that its cities "needed luck or location to become industrial centers." Likewise, the people who developed those centers "needed luck or cunning or driving strength or inventive skill to succeed." Each of these factors was present in Richmond in 1890.

Twenty-five years earlier, much of the city lay in ruins, its factories, warehouses, rail turntables, bridges and many of its residences little more than smoldering hulks, all the victims of a brutal civil war. With slavery abolished, the top source of capital and wealth in the city before the war had evaporated. It would be difficult to find another American city that suffered as badly from war as had Richmond.

Yet that combination of location, luck, cunning, drive and inventiveness described by Weisberger began to turn around the devastated city within a matter of years. Key to that reversal of fortune was a new way for people to consume tobacco.

Until the mid-19th century, most people chewed tobacco, dipped snuff or smoked it in pipes and cigars. Users in large numbers, however, began to shift to seemingly milder cigarettes, which had to be hand-rolled and were relatively expensive. So the advent of the cigarette-making machine after the Civil War revolutionized the tobacco industry. With one machine able to roll more than 100,000 cigarettes a day, the price of the product plunged. Tobacco companies also began an aggressive advertising campaign. The combination of cheap cigarettes and clever marketing resulted in a rapid growth in smoking in the United States and beyond.

Although cigarette manufacturing got its start in North Carolina, Richmond was not far behind, opening its first plant in 1874. Lewis Ginter led the way. Born in New York but raised in Richmond, Ginter gained and lost two fortunes before launching into the increasingly lucrative tobacco business in the early 1870s.

Starting with a handful of young women who could hand-roll several hundred cigarettes a day, he began to make a profit almost immediately. Within a few years, he invested in cigarette-making machinery, and his business took off. By 1880, Ginter employed more than 4,000 men and women. Soon Richmond became the country's leading cigarette manufacturer.

Factories also began to spring up in response to an unending demand for other tobacco products. Even though cigarettes were the No. 1 moneymaker, snuff, chewing tobacco and pipe tobacco had a substantial consumer market.

Infusions of Northern capital provided much of the financial underpinning for new plants that also turned out flour, whiskey, paper, locomotives, soap, spices, fertilizer, boats, iron and textiles in huge numbers.

Key to this growth in industry was the fact that Richmond had become a major rail center. Railroads, which had suffered terribly during the Civil War, were expanded and greatly improved. Products from Richmond's factories were easily shipped from the crossroads of two major rail lines, running north to south and east to west. In addition, every year millions of tons of coal from newly opened mines in Southwest Virginia passed through the capital city to ports in Hampton Roads. Along the Eastern Seaboard, goods from the Deep South made their way rapidly to the North, meeting trains carrying cargo from Northern factories to the South, all through Richmond.

With each of these postwar developments in manufacturing, commerce and transportation, Richmond started experiencing unprecedented growth and prosperity, which were manifested in many ways.

For one, the city began to expand physically because of a growing population and improved transportation. Until the late 1880s, Richmonders got around either on foot or by horse. The city was compact, with relatively short distances from one part to another. Wealthy families lived downtown, not far from the working classes. Poor whites and blacks tended to reside on the east side in cheaper housing, downwind from thick black smoke pouring from Richmond's factories and coal-fueled furnaces in homes.

The fundamental layout of all American cities began to change, however, when Richmond became the world's first city to introduce electric streetcars as public transportation in 1888. Now people could quickly go to and from the bucolic countryside nearby, escaping the constant sights, smells and sounds of a bustling and increasingly crowded manufacturing city.

Streetcars made the land surrounding Richmond available for development and lengthened the distance between a person's home to his or her place of work. It also helped lead to something else – racial and economic segregation.

With the spread of streetcar lines, whites, especially the well-to-do, began to leave downtown Richmond and settle in suburbs such as Bellevue and Ginter Park, commuting to and from work by streetcar. People of lesser means continued to live in town. This phenomenon occurred in cities throughout America, leading eventually to sprawl and increased division of populations by race and economic status.

By 1890, Richmond had all of the elements of a modern city. Electricity powered its streetcars and lighted an increasing number of businesses and homes. Big factories churned out products that were marketed and sold throughout the country and beyond. Wholesale businesses supplied any number of products for retail shops in small towns throughout the mid-Atlantic. Large retail stores catered to the wealthy and a budding middle class.

Richmond's population had grown to more than 80,000, making it the second-largest city in the South next to New Orleans.

With the 20th century fast approaching, however, Richmond ironically began to embrace its past, almost obsessively. Whites in Richmond and the rest of the South increasingly accepted a simple version of history: Everything had been better in the past, especially before the Civil War. As one 20th-century historian observed, white Southerners came to accept a "sort of ecstatic, teary-eyed vision of the Old South as Happy-Happy Land." By extension, the men who fought and died to defend that happy land against Northern aggression were heroes and deserved public recognition.

In May 1890, 100,000 people gathered in Richmond to dedicate a gigantic statue of Robert E. Lee, the first of five statues eventually erected to honor Confederate heroes along a handsome avenue pointing west from the downtown. Named Monument Avenue for its iconography honoring the Confederacy, it would be lined with magnificent homes built mainly by the people who had prospered from the new Richmond.

Richmond had emerged from the smoke and ashes of the Civil War in no small part because of infusions of Northern capital. At the same time, this expanding modern city was memorializing a lost cause that had been devoted in large part to the preservation of slavery. It was a paradox that would last for a long time.

1915

The past and future collide: Growth and division marked a city that expanded its footprint, industrialization – and segregation

The speed at which the United States changed in the late 19th and early 20th centuries astonished many observers. Factories and cities rapidly replaced farms and villages. By 1915, fewer than 4 in 10 workers made their living in farming, a far cry from Thomas Jefferson's vision of America where "every one may have land to labor for himself." More and more of those workers came as immigrants from eastern and southern Europe, mostly Catholics and Jews.

With a population larger than any European country except Russia and with exports greater than Great Britain's, the United States was the foremost industrial country in the world. It had managed to stay out of the brutal war that had been raging in Europe between the Allied and Central powers for a year. Despite ongoing problems with a blockade imposed on the Allies by the German U-Boat fleet, American factories saw their production increase dramatically to keep up with Allied demands. By now the U.S. was arguably the wealthiest nation on earth.

In some ways, Richmond exemplified that transformation. Its population increased, though not with the new wave of immigrants. Rather, people from rural Virginia and North Carolina, black and white alike, moved to the community in large numbers seeking good-paying jobs in the city's humming factories.

Richmond also began to add citizens in a series of annexations. Officials believed that the city must avoid overcrowding and expand to remain prosperous. That in turn led to a series of mergers with neighboring communities such as Manchester.

The city limits also continued to expand over surrounding farmland because of another revolutionary new mode of transportation: the automobile.

Since the first prototype was unveiled nearly 25 years earlier, the automobile experienced slow but steady growth. Manufactured in small plants scattered throughout the country, these self-propelled vehicles were expensive and, therefore, owned mainly by the wealthy. From 1912 to 1923, Richmond was home to the Kline Kar Company, which operated a factory on the Boulevard (on the site of the current Greyhound Bus station). Like most early automobiles, Kline Kars were expensive, and during the company's decade of operation in Richmond, only about 2,500 were manufactured.

Another vehicle, made hundreds of miles away, would not only drive the likes of Kline Kars off the road, it would change America forever. When Henry Ford introduced his affordable and reliable Model T, sales were far greater than even he anticipated. Soon the Model T was transforming the automobile from a novel luxury to a necessity for millions of people of all ages, ethnic backgrounds and a growing middle class. Look at almost any photograph of downtown Richmond in the several years after 1914, and the cars on the streets are mostly Model T's.

There were plenty of things to draw people to the heart of the city, whether by automobile or streetcar. In Richmond's thriving downtown, people could dine at a variety of restaurants and shop at a number of general and specialty stores. Two department stores – Miller & Rhoads and Thalhimers – were examples of a new type of merchandising created to bring the products of industry to the people at lower prices than found at specialty shops.

Despite Richmond's growth in the early 20th century, other Southern cities such as Atlanta, Nashville, Memphis and

Birmingham grew faster. Better connected with railroads and positioned geographically, they could take greater advantage of the nation's expanding economy than Richmond.

Those cities also seemed more attuned to the future. As historian Marie Tyler McGraw noted, while other Southern cities were dedicated to emulating the North's industrial and commercial might, "Richmond, the old industrial city, had no peer in collecting documents, erecting monuments and planning memorials to the Confederacy." With the South's largest home for Confederate veterans, a recently dedicated memorial to the Confederate soldier on the Boulevard named Battle Abbey, numerous statues standing in prominent places and other iconic imagery commemorating the Southern cause, no other city south of the Mason-Dixon Line could match Richmond's continued fixation with the past.

One would be hard-pressed to find another country that allowed the losing side in a civil war to celebrate and memorialize its leaders. The South may have lost the Civil War, but by 1915, it seemed to be winning the memory war in the capital of the Confederacy.

Attempts by Richmond's African-American community to counter this movement proved fruitless. When they learned that the film "The Birth of a Nation" would be showing at one of the city's 14 movie theaters in the summer of 1915, a delegation of leading black citizens unsuccessfully urged that it not be allowed to open. Based on the novel "The Clansman," director-producer D.W. Griffith's film, among other things, portrayed the Ku Klux Klan as a gang of heroes, black men as rapists, and even condoned lynching.

The first two decades of the 20th century represented the lowest point of race relations in Richmond. State-imposed poll taxes, gerrymandering and rigged elections ensured white supremacy in the political process. So-called Jim Crow laws segregated public transportation, accommodations, hospitals, schools, theaters, drinking fountains and bathroom facilities. The Supreme Court's Plessy v. Ferguson decision in 1896 upheld laws requiring "equal but separate accommodations for the white and colored races." It did not take long for accommodations for blacks to be anything but equal.

Segregated neighborhoods had evolved for several decades, but they became more distinct in the early 20th century. For African-Americans, Jackson Ward was the center of black commerce, worship and entertainment. As a thriving business community, it was home to banks, insurance companies and numerous commercial enterprises that catered to African-Americans, leading people to call it the "Black Wall Street of America." It was also referred to as the "Harlem of the South" because of its thriving theaters, clubs and the number of entertainers who performed or grew up there.

Jackson Ward boasted a small middle class, including businessmen, lawyers, teachers and preachers, all well-educated and influential. A few African-Americans were people of wealth, including Maggie Lena Walker, who made history by chartering a U.S. bank.

No matter how wealthy or educated African-Americans in Richmond were in 1915, they still were denied the full benefits of citizenship that white citizens enjoyed, at least white males. And in the decades the followed, the vestiges of slavery would still not disappear.

1940

THE WAR EFFORT:
HAVING WEATHERED THE DEPRESSION,
THE CITY GEARED UP FOR –
AND PROSPERED THROUGH –
WORLD WAR II

A s the 1930s came to an end, the people of Richmond could look back on the decade with a measure of relief.

Ten years earlier, the stock market crash ended seven decades of steady American economic growth and prosperity. By 1932, American industry was operating at less than half of its 1929 volume. Blue-chip stocks had plummeted. Crop prices collapsed. A staggering 25 percent of the labor force was unemployed. American cities with economies dependent on heavy industry suffered the most.

Although it was not immune from the national economic disaster, Richmond held its own in the 1930s because of its diversified economy. Cigarette production declined slightly. Many smokers who had bought premium brands such as Lucky Strike, Camel and Chesterfield switched to cheaper cigarettes and the roll-your-own varieties that were produced in Richmond. DuPont's giant rayon plant south of town actually produced at levels higher than before the crash. As the capital of Virginia and as a medium-sized city, Richmond had a solid core of state and local workers who were seldom laid off.

It was impossible, however, for the city to remain impervious to the Great Depression. In 1931, factories and the service industry began to lay off workers. Construction slowed. The hard times were devastating for marginal workers and people with limited resources, especially African-Americans. Yet Richmond got through the worst economic crisis in American history in better shape than most cities. By 1937, it was the nation's fastest-growing industrial center, and all of the city's economic indexes were higher than they were before the stock market crash of 1929.

When Franklin D. Roosevelt was elected president in 1932, he promised a New Deal for the American people with a wide array of federal programs and services aimed at restoring the economy. But these bold initiatives ran counter to Virginia's tradition of balanced budgets and limited government. As a result, New Deal spending in Virginia was the lowest of any comparable state.

By the end of the 1930s, events abroad began lifting the U.S. economy from depression more than any programs of the New Deal. When war broke out in Europe in 1939, neutrality remained America's policy, but Roosevelt started preparing the nation for eventual armed conflict with the Axis powers. As a result, the United States began moving from New Deal economics to war preparations, much to the benefit of Richmond.

Despite the declarations of American neutrality, U.S. factories began supplying the Allied forces with war-related products and materials. Much to the benefit of Richmond, cigarettes experienced a significant increase in production in response to increased demand from Allied service members. The next-largest industry – paper and paper products – started round-the-clock production in 1940, as did printing and engraving. The large DuPont plant turned to war production, making parachutes, munitions and a host of related products. Reynolds Metals, which had moved its corporate headquarters from New York to Richmond in 1938, began manufacturing aluminum for warplanes and military vehicles.

Despite the industrial expansion in the United States, most Americans were reluctant to become involved in the war in Europe. Most Richmonders, however, sympathized with the Allied nations, especially Great Britain, and did not object to the next steps taken by the president.

Roosevelt moved rapidly to arm the nation and help its friends. In May 1940, he asked Congress for a huge increase in spending to enlarge the armed services and to provide them with better arms and equipment. A month later, the president authorized the release of surplus military equipment and ships to the British. In September, Congress passed the first peacetime military draft in American history, requiring all men from ages 21 to 35 to register for possible service in the armed forces.

Richmond readily joined the national endeavor toward preparedness. The city had long wanted a deep-water terminal, and with the prospects of war mounting and an infusion of federal money, a 1,200-foot wharf wall and two fireproof warehouses were dedicated in October. A little more than a year later, the terminal proved invaluable for the giant supply depot built by the Army at Bellwood.

Two months after the passage of the Selective Service Act, a local draft board began inducting men for military service. Twenty miles south of Richmond, World War I's Camp Lee was rebuilt and expanded for training soldiers. Even though the United States would not enter the war for another year, the streets and sidewalks of Richmond soon became crowded with soldiers on weekends. Volunteer organizations worked with city officials to keep the soldiers entertained by sponsoring dances and socials. But this was the segregated South.

The military services would remain segregated until after World War II, and black military personnel taking leave in Richmond found that Jim Crow was entrenched in the former capital of the Confederacy. It was an eye-opening experience for African-American service members who had been raised in the North. Movie theaters, restrooms, restaurants, churches, schools, public transportation and even the Red Cross were all segregated. Many young black soldiers would question the irony of fighting to defend American democratic principles against German and Japanese tyranny when those very ideals were being ignored and violated in their own country.

As 1940 ended, Richmonders hoped that their nation would remain at peace. Yet in a matter of months the nation would be plunged into a global war. As they had during the Civil War, the city's industries shifted into high gear. The defense buildup and the ensuing war effort would raise Richmond, as well as the entire commonwealth, to unprecedented levels of prosperity and employment. Among Southern states, Virginia ranked second only to Texas in the value of war contracts.

The war effort allowed Richmond to grow and prosper. The federal government became Virginia's largest employer and emerged as a key factor in the economy of its capital city, although tobacco remained king. As agriculture became more mechanized during the war, farmers by the thousands were freed for work in factories and in the service industries.

Little did anyone know that within 25 years, two mainstays of life in Richmond – tobacco and segregation – would come under attack, changing the city forever.

1965

THE TIMES CHANGE:
FROM THE CIVIL WAR'S CENTENNIAL
TO CIVIL RIGHTS, A CITY REMAINED
CAUGHT BETWEEN OLD AND NEW

On Friday, April 9, 1965, Governor Albertis Harrison and his wife, Virginia, rose early, ate breakfast in the dining room of the Executive Mansion, and by 8 o'clock they climbed into the back seat of a state car. They were headed on a 90-mile trip to Appomattox, where he would deliver a speech.

Their car pulled out of the Capitol grounds and turned right onto 14th Street. Within minutes they passed near the warehouses and factories of Tobacco Row and were speeding across the 14th Street Bridge, soon to join Highway 360. What was on Harrison's mind? Did he practice his speech for the big event later in the day? Did he stare out the window, wondering what Richmond must have looked like 100 years ago?

Instead of viewing a city once devastated by war, he saw a vibrant landscape.

Since World War II, cities in the South had grown faster than those in any other region in the United States. Richmond's population had risen to 230,000 thanks to a good supply of low- to moderate-income jobs. The area outside the city limits had grown nearly 25 percent in a decade, pushing the metropolitan area's population to more than half a million. Small and midsize tract houses began to pop up like mushrooms on the outskirts of the city. The GI Bill and high employment rates made homeownership possible for many people who dreamed of raising their families in the bucolic suburbs.

Something less obvious also helped explain Richmond's growth: air conditioning. Between 1900 and 1950, the South experienced a net loss of 10 million people. But by 1965, the region was seeing net gains in population. The South also was becoming more urbanized than other sections of the country, and these growth patterns were closely tied to the spread of air conditioning in the years after World War II. With climate control available year-round, corporations were more willing to move their headquarters and operations south of the Mason-Dixon Line, where labor was also cheaper.

As it had for decades, Richmond boasted a diverse economic base. Federal, state and local government employees numbering in the thousands commuted to work from their suburban homes to downtown. City-center served as the home office for three large banking corporations, and it was home to one of the nation's 12 Federal Reserve Bank branches. Several major corporations listed Richmond as their headquarters. Two large department stores, Thalhimers and Miller & Rhoads, anchored a thriving retail scene downtown. The John Marshall and Jefferson hotels provided good accommodations for out-of-town guests and served as the regular meeting places for the city's largest service clubs. The Medical College of Virginia continued to expand its physical plant within sight of the Executive Mansion, state Capitol and imposing City Hall building.

Almost daily, streets and sidewalks were crowded with workers and shoppers, not to mention tourists who had come to town to visit the ultramodern domed Civil War Centennial visitor center, which had opened with great fanfare in 1961. The last two years of the commemoration, however, had been more subdued.

Ironically, the centennial kicked off just as the struggle for civil rights in the South intensified. The NAACP asked the American public to use the commemoration as a way "to fulfill the dreams of the Founding Fathers by granting rights to every American citizen." The centennial in Virginia, however, had been mostly the work of white men determined to portray the South as keepers of a noble cause. Materials prepared by the Virginia

Centennial Commission did not mention blacks or delve into the issue of slavery.

After Governor Harrison arrived at Appomattox to mark the 100th anniversary of Lee's surrender, the speech he delivered reflected views that ran counter to the profound changes that were occurring in American race relations. Addressing a subdued and modestly sized crowd, the governor proclaimed that "Virginians could recall the surrender of 1865 without bitterness because of the passage of time, but also because the beliefs and principles for which the Confederate forces fought for are still with us."

Yet Virginia's resistance to integration was crumbling. Within a matter of months of the Appomattox ceremony, President Lyndon B. Johnson signed the Voting Rights Act into law. Speaking to Congress, he declared: "It is really all of us, who must overcome the crippling legacy of bigotry and injustice. And we shall overcome."

Little by little, white supremacy, which had been reinforced by Lost Cause mythology, began to unravel. Within a matter of years, a new ward system resulted in the creation of a black majority on the Richmond City Council. It, in turn, elected Henry L. Marsh III, a lawyer active in civil rights litigation, as the city's first black mayor. Another Richmond attorney, L. Douglas Wilder, became the first African-American elected to the Virginia Senate, paving the way for his eventual distinction as the nation's first elected black governor.

While the days of white supremacy began to fade, thanks in no small part to the actions of the federal government, another federal action would also have far-reaching consequences in Richmond. Tobacco had long been the center of the city's economy. In 1965, American consumption of cigarettes continued to rise, as did sales abroad. Forty-two percent of the American people were considered as regular smokers. But a year earlier, the U.S. Surgeon General issued a report warning the public that cigarette smoking caused lung cancer and probably led to heart disease.

The tobacco companies responded quickly and forcefully by denying the validity of the report and developing strategies to fight back. Fight back they did, but in the long run, it was a losing battle. Cigarette smoking was at its apogee in 1965, but from then on, more and more Americans began to kick the habit.

A tobacco-based economy and issues of race were crucial components of the social, political and economic fabric of Richmond for most of its history, and would persist well beyond 1965. When Governor Harrison returned to Richmond from the ceremonies in Appomattox on April 9, little could he or anyone else know that the city would begin to face challenges that rivaled those of the post-Civil War years.

The Richmond of old – the bastion of the Lost Cause – had not died. Fragments of it could be glimpsed on Monument Avenue and at the Battle Abbey on the Boulevard. But the Richmond of old was being overlaid by another city – a more diverse, more suburbanized, more American community.

PART X
ALL IN THE FAMILY

As the average size of nuclear families in America has diminished over the last century, so has the number of our first cousins. I have had seventeen first cousins, fourteen of whom are still living. I know each by name, who they married, where they live, and what they do or did for a living. Remembering how many children they had and their names, however, escapes me. It takes my wife, Cammy, with her steel trap mind, to supply that information. She, on the other hand, has only four first cousins. Our three grandchildren will have only one or two each.

To me, cousins tend to be more like friends and acquaintances than relatives. You didn't have to fight over space in a room you shared with them when you were growing up. Absent is any semblance of sibling rivalry or concern over who is your parent's favorite child.

Like most of our cousins, we know and feel closer to some than others, a process that can waft and wane over the years. Some of my cousins who I had little contact with when we were growing up have become good friends in adulthood.

One of them is John ("Johnny" to me) Bryan. He was the son of my Uncle Tom, a prominent physician in Nash-

ville, who counted Country Music stars among his patients. His mother, my Aunt Margaret, was a remarkable southern woman who embraced feminism all of her adult life.

Soon after we moved to Richmond in 1988, we met up with John and his wife Janet along with their two children, Kelly and Thomas, who helped welcome us to our new city. As we settled into our new home, It didn't take me long to realize how respected my cousin was in this community. He served as director of development for the School of the Arts at Virginia Commonwealth University for some two decades and later was the founder of CultureWorks, a coalition of various business and community leaders in support of the arts in Richmond. I frequently found myself bragging that John Bryan was my cousin.

An artist himself, Johnny combines his love of painting with his passion for fishing. His artwork has been the subject of solo exhibitions in New York City, Richmond, Nashville, and numerous other communities.

I also discovered that Johnny is quite a good writer, having placed articles in Parade Magazine, *the Delta Airlines in-flight magazine* SKY *and* Sports Illustrated. *In addition, he has published numerous commentary pieces in the* Richmond Times-Dispatch *over the years.*

Therefore, similar to what I did in the first volume of Imperfect Past, *in which I included my daughter's exceptionally moving piece on the Sandy Hook School massacre, I am honored to provide space in this volume to include five pieces written by John.*

76

BIZ 101: HUG AN ARTIST

Ever heard of The Conference Board? Headquartered in New York City and with offices around the world, The Conference Board is a global leader for business research and strategies.

Two years ago I met The Conference Board's president and CEO, Jonathan Spector. He told me he was advising corporate executives that being able to think differently would help them survive the recession, and the best way to think differently was to embrace artists -- people whose minds are wired differently. Thinking differently, he told me, gives corporate executives a leg up on their competitors.

This belief is the cornerstone of The Conference Board's newly-launched national research initiative: "Creative Conversations." The idea is to put a small number of business executives and artists in a room together for an entire day and see what happens.

The Conference Board selected Richmond as the first of three cities (along with San Diego and Philadelphia) in which to facilitate Creative Conversations. They'll publish the results and share them with business, education and arts communities.

The Conference Board's partner in this research is Americans for the Arts. Headquartered in Washington, D.C, AFTA is the nation's leading organization for advancing the arts and arts education. Nonprofit Times lists AFTA President and CEO Robert L. Lynch among the 50 most influential people in the nonprofit world, along with such leaders as Bill Gates and the heads of the Rockefeller Foundation and the Pew Charitable Trusts. I came to know Lynch through my work at CultureWorks here in Richmond.

ville, who counted Country Music stars among his patients. His mother, my Aunt Margaret, was a remarkable southern woman who embraced feminism all of her adult life.

Soon after we moved to Richmond in 1988, we met up with John and his wife Janet along with their two children, Kelly and Thomas, who helped welcome us to our new city. As we settled into our new home, it didn't take me long to realize how respected my cousin was in this community. He served as director of development for the School of the Arts at Virginia Commonwealth University for some two decades and later was the founder of CultureWorks, a coalition of various business and community leaders in support of the arts in Richmond. I frequently found myself bragging that John Bryan was my cousin.

An artist himself, Johnny combines his love of painting with his passion for fishing. His artwork has been the subject of solo exhibitions in New York City, Richmond, Nashville, and numerous other communities.

I also discovered that Johnny is quite a good writer, having placed articles in Parade Magazine, *the Delta Airlines in-flight magazine* SKY *and* Sports Illustrated. *In addition, he has published numerous commentary pieces in the* Richmond Times-Dispatch *over the years.*

Therefore, similar to what I did in the first volume of Imperfect Past, *in which I included my daughter's exceptionally moving piece on the Sandy Hook School massacre, I am honored to provide space in this volume to include five pieces written by John.*

Symphony) together showed brief videos of their music and then discussed their ways of creating and working with their musicians. We saw that they have much in common that can relate to strengthening a business.

"Both types of music are powerful and they bring people together," Smith said. "Both feed on the energy of those who are experiencing it. The idea of a live performance is absolutely essential -- that human touch."

Although the business executives and artists recognized the benefits of their interaction, both groups agreed that there is a need for a new transaction model. (The longtime, traditional transaction model is straightforward: The arts ask businesses to give money to make the arts better.)

The Martin Agency's John Adams identified the challenge: "The biggest impediment is that businesses think they don't need anything from the arts. Artists haven't done a good job articulating about this. I know what a ropes course will do for my company, but I have no idea what an art retreat will do."

We spent the afternoon visualizing new ways for businesses and the arts to interact -- ways that might trump and replace our long held transaction model.

The Conference Board wants Richmond to proceed with three steps. First, we'll explore and test new transaction models. Second, we'll pilot some closely related lines of research for The Conference Board. And third, we'll put in place systems to further explore potential benefits from business-arts relationships.

What did The Conference Board learn at the Richmond launch of its Creative Conversations? Five things, according to Spector.

First, there is a clear desire to bring the arts and business communities together. Second, the transaction model needs improvement. Third, the arts need to look for better ways to deliver value to businesses. Fourth, the local dimension is critical: RVA is just the right size for all of us to feel ownership. And fifth, this construct of a Creative Conversation can work.

We at CultureWorks attracted and helped coordinate this national research spotlight on RVA's business and arts communities. We now embrace our responsibility to help leverage this for even stronger arts and culture and an even more robust economy -- both helping to make lives better.

The Pioneers

On November 27, artists and business leaders met for a creative conversation in Richmond:

John Adams Jr., CEO, The Martin Agency

Jonathan Austin, juggler and magician

Beth Bailey, owner, The Pediatric Connection

Heather Bailey, aerialist and kinetic artist

Dave Brockie, musician, president, Slave Pit Inc.

John Bryan, president, CultureWorks

Rob Carter, professor emeritus, graphic design, VCU

Alejandro Cedeno, v-p global innovation, MeadWestvaco

David A. Christian, CEO, Dominion Generation

Thea Duskin, co-founder, Ghostprint Gallery

Lynnelle Ediger-Kordzaia, artistic director, American Youth Harp Ensemble

Lauren Fagone, dancer, The Richmond Ballet

Steven B. Glass, resident potter, Virginia Museum of Fine Arts

David Grant, consultant, The Conference Board

D.L. Hopkins, artistic director, African American Repertory Theater of Virginia

Jennifer Hunter, senior v-p, Altria Client Services

Kenneth S. Johnson, CEO, Johnson Inc.

Hugh Joyce, president, James River Air Conditioning Co.

Jon C. King, CEO, Exclusive Staffing Companies

Robert L. Lynch, CEO, Americans for the Arts

Thurston Moore, chairman emeritus, Hunton and Williams; president, VMFA

Tayloe Negus, principal and Virginia office leader, Mercer

Darcy Oman, CEO, The Community Foundation Serving Richmond & Central Virginia

Kevin Orlosky, director of programs, Art on Wheels

James T. Parrish, co-founder, James River Film Society

Emily Peck, director private sector initiatives, Americans for the Arts

Gary L. Rhodes, president, J. Sargeant Reynolds Community College

Douglas Roth, senior v-p, BB&T

Eric Schaeffer, artistic director, Signature Theatre

Tom Silvestri, publisher, Richmond Times-Dispatch

Myra Goodman Smith, CEO, Leadership Metro Richmond

Steven Smith, music director, Richmond Symphony

Jonathan Spector, CEO, The Conference Board

Gordon Stettinius, photographer, founder, Candela Books and Gallery

Ed Trask, muralist

Samson Trinh, music director, Upper East Side Big Band; Henrico music educator

Mara Walker, chief operating officer, Americans for the Arts

Scott Warren, co-founder and director, Warren Whitney

Mary Wright, associate director, Workforce Initiatives

77

How Some of Trump's Advice Can Advance the Arts

I suspect that many of my fellow artists and arts advocates have no interest in reading any of Trump's books - and so I herewith provide for them five rules distilled from his much larger list that can be helpful for the arts.

I recently read President Donald J. Trump's book, *The Art of the Deal*, which, written 30 years ago, remains the runaway best seller among his 15 books. He has never shown evidence of being an advocate for the importance of the arts - as president he is even calling for abolishing the National Endowment for the Arts - so it is ironic that while reading his book, I realized that many of the fundamental principles and strategies that he touts can be wonderfully instructive for the arts.

I suspect that many of my fellow artists and arts advocates have no interest in reading any of Trump's books - and so I herewith provide for them five rules distilled from his much larger list that can be helpful for the arts. The list also contains directives that I certainly don't recommend, such as "fighting back very hard" and "truthful hyperbole."

(I of course realize that this whole notion is loaded with irony, and also note the irony that among the more than 100 books written by persons who have held the office of president of the United States, only two contain the word "art" in their titles - both by Trump. The other one is *The Art of the Comeback*.)

Below are five of the book's themes. Trump swears by them, uses them almost as religion, has them embedded in his wiring, takes them to the bank. He of course relates them to real estate deals, but they can be effective indeed when applied to the arts.

***

(1) Aim high and think big.

Artists and arts organizations that don't do this are missing opportunities. Trump says, "I aim very high, and then I just keep pushing and pushing. ... Sometimes I settle for less, ... in most cases I still end up with what I want."

Two local examples of this approach are VCU's Institute for Contemporary Art and SPARC's "Live Art." Steven Holl is the world's best architect, and VCU aimed high and got him! Richmond is not a major-market city, but because of VCU's high aim, we're getting a major-market architectural gem.

Four years ago, when SPARC's Erin Thomas-Foley and Executive Director Ryan Ripperton, its executive director, decided to stage a performance by a huge bunch of kids of all abilities, they thought big when determining the venue: the most glorious stage in town. The first two years were at the Carpenter Theatre and the recent two moved to the much-greater-capacity Altria Theater. Just ask those SPARC performers whether big thinking produces big results.

(2) Controversy sells.

Do something outrageous. A few years ago the Richmond Symphony found itself smack in the middle of a front-page controversy when it was told that its selection as The Community Foundation's $100,000 Impact 100 winner was a mistake. Symphony Executive Director David Fisk's graciousness and acumen turned the controversy-spawned publicity into replacement donations totaling $100,000 and more - as well as good will and an even broader public focus on the Symphony's goal: a big tent for performances for diverse audiences at diverse venues.

Studio Two Three does lots of good stuff, but the media's attention was immediately magnetized when Executive Director Ashley Hawkins announced the use of a steamroller to make giant woodcut prints of a map of Richmond. Trump says, "Most reporters have very little interest in exploring the substance of a story - they look instead for the sensational."

(3) Get the word out.

Trump says, "You can have the most wonderful product in the world, but if people don't know about it, it's not going to be worth much ... YOU need to generate interest, and YOU need to create excitement."

I don't know how much money VMFA Executive Director Alex Nyerges budgeted to market the 2011 Picasso exhibition, but boy it was worth it! It resulted in tens of thousands of new VMFA members and our whole community took notice of our great museum.

(4) Leadership is the key.

Trump: "Leadership is perhaps THE key to getting any job done."

Witness one gargantuan arts result of the leadership of Jack Berry and Lisa Sims at Venture Richmond: hundreds of thousands of persons convening downtown each year for the Richmond Folk Festival - all of our community's diverse demographics tapping their toes together.

(5) Persistence can cause success.

There may be no better example of persistence than Jenni Kirby, who started Crossroads Art Center 15 years ago from scratch and now presents the works of 225 artists and welcomes 1,000 attendees to the bi-monthly Open House - and was recently named Richmond's Retail Merchants Association's 50th Anniversary Retailer of the Year.

Trump: "I was relentless, even in the face of the total lack of encouragement, because much more often than you'd think, sheer persistence is the difference between success and failure."

***

To again clarify: There are many of Trump's themes and directives with which I don't agree. So if you read the book, be your own guide.

Interestingly, there are two brief passages in the book that are actually about art. I think they're poignant.

Early on, Trump relates his encounter with a noted artist (unnamed) who spends two minutes splashing paint on a blank canvas and then brags to Trump that he's just made $25,000; collectors were eager for his art. Trump's insight: "Most successful painters are often better salesmen and promoters than they are artists."

Midway through the book Trump tells about purchasing the Bonwit Teller building in Manhattan - and demolishing it along with its bas-relief Art Deco sculptures, for which he continues to be castigated by the arts community.

He later regretted destroying the sculptures: "I still think that a lot of my critics were phonies and hypocrites, but I understand now that certain events can take on symbolic importance."

So there you have it. My personal bleeding heart compelled me to read this book in order to better understand our president. And although I haven't changed my thoughts about his absolutely deplorable words and actions, I do now have better insight. What I didn't expect was for the book to contain nuggets of wisdom that can be applied to the arts.

Richmond *Times-Dispatch,* July 9, 2017

78

50 YEARS OF AQUARIUS

I t was the emergence of political correctness that caused us to understand that we should think about our words and actions, and proactively make choices that reflect kindness and understanding.

Something dawned on me recently when I heard my radio's oldies station sing, "This is the dawning of the Age of Aquarius." The Fifth Dimension released that song in the year I left my teens, the year of the dawning of my adulthood: 1969. Although created for the musical "Hair" a couple of years earlier, it was The Fifth Dimension's version that won the Grammy for Record of the Year.

Lots of us embraced that song's message as a herald of an age when "love will steer the stars."

We've now entered the 50th year since that dawning. I wonder if love has indeed steered the stars, and if so, to what avail?

It seems like everywhere you look you can see examples of love not steering the stars, but I see three examples of love's influence on the stars.

***

Example One: Our society has vocally and legally embraced the belief that marginalized persons - persons who are among minorities, persons without power, "the least of these" (just about all categories of persons who are not healthy, Caucasian, male, and heterosexual) - deserve to be recognized, accommodated, empathized with, and, if you will, loved.

Back in 1969 who would have dreamed that love would steer the stars to the Americans with Disabilities Act? Or to same-sex marriage? Or to all sorts of other legalities that imply love and understanding for formerly marginalized persons?

Example Two is philanthropy. According to Michael Jones' "The Growth of Nonprofits" in the Bridgewater Review, 1970 is when the formation of new nonprofit organizations - organizations whose missions are to make lives better - started to blossom.

Today our country has more than 1.5 million nonprofits - thousands right here in Richmond. These are organizations fueled by financial gifts from you and me and just about everyone.

It seems that everyone these days makes charitable gifts - whether through social media, special events, community giving days, or responses to all of those envelopes that stuff our mailboxes. Over the past 50 years philanthropy - an evidence of love - has become a pervasive part of our culture.

Example Three is political correctness - a vilified term that simply means, as per Wikipedia, "avoiding language or behavior that can be seen as excluding, marginalizing, or insulting groups of people." PC means using words and actions that indicate kindness and empathy.

But back in 1969, we all made cavalierly unthinking use of language that was hurtful and that caused pain. It was the emergence of that phrase - political correctness - in the 1980s that caused us to understand that we should think about our words and actions, and proactively make choices that reflect kindness and understanding.

***

Are these three examples truly the result of love steering the stars? Or have they resulted from other things - perhaps money or politics? I don't know, but my guess is that if love had made a list back in 1969, those three things would have been on it.

What might steer the stars during the coming 50 years? This year's Grammy-winning Record of the Year has a different message from 1969's "Aquarius." It's Bruno Mars' "24K Magic" - a wonderful example of an egocentric, money-and-glitter, party song. I still laud that grand party song, The Isley Brothers' Grammy-Hall-of-Fame-honored "Shout," but I'm not sure how well it would have steered the stars.

My hope is that love will continue to have a role in steering the stars. I see ongoing evidence in Richmond.

Take something that doesn't happen anywhere except in Richmond: our Acts of Faith Festival. It's an annual gathering of our theater community to present faith as a theme of many productions.

The participating theaters have had diverse affiliations: Baptist, Muslim, Jewish, gay, Shakespearean, Equity, community, and on and on.

And what about our smorgasbord of public awards for persons and organizations that have allowed love to steer their stars in making things better? Such as the YWCA's recently announced Outstanding Women Awards: nine women whose work and lives have made other lives better. Or the Valentine's recently announced Richmond History Makers: six honorees whose work has improved lives throughout the region. Good for Richmond that we publicly celebrate this evidence of love steering the stars.

All of which begs a definition of love. I believe that it's somewhere in the ballpark of showing kindness and causing a smile.

One of my recent donations was to an online Kickstarter campaign for singer/actor Jason Marks' "Becoming Santa Claus" - his quest to raise money to assemble an absolutely glorious Santa costume so he can do an ever better job of "giving joy to people everywhere." That's one Santa line I'll be in.

I recently met with another Richmonder whose persona is kindness and smiles: juggler/magician/entertainer Jonathan Austin. We smile with him each year at Easter on Parade. Did you know that he does more than 200 contracted gigs each year for diverse groups ranging from first-graders to corporate board members to White House attendees to Muslim birthday celebrants to you name it?

Jonathan's popularity is magnetized by his innate interest in understanding, empathizing with, and delivering kindness and smiles to whomever he encounters. (Want a guaranteed happy dining experience? Jonathan does table-to-table at Joe's Inn Bon Air on Wednesday evenings.)

All of which raises what may be the key question: Is love the best pilot for steering a country's stars to greatness? The words and actions of our nation's leaders indicate vastly different answers.

"No more falsehoods or derisions," is another of the lyrics from "Aquarius." The song's most famous line is of course, "Let the sunshine in." It's raining outside as I type this. I vote for sunshine.

Richmond *Times-Dispatch*, February 18, 2018

79

CELEBRATING OUR FATHERS' BEST QUALITIES
EXAMPLES OF GRACE

"Our Pearl Harbor" is how U.S. Surgeon General Jerome Adams described the arrival of COVID-19.

Seventy-five years ago, my father, Tom, spent Father's Day on Okinawa in Japan doctoring sick and wounded soldiers of World War II's last great battle (as described by my cousin, Charles F. Bryan Jr., in his April 15 Commentary piece.)

Today two of my father's grandchildren (my children) - Kelly and Thomas - are spending Father's Day helping in our new war against COVID-19: Kelly as a nurse and Thomas at an Amazon fulfillment center. Kelly helps sick people; Thomas helps the rest of us stay home.

Kelly and Thomas are different from my father, but I've identified four of his qualities that I see in them - qualities that contributed to his value on Okinawa and to their value in Virginia.

I'll start with courage, although all three would call it "just doing my job." WWII doctors were shielded as much as possible from direct exposure to the enemy, but Daddy was awarded a Bronze Star because of an extraordinary voluntary action. "Just doing my job" or courage?

Kelly works 12-hour shifts in the acute care unit of VCU Medical Center Critical Care Hospital. She not only continually risks exposure to a lot of dangerous things that most other nurses face (physical attacks from patients, drenchings from bodily fluids, etc.) but also to COVID-19. "Just doing my job" or courage?

Thomas works more than 50 hours each week alongside 2,000-plus employees who continually touch the same surfaces and penetrate personal distance zones. Amazon does have safety rules, such as taking employees' temperatures and firing employees who blatantly disregard social distancing, but still: "Just doing my job" or courage?

A second quality is modesty - an attribution that all three would decline. When I asked Daddy about his Bronze Star, all he would say was that he took a Jeep and picked up some soldiers who had been fired on by snipers. After he died, I discovered the harrowing details of his heroism. Modesty.

Likewise Kelly and Thomas receive commendations, but never mention them.

Nurses can get DAISY Awards for clinical excellence and compassion, and recently I asked Kelly whether she ever has gotten one. Her reply simply was, "Yes, I've received a few. Why?" Modesty.

Same with Thomas. From time to time he'll give me a preloaded gift card that he says was "handed out" at Amazon. Recently I asked him if those cards are commendations for good work or simply random giveaways. His only reply: "Depends. Why?" Modesty.

Third is unpretentiousness. Daddy never wanted or needed to wear a Rolex, buy designer clothes, drive a status-symbol car, or display his honors and awards. Surely his lack of pretension was an endearing quality in his relationships with fellow soldiers.

Likewise, Kelly and Thomas both are adverse to pretentiousness - not only with obvious things like clothing and cars, but also things that directly relate to working with colleagues: Kelly never flaunting her academic excellence (including finishing No. 1 in her graduating class at the University of Richmond's School of Professional and Continuing Studies) and Thomas never flaunting his Amazon expertise and seniority - more than five years, and one of only two persons to survive his 20-member recruitment class.

Apparently both, like Daddy, have no need or desire to use pretention to signify their value.

And fourth is a double quality: kindness and empathy, especially for "the least of these." I once asked Daddy about Japanese atrocities in the Pacific. His reply was that he never saw any and that he mostly saw good things as confirmed, for example, by seeing soldiers give cigarettes to Japanese prisoners.

After the war in a then-segregated Nashville, he broke a strict "color line" by performing surgery on a black girl whom he quietly had admitted to the city's largest white hospital.

And although Daddy's patients included governors, celebrities and VIPs, he quietly gave his time to treat underserved patients, such as those from the Nashville jail and the state prison. I remember how distraught he was one evening when he came home from treating a prison inmate who had been beaten.

I suspect that all nurses who work in huge metropolitan hospitals have occasion to care for VIPs and celebrities, but Kelly speaks most caringly about the forlorn, the downtrodden, the mentally ill, the dysfunctional, and those consumed by poverty or addiction. Kindness and empathy.

I see this kindness/empathy quality in Thomas right here in our own family. My brother-in-law, Tony Gilmore, who had Down's Syndrome, was our houseguest for a few weeks every summer, from before Thomas was born until Tony's death a few years ago. From toddlerhood through adulthood Thomas, probably even more than the rest of us, loved being with Tony: playing with Tony, laughing with Tony, caring for Tony, simply being with Tony.

And today Thomas, perhaps even more than the rest of us, exhibits that same kindness and empathy for Kelly's daughter, Angelina, who is on the autism spectrum. He always is eager for opportunities to play with her, laugh with her - be with her.

Empathy/kindness: my favorite double-good quality to honor on Father's Day, whether celebrating it in my father's 75-years-ago service on Okinawa, or in his two grandchildren who are on the front lines of today's war.

I wonder if Father's Day might be an annual opportunity for us to recognize and celebrate our fathers' best qualities as we observe them in persons whom we know now - especially our children.

Richmond *Times-Dispatch,* June 21, 2020

80

THE FIGHT OF THE CENTURY
LESSONS LEARNED FROM 1971

He made unprecedented use of the media and public spotlight to energize his supporters, engage the masses and attract a record turnout.

His narcissistic arrogance complemented an infectious charisma that he exuded among cheering crowds at every appearance and rally. His prediction of certain victory was buoyed by his love of the camera, his name and face in print, and the unfettered adoration from his fans.

And as the climactic contest finally got underway, it looked like a victory. But there came a devastating final-phase surprise, and he was vanquished.

No, not Trump-Biden, but Ali-Frazier: March 8, 1971, 50 years ago, Muhammad Ali lost to Joe Frazier in "The Fight of the Century," thanks in large part to a last-round knockdown.

I saw it live via closed circuit at the Charlotte Coliseum. *Sports Illustrated* still calls it "The Biggest Sporting Event in History." Through all of these years, I often have wondered whether that event would have any enduring relevance.

And then came Donald Trump. And his campaign against Joe Biden. And its aftermath.

We learned a few things from "The Fight of the Century" and its aftermath - learnings that perhaps can benefit us today.

First, we learned that a single person with a big enough voice and ego and charisma can energize unparalled numbers of participants (300 million worldwide viewers then, 160 million voters now) and transform a previously routine event into one that seems existential.

Those viewers from a half-century ago - many who, like me, were first-time boxing enthusiasts - stuck around for years and produced a fresh heyday for boxing. Just four months later, Ali crowded the Houston Astrodome for his fight against sparring partner Jimmy Ellis.

Record turnouts for other fights, even without Ali and Frazier, continued for many years. Might the wake of Trump-Biden include record voter participation for many years to come, even for nonpresidential elections? The record turnout for the Georgia U.S. Senate runoffs might be a leading indicator.

Second, we learned that lesser-used methods of participation (closed-circuit viewing, mail-in and advance voting) dramatically can enhance an event's reach.

Closed-circuit viewing of Ali-Frazier, and mail-in and advance voting for Trump-Biden, newly were expanded with fresh bells and whistles and reached vast new audiences. Ali-Frazier taught us that expanded participation methods can endure and be productive and make things better for everyone. Might the same now be true for expanded voting methods?

Third, we learned from Ali-Frazier and its aftermath that intense polarization can dissipate and even disappear. Ali used unbridled vitriol to castigate the soft-spoken Frazier. Half the nation viewed Ali as a radical, loudmouthed, hate-spewing Muslim, and Frazier as the embodiment of decency and patriotism.

Communities everywhere bristled with intense arguments, and it was impossible to find an unbiased opinion. But during the following years, the polarization lessened and eventually disappeared - all coinciding with Ali's own gradual abandonment of inflammatory speech. Might it be possible for former president Trump to likewise defuse today's polarization?

Fourth, that 50-years-ago event taught us that it's possible to be a good loser - even when the loser has bet everything on the event. There indeed was room for Ali to claim that The Fight was rigged, that it had been stolen.

The scorecards revealed that Ali had won 10 of the fight's 15 rounds on at least one of the three judges' scorecards. Half the crowd booed the result. But Ali's words and actions eventually signaled agreement with the decision - an agreement for which he gained respect, even from those who had hated him.

If Trump were to embrace his loss, might that, as with Ali, attract a degree of respect from his detractors and an even greater respect from his base?

And finally, we learned that a soft-spoken winner can be productive and effective, and gain admiration from those who rooted against him.

Frazer was a gracious winner, an effective champion and a good role model for the boxing profession's long-tarnished reputation. On March 8, 1971, there were many of us who held undeserved disdain for Frazier based on Ali's hate speech.

But we learned to like Frazier as a person and admire him for the workmanlike professionalism he brought to boxing. Might the same be possible for now-President Joe Biden?

Of course this is not 1971, Trump and Biden are not Ali and Frazier, and The Fight didn't result in an armed insurrection.

Ali was 29 and had an entire adulthood ahead of him to build character; Trump is 74 and has a character that already is well-baked. And today we are confronted with a global "Fight of the Century" of our own, and it is far more consequential than anything in competitive sports - even "The Biggest Event in Sporting History."

Nevertheless, on this 50th anniversary of that grand Monday evening when I was sardined among a smiling and friendly half-white, half-Black, electrified audience in Charlotte, I can't help but reflect on that unparalleled event and the unanticipated healing that took place over the years to come.

Postscript - I completed this piece on January 21, the day after Biden's inauguration and his revelation that Trump left him a "very generous letter."

Richmond *Times-Dispatch,* March 7, 2021

ABOUT THE AUTHOR

CHARLES FAULKNER BRYAN, JR.

Charles Faulkner Bryan, Jr., was born and raised in McMinnville, Tennessee. He is a distinguished military graduate of the Virginia Military Institute, and he received his Ph.D. in history from the University of Tennessee. He served as an officer in the United States Army for two years during the Vietnam War.

Bryan was awarded a one-year post-doctoral fellowship in historical editing with the Andrew Jackson Papers, a University of Tennessee project located at The Hermitage in Nashville. He was then appointed as assistant editor of the project and edited Jackson's correspondence during the War of 1812, which appeared as part of Volume 2 of *The Papers of Andrew Jackson*, published by the University of Tennessee Press.

Bryan was appointed as the first executive director of the East Tennessee Historical Society in Knoxville. Five years later, he became executive director of the St. Louis Mercantile Library, one of the country's richest research collections on the history of the American West, railroading and river transportation.

In 1988, Bryan was named President and CEO of the Virginia Historical Society. Founded in 1831, the VHS is the repository of a large and rich collection of books, manuscripts, photographs, artwork, and museum objects that support the study and interpretation of Virginia and American history. The institution (now named the Virginia Museum of History and Culture) sponsors conferences, lectures, and exhibitions as part of its mission to promote a broader understanding of Virginia history.

During his tenure, Bryan oversaw capital campaigns that raised more than $110 million. Those efforts resulted in quadrupling the size of the VHS's headquarters building and a significant expansion of educational programs statewide.

In recognition of those endeavors, Bryan has been the recipient of numerous awards. In 2008 the Virginia General Assembly named him its Outstanding Virginian for "his remarkable service to the citizens of Virginia [and for his] inspirational leadership in making the Virginia Historical Society one of the leading historical institutions in the nation." He holds honorary doctorate degrees from Virginia Commonwealth University and Randolph-Macon College. He served as president of the American Association for State and Local History and of the Independent Research Libraries Association. He also serves on the board of the Smithsonian's National Museum of American History.

He has considerable teaching experience, having had appointments as adjunct associate professor of history at the University of Missouri–St. Louis and the University of Tennessee. He has published extensively on history museum management and the American Civil War. With Nelson Lankford, he edited the Civil War best-seller *Eye of the Storm, A Civil War Odyssey* and a follow-up volume *Images from the Storm,* based on diary of a Union soldier, Robert K. Sneden, published by the *Free Press*, a division of Simon & Schuster.

He and his wife of 52 years, Cammy, reside in Richmond. They have two married children and three grandchildren.

USING THIS BOOK FOR YOUR BOOK CLUB
OR IN A CLASSROOM

For the first volume of *Imperfect Past,* I developed a number of questions to be discussed in the classroom or in a book club. Many readers have told me that the questions I suggested did, indeed, lead to lively dialog. On occasion, the discussions became heated, particularly when the topic related to politics.

Below are some questions that can lead to a good discussion on various topics. Feel free, however, to develop your own questions.

(1) The word "hero" is applied to people for a variety of reasons, sometimes even when a person really does not deserve that recognition. Who are some heroes in this volume and why do you think the label applies to them?

(2) Certain events or developments can change the course of history. Rank in order of importance the following turning points in history and explain your reasons for each.

a. the "Columbian Exchange"

b. The development and rollout of the Boeing 757

c. The discovery of germs and the eventual implementation of the "germ theory"

d. The election of Franklin Roosevelt and subsequent rolling out of the New Deal and presidency during World War II

e. The failure of the southern states to win the Civil War.

(3) Has lying by public officials become so common that the American citizenry are almost numb to it? Cite and discuss some examples how lying, both little and big lies, have come back to haunt the American people.

(4) In what ways has the Coronavirus pandemic resembled previous pandemics? In what ways has it differed?

(5) John Adams certainly should be regarded as one of our nation's "Founding Fathers" for the crucial role he played in helping gain American independence. Yet when he served as the second president of the U.S. his actions did not live up to the principles he had espoused earlier. Today, most historians rank him as a mediocre president. Is that fair, or should he be ranked higher?

(6) Historians have usually given high marks to presidents who were successful when confronted with crises that varied in degrees of seriousness. Which five presidents would you choose who successfully faced a crisis (or crises)? Why did they succeed? Was it luck, people skills, powers of persuasion, or was it something else?

(7) In the essay "Remembering My Three Fathers," you learn that my father died of a massive heart attack when I was only eight years old. In what ways did my grandfather and father-in-law fill the holes left by the loss of my father?

(8) Both my cousin John Bryan and I had encounters with Muhammad Ali, one of us in person, the other virtually. From what you know about Ali, did your image of him change?

(9) Herbert Hoover did more than any previous president to stem the tide of an economic downturn. His presidency, however, has been regarded at best as below average. Is that a fair assessment?

(10) As described in the essay "A Moving Experience: The Exquisite Trauma of Downsizing," moving is "one of life's most traumatic experiences, ranking only behind the death of a loved one and divorce." How did your last move go? Describe your experience.

(11) In the 18th-century, Thomas Malthus argued that the world's population would continue to surge until disease, famine, or natural disaster reversed the trend. This assertion never became reality. Why?

(12) In my essay on television, I list a number of my ten favorite television programs. What are yours and why?

(13) The late author John Egerton argued that "there are essentially three kinds of history: what actually happened, what we are told happened, and what we finally come to believe happened." How does Egerton's premise relate to the Civil War and the Cult of the Lost Cause?

(14) In what ways was the Revolutionary War to Great Britain what the Vietnam War was to the United States?

(15) In the 1940's, British historian Arnold Toynbee contended that Virginia's most distinguishing characteristic was its resistance to change. Can you demonstrate that with examples cited in this volume?

(16) What made the 1824 presidential election one of the most controversial in American history, resulting in Andrew Jackson losing to John Quincy Adams in what the former call it a "corrupt bargain?"

(17) Three presidents have been impeached on grounds that they committed high crimes and misdemeanors, yet none has been convicted. Why is that? And which of those three committed the most serious offense?

(18) Is Donald Trump a demagogue? If you say "yes," Choose your faves and get alerts about your favorite artists, teams and venues! Here's how: what is your proof? The same question applies If you say "no."

(19) What made the "Christmas Truce" of 1914 such a poignant story of World War I?

INDEX

NOTES

NOTES